FOCUS ON CANADA

JOHN WASHINGTON

ANDREW BURGHARDT

GALE HITCHCOX

PETER CHRISTIAN

McGRAW-HILL RYERSON LIMITED
Toronto, Montreal, New York, St. Louis, San Francisco, Auckland, Beirut,
Bogotá, Düsseldorf, Johannesburg, Lisbon, London, Lucerne, Madrid, Mexico,
New Delhi, Panama, Paris, San Juan, São Paulo, Singapore, Sydney, Tokyo

FOCUS ON CANADA

ISBN 0-07-082309-X

12345678910 BP 7654321098

Printed and bound in Canada

Cover Photo: George Hunter
Cover Design: Bev Atkinson
Maps and Illustrations: Frank Hammond

Canadian Cataloguing in Publication Data

Main entry under title:

Focus on Canada

Includes index
ISBN 0-07-082309-X

1. Canada. 2. Canada — Description and travel —
1950- * I. Washington, John, 1936-

FC75.F63   917.1'02   C77-001414-3
F1016.F63

CONTENTS

PREFACE

The geography of Canada is complex because the country is not only vast but also remarkably diverse. In writing this textbook, the authors have attempted to focus both *thematically* and *regionally* on Canada in order to provide students in the early secondary school grades with a clearer understanding of the land in which they live.

This book is divided into three parts. Chapters 1-4 of *Part One: Where We Live* develop essential themes necessary for a basic comprehension of Canada's size and location, historical perspective, physical characteristics, population mix, and varied economy. Chapters 5-10 of *Part Two: Regional Diversities* are devoted to the study of the many ways in which the human and natural elements have interacted to develop distinct geographical regions in the country. The individual "personality" of each of these regions and their unique problems are clearly brought out. Chapter 11 of *Part Three: From Sea to Sea — and Beyond* describes how the diverse regions of Canada are held together by common transportation bonds; Chapter 12 sums up Canada's relationship with the other members of the "global village."

Each of the twelve chapters contains a wide range of suggested activities for the student. These activities range from *written* questions and exercises intended for recapitulation of topics covered to *enrichment* or research activities that may involve group work among students for a period of time. The activities are designed to consolidate student comprehension of essential factual information with some basic geographical concepts.

Canada has often been compared to a mosaic — a picture composed of many many coloured stones. The chapters in this text are like the stones in a mosaic, since they can be viewed either singly or collectively to create a picture of Canada. It all depends on how you adjust the focus.

Focus on Canada is highly visual and graphic. This book contains a wealth of maps, graphs, diagrams, and charts, together with numerous exciting and relevant photographs. Newspaper clippings and interesting material from magazines create interest in a number of issues covered in the text.

We want to thank the following people for the help they gave us: Christopher Daniels, Industrial Analyst at the Canadian Imperial Bank of Commerce; Robert A. Hughes of the Public Relations Department at Gulf Oil; Marilyn Andrews; and Rosina Daillie and Dave Marshall of McGraw-Hill Ryerson.

January, 1978.   *The Authors*

PART ONE:
WHERE
WE LIVE

1 CANADA:
LAND OF DIVERSITY

Have you ever tried to draw a map of Canada? If you have, you know something of the complexity of Canada's physical geography. This complexity appears in all aspects of the natural environment — the geology, landforms, climate, natural vegetation, and soils. But this complexity is not surprising: after all, Canada occupies the northern half of the world's third largest continent. And, with a total land area of 9 937 660 km², Canada is the second largest country on the globe. Our country stretches

Figure 1–1:   Time Zones in Canada

Canada Year Book 1974

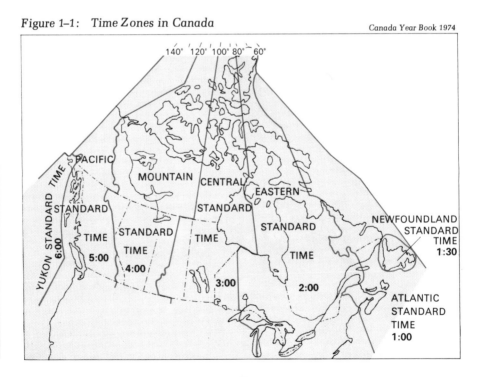

2

westward from Cape Spear, Newfoundland for 5630 km through seven
time zones to Mount St. Elias in the Yukon Territory. From Pelee Island in
Lake Erie, Canada extends 4830 km northward to Cape Columbia on the
northern tip of Ellesmere Island.

Canada's physical geography is easier to get to know if you understand its overall pattern. Examine the diagram that shows Canada as a

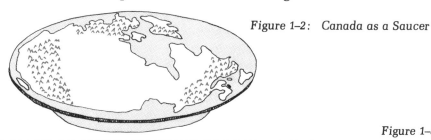

Figure 1–2: *Canada as a Saucer*

Figure 1–3: *Drainage in Canada*

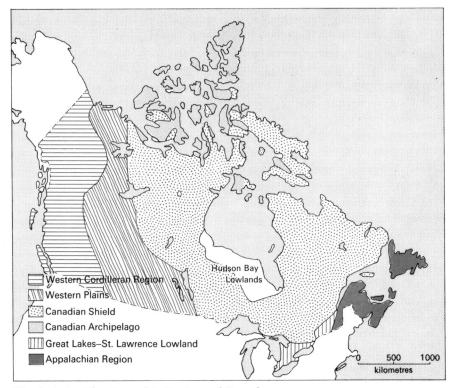

Figure 1–4: *Physiographic Regions of Canada*

giant saucer (Figure 1-2). The Canadian Shield forms the central portion, while three major mountain ranges stand at Canada's northeastern, eastern, and western edges, and the Canadian-United States border lies to the south.

Water has tremendous importance in the geography of Canada. The mountain ranges at the edges of the country rise from the floors of the three great oceans — the Arctic, Pacific, and Atlantic. Canada has nearly 95 560 km of coastline. The coastline is so long because of the incredible number of headlands and bays. (For instance, the Great Lakes–St. Lawrence River system and Hudson Bay, add greatly to the length of the Canadian coastline.) Included in the length of the coastline is the large number of islands which are actually mountains rising from the ocean floor.

Even in the interior of the country, the combination of land and water is a significant aspect of the landscape. Nearly 8% of Canada's area is covered by fresh water lakes: they number in the hundreds of thousands. The large lakes, such as Great Bear, Great Slave, Winnipeg, and the Great

Lakes, are so large that they would probably be called seas in other parts of the world (Figure 1-3).

Obviously, Canada's geography is diverse. However, geographers have simplified the process of understanding these landscapes by dividing the country into a number of physiographic regions, each of which displays distinct physical characteristics (Figure 1-4). In the following pages, the basic characteristics of each of these regions will be examined. These regions are the Canadian Shield and the three major lowland areas of Hudson Bay, the Great Lakes–St. Lawrence, and the Western Plains (which make up the interior of the country), then the great mountain ranges of the Canadian Arctic Archipelego, the Appalachians, and the Western Cordillera that form the outer rim of Canada.

THE CANADIAN SHIELD

Look at the map showing the locations of the world's shields (Figure 1-5). Each of the world's continents has at its core a mass of hard, old, crystalline rock known as a *shield*. In North America the shield is often identified as the Canadian Shield because it underlies more than half of

Figure 1–5:   *Shields of the World: The shields and adjoining platforms that form the ancient centres (nuclei) of continental "growth."*

Introduction to Historical Geology. Moore, pp. 4-5, 66. Used with permission of McGraw-Hill Book Company

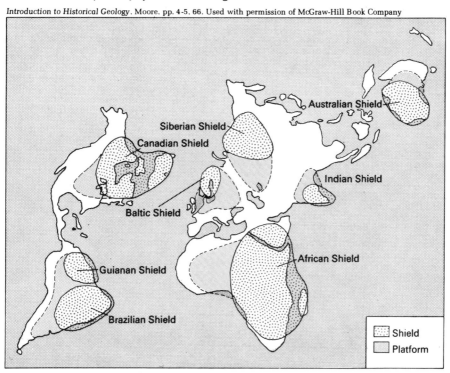

Canada. The area of the Canadian Shield (also called the Precambrian Shield) is 4 789 650 km².

By measuring the amount of radioactive materials remaining in the rocks of the Shield, scientists have established that they date from 3.5 billion years ago and are among the oldest rocks on the earth. To reconstruct the geological origins of the Canadian Shield has for a number of reasons been a monumental task for geologists. Not only is the area of the Shield extensive, but also in many places it is covered with *geologically recent* sedimentary deposits that now hide the Shield from view. The second major problem is that the Precambrian era is far removed from the present time and of a very long duration, enabling successions of mountain ranges to appear, then completely erode away.

The oldest rocks of the Canadian Shield belong to the Archeozoic period which dates back to about 4 500 million years ago (see Table 1-1). Most of these rocks were formed when layers of sediment became com-

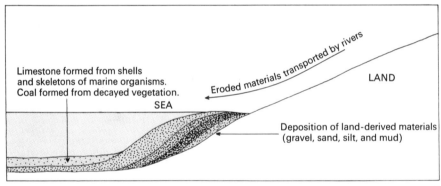

Limestone formed from shells and skeletons of marine organisms. Coal formed from decayed vegetation.

Eroded materials transported by rivers

LAND

SEA

Deposition of land-derived materials (gravel, sand, silt, and mud)

Figure 1–6:   *Formation of Sedimentary Rock*

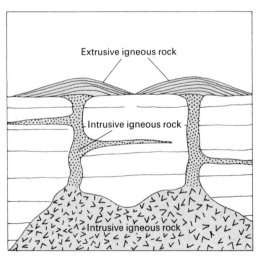

Extrusive igneous rock

Intrusive igneous rock

Intrusive igneous rock

Figure 1–7:   *Formation of Igneous Rock*

TABLE 1-1
Geological Time Scale

Era	Period	Epoch	Duration (millions of years)	Began (millions of years ago)
CENOZOIC "Age of Mammals"	Quaternary	Recent started 11 000 years ago		
		Pleistocene	1	1
	Tertiary	Pliocene	10	11
		Miocene	14	25
		Oligocene	15	40
		Eocene	20	60
		Paleocene	10	70
MESOZOIC "Age of Reptiles"	Cretaceous		65	135
	Jurassic		45	180
	Triassic		45	225
PALEOZOIC "Age of Amphibians" "Age of Fishes" "Age of Invertebrates"	Permian		45	270
	Pennsylvanian		60	330
	Mississippian		20	350
	Devonian		50	400
	Silurian		40	440
	Ordovician		60	500
	Cambrian		100	600
PRECAMBRIAN	Proterozoic		1100	1700
	Archeozoic		2800	4500

pacted into *sedimentary rock*, or when molten material from numerous volcanic eruptions cooled and solidified into layers of lava. In some places the molten lava fell into water that cooled it in rounded lumps, producing what is known as "pillow lava." Both the layers of sedimentary rock and lava were then subjected to a great deal of folding and faulting during periods of mountain building. As a result the rocks were under great stress and heat for long periods of time and thus they were

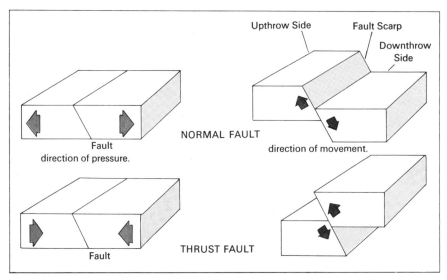

Figure 1–8: Faulting, and Landforms Produced by Faulting

Figure 1–9: Folding, and Types of Folds

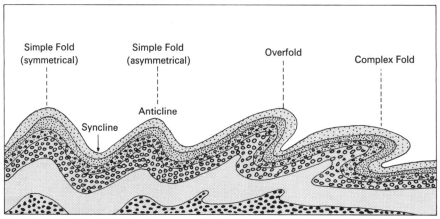

changed or metamorphosed into new forms of crystalline rock known as *metamorphic rocks*. While this process of "mountain building" was taking place, upwellings of molten material from within the earth's crust occurred on the surface of the earth. This molten material gradually cooled to form rocks known as *igneous rock*, of which granite is an example.

The rugged landscape of the Canadian Shield did not last under the attack of the forces of erosion, so the mountains of solid rock were eventually worn away. The nearly smooth landscape that was produced,

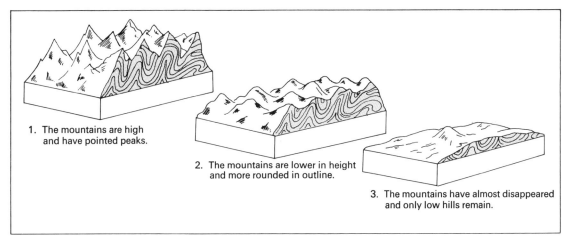

1. The mountains are high and have pointed peaks.

2. The mountains are lower in height and more rounded in outline.

3. The mountains have almost disappeared and only low hills remain.

Figure 1–10: *Stages in the Development of a Peneplain*

called a *peneplain*, provided a base on which new layers of sedimentary and volcanic material were deposited. The process of mountain building, accompanied by the "intrusion" of "fresh" masses of granite, occurred again. Prolonged erosion wore away these mountains too: the entire landscape was leveled once again.

During the latter part of the Precambrian Era known as the Proterozoic Period, sedimentary deposits accumulated in the depressions on the peneplain surface, while in other places molten material solidified to form granite. As had happened before, the rocks were deformed by folding and faulting during periods of renewed mountain building. Mountain ranges appeared along the eastern shore of Hudson Bay (Belcher Range), around Great Slave Lake (Great Slave Range), and in long bands from Ungava Bay to Anticosti Island in Quebec and Labrador (Labrador Range) as well as from the locations of Montreal in the north and Kingston in the south through to Minnesota (Killarney Range). It is believed that these mountains underwent the same processes of *peneplanation* as had the mountains of earlier times. Eventually the Shield was worn away: all that remained at the surface were the roots of ancient mountains.

Today the Shield has a saucer shape: the depressed centre is occupied by Hudson Bay. The lands surrounding this large body of water are low and flat and are covered with muskeg and large swamps. The surface of the Shield rises to the east as a result of uplifting occurring in recent geological times. Along the northern coast of Labrador, the surface has been uplifted to a height of 1880 m to form the Torngat Mountains. The outer edge of the Shield decreases in height in the southern sections

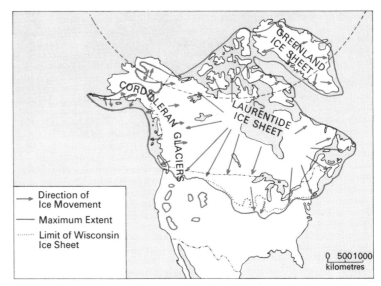

Direction of
Ice Movement

Maximum Extent

Limit of Wisconsin
Ice Sheet

0 500 1000
kilometres

Figure 1–11:   Pleistocene Extent of Glaciation in North America
The Physical Environment, S. Inch and W. G. Stone, p. 136. McGraw-Hill Ryerson, 1972

View of the Canadian Shield north of Lake Superior. Notice the heavy forest, the numerous lakes and rivers, and the hard granitic outcrops in the background.

Ontario Ministry of Transportation and Communications

and is overlaid by the sedimentary deposits of the St. Lawrence–Great Lakes Lowlands. West of Lake Huron the Shield rises again to a height of about 500 m.

Despite the differing degrees of hardness of the underlying rock, the Shield has a monotonous appearance. From the air, the land appears level; pilots might think that the ground is flat. However, if pilots flew nearer to the ground, they would find out that the surface was rough and uneven, a mixture of low hills and ridges separated by areas of muskeg. This unusual landscape has resulted from the repeated glaciation during the Pleistocene Epoch, approximately one million years ago (Figure 1-11). The moving ice bulldozed away the loose materials on the surface and pushed them from the Shield onto the neighbouring regions. The drainage patterns were completely modified by the actions of the ice so that today the area is poorly drained. The surface is dotted with numerous lakes that are often joined by fast-flowing rivers.

THE HUDSON BAY LOWLANDS

The southern shore of Hudson Bay as far east as James Bay forms a distinct physiographic region of Canada. This low, swampy area of sedimentary rock, covering an area of 323 750 km², contrasts to the landscape of the surrounding Shield. Here, coral reefs, limestones, and sandstones of the Paleozoic Era have been deposited on the flat and weathered surface of Precambrian granite and gneiss. These older sedimentary rocks and the more recent sediments deposited over the area during the end of the last glaciation are proof that the centre of the Shield was a lowland throughout most of the earth's geological history.

Despite this region's large size and relatively southern location in the country, the population of the Hudson Bay lowlands is extremely small. The combination of *permafrost* (permanently frozen soil) and poor

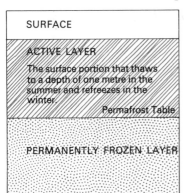

Figure 1–12: Permafrost

drainage had made transportation difficult; as a result, the area has remained a mixture of coniferous trees, barrens, and swamp. Part of the northern area has been designated as Ontario's Polar Bear Provincial Park to preserve the natural habitat of these great white bears. The southern parts of the Hudson Bay Lowlands are underlain by Cretaceous deposits containing lignite and clay, especially on the west side of the Abitibi River. The lignite lies in two seams covered and separated by the clay. Both the clay and lignite can be mined by the open-pit process. The lignite can be burned to generate thermal electricity; the clay is suitable in the manufacturing of fire brick used for lining furnaces and chimneys, where resistance to great heat is required.

THE GREAT LAKES–ST. LAWRENCE LOWLANDS

With an area of only 110 851 km², the Great Lakes– St. Lawrence Lowlands is the smallest of the physiographic regions of Canada. The region is characterized by the nearly flat Paleozoic sedimentary rock that forms its base. Millions of years of erosion have created the largest fresh-water area on the earth. The Great Lakes drain into the Atlantic Ocean through the St. Lawrence River. This lowland is divided into two major sectors by an outcropping of rocky land (a spur) of the Shield near Kingston, Ontario, known as the *Frontenac Axis*. (See Figure 7-1).

About 300 million years ago the Great Lakes area was covered by a shallow tropical sea. The sediment at the bottom of the sea became compressed and cemented into layers of sedimentary rock that rested one upon the other like a stack of saucers to form a geological structure known as the Michigan Basin. Thus, all the rock formations of southern Ontario dip westwards towards Lake Michigan. The outer edges of some of the more resistant layers of rock protrude as escarpments. The largest and most well-known is the *Niagara Escarpment*, which extends right across the peninsula of southern Ontario from the Niagara River to the Bruce Peninsula and the Manitoulin Islands.

The surface of the bedrock has been carved and molded by the ice sheets that covered the area four times during the last one million years (Figure 1-11). The ice sheet scoured the surface and tonnes of rock were ground into very fine material that was subsequently pushed into great piles of debris known as *moraines* (Figure 1-13). In addition to the various types of moraines (lateral, medial, ground, and terminal), another type of glaciated feature in southern Ontario is the low hill known as a *drumlin*. These hills were formed when the glaciers overrode existing moraines and reworked them into a cluster of hills.

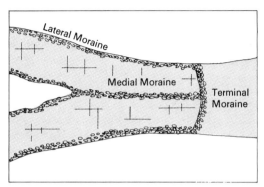

Figure 1–13: Moraine

Moraine is the load of stones, clay, and rock debris transported and then deposited by glaciers or ice sheets. A lateral moraine occurs at either side of a glacier between the ice and the valley walls. A medial moraine is found at the valley centre, where two glaciers or lateral moraines meet. A ground moraine forms along the bottom of a glacier. A terminal moraine occurs where the "snout" of a glacier has remained for a period.

Perhaps the most dramatic effect of the glaciation on this part of the North American continent was the creation of the Great Lakes themselves (Figure 1-14). Geologists believe that the great weight of the ice was sufficient to depress the bedrock — and when the ice moved, the erosion that occurred deepened the depression even further. When the ice began to melt (the end of the Pleistocene Epoch), large quantities of water were released. This water was unable to drain away down the St. Lawrence Valley to the ocean because the route was blocked by the still-unmelted northern portion of the glacier. As a result, the trapped water created the original Great Lakes, which were very large and deep. When the St. Lawrence Valley was finally free of ice, the waters of the lakes fell to their present levels, exposing expanses of former lake bottom as flat areas of sand and clay. Thus, the area south of the Canadian Shield known as Southern Ontario exists today as a peninsula whose boundaries

Figure 1–14: *Formation of the Great Lakes*

Geological Survey of Canada

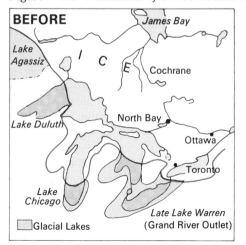

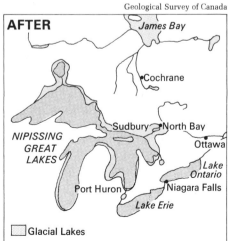

A large drumlin south of Campbellford, Ontario.

Geological Survey of Canada. Ottawa

are defined by the shorelines of Great Lakes. Within this peninsula, the landscape is not flat and monotonous as one might expect of a lowland but is in reality a complex mixture of morainic hills, old shorelines, and former lake beds.

East of the Frontenac Axis is the St. Lawrence Lowland section of the region. In the northwest of the St. Lawrence Valley, the sedimentary rocks fault against the Canadian Shield, while the southeastern boundary is formed by Logan's Line, a zone of *thrust faults* (Figure 1-8) which separate the lowlands from the Appalachian region. The floor of the St. Lawrence Valley consists of sediments deposited when a succession of seas existed in this area during the early Paleozoic Era (Fig. 7-1).

Mount Royal, St. Bruno, St. Hilaire, Rougemont, and Johnson are five of the Monteregian Hills that lie along a curved line to the east of Montreal. These hills are only a few square kilometres in area, but they rise to more than 300 m above sea level from the floor of the valley. Geologists believe that at some period between the Devonian and the Tertiary, masses of igneous rock were intruded through the sedimentary layers in the St. Lawrence Valley. The softer, less resistant rocks were subsequently eroded away, thus exposing the more resistant granite. These intrusions of granite now appear as a series of hills rising abruptly from the valley floor.

THE WESTERN PLAINS

The Western Plains of Canada is part of the Great Plains Region of North America that stretches from the Gulf of Mexico to the shores of the Arctic Ocean. For many people the very name Western Plains or The Prairies generates mental visions of a flat landscape with waving grasses extending to the horizon in every direction. The vision may contain an element of truth, but in reality the Western Plains contain a number of interesting and varied topographical features.

Like the other lowlands of Canada, the Western Plains region has been an area of relatively low elevation throughout most of the earth's history. This area was once covered by shallow seas where sediment accumulated in a shallow depression and hardened into layers of rock during the Paleozoic and Mesozoic Eras. In more recent geologic time, glaciers from the Western Cordillera and the Canadian Shield have swept across the surface of the Western Plains gouging and moulding the landscape. When the ice melted at the end of last Ice Age, the piles of debris which had been pushed remained as hills, while the depressions or hollows were filled with melt water.

The Prairies actually rise from east to west in a gentle slope. The first prairie level, *the Manitoba Lowland*, is actually the bottom of the ancient glacial lake, Agassiz, which once covered an area larger than all of the five Great Lakes. This natural basin is now occupied by Lakes Winnipeg, Winnipegosis, and Manitoba, plus numerous smaller ones. The interlake areas are overlain by stony soils and sand, the remains of the glacier which once flowed across the area. Many of the shallow lakes are drying up and as a result creating a large plain. The southern part of this plain is drained by the Red River which flows north into Lake Winnipeg. The Red, Assiniboine, and Rat Rivers often cause serious spring floods. Soils here have developed from the accumulation of silt and clay deposits on the bed of the old lake, and are dark and rich (Figure 1-15).

Proceeding west from the Manitoba Lowland, a range of hills approximately 100 m high marks the boundary between the first and second prairie levels. This is a narrow region and is not continuous. Beyond this

Figure 1–15: Cross-Section of the Prairies

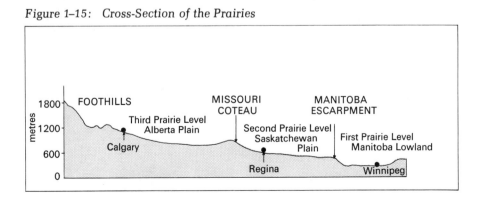

narrow boundary lies the *Saskatchewan Plain* or second prairie level. It is more extensive and climatically drier than the first. This area has gently rolling relief, consisting of plains covered with clay among ground moraine. At the western side of the Saskatchewan Plain, the *Missouri Coteau* marks the eastern edge of the third prairie level. The Missouri Coteau cuts diagonally across southern Saskatchewan and runs parallel to two morainic belts, but the Missouri Coteau is not as high or marked as the Manitoba Escarpment.

The *Alberta Plain* is the third level, a plateau rising from 800 to 1200 m at the foothills of the Rockies. In the south, visible from the Trans-Canada Highway, a number of upland areas rise about 450 m above the surrounding plain. These uplands are the Cypress Hills, Wood Mountain, and the Milk River Ridge. They are thought to be remnants of an earlier erosion surface, as are the Watt and Caribou Mountains in northern Alberta. The rest of the Alberta Plain is characterized by greater erosion and slope development than are found in the other two areas. In the valleys of the Red Deer, Milk, Frenchman, and Big Muddy Rivers the less resistant river beds have undergone extreme erosion by wind and water. In this area, the badland area of central Alberta, are found the curiously shaped features known as *hoodoos*.

View of the eroded landscape of Southern Alberta, part of the Western Prairies.

National Film Board of Canada

To the west of the third prairie level are the foothills, the prelude to the spectacular glacial peaks of the Rocky Mountains.

THE CANADIAN ARCHIPELAGO

The Canadian Archipelago is the group of islands north of the Arctic Circle. This remote region contains masses of rugged Precambrian crystalline rock. Its surface is topped with Paleozoic sedimentary strata formed roughly from 600 million to 400 million years ago. However, these rocks today show the effects of the great mountain-building forces that move the earth's crust. The stresses and strains of the movements of the earth's crust have broken the crust along two intersecting sets of parallel joints and faults. Now these land areas stand out as a series of islands arranged in rows; these islands are separated by down-faulted sections that have become sounds, straits, channels, and gulfs.

The southern islands close to the mainland are flat, treeless lowlands. To the north of these lowlands are the mountainous islands of the Innuitian Region. This area consists of sedimentary rocks which have been subjected to several periods of folding. The folds appear today to be highest on the east but slope down to the west. This range of fold mountains extends for a distance of 1280 km from the southwest to the northeast across the Queen Elizabeth Islands to Ellesmere Island.

THE APPALACHIAN REGION

The Appalachian Region consists of the Atlantic provinces and the portion of the province of Quebec that lies to the east of Logan's Line. The landscape is an attractive mixture of old, worn mountains and lowlands that have been scraped by glaciers and carved by the sea or by meandering rivers. The bedrock of this region is a complex mosaic of igneous, sedimentary, and metamorphic rocks that have resulted from a long history of geological activity.

At the end of the Ordivician period about 440 million years ago, a series of mountains were folded up along a northeast-southwest line. Then, about 350 million years ago during the Devonian period, these folds underwent a re-elevation. This physical region takes its name from the great Appalachian Orogeny or mountain-building period that crumpled the earth's crust from Alabama to Newfoundland. This great disturbance occurred at the end of the Paleozoic era about 300 million years ago and produced a series of fold mountain ranges 600 km wide and 2400 km long. The shape of the Gaspé Peninsula, the elongated

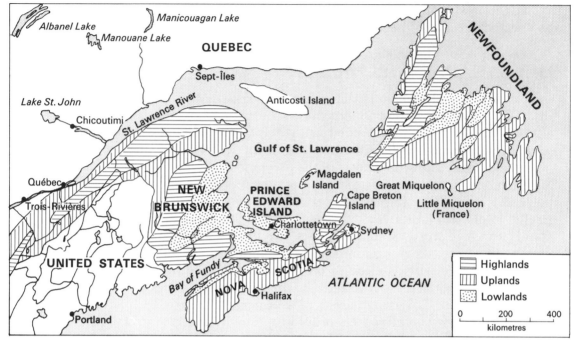

Figure 1–16: *Physiographic Regions of the Atlantic Provinces (Appalachian Region)*

outline of Nova Scotia, the direction of the Long Range of Newfoundland, and the intervening depressions or bays all reflect the influence of the original folds (Figure 1-16).

THE WESTERN CORDILLERA

The Western Cordillera is Canada's portion of the "Ring of Fire," that zone of active volcanoes and earthquakes that surrounds the Pacific Ocean. The region is composed of two parallel mountain systems, the *Rockies* on the east and the *Pacific Mountain System* on the west, separated by a system of *intermontane plateaus*. The Western Cordillera contains some of Canada's most spectacular landscapes of high mountains, with snow-capped peaks, slopes covered by gigantic coniferous trees towering over glacial valleys. Nearly 1500 km² of the region has an elevation above 3000 m with some individual peaks even higher. At 6045 m, Mount Logan in the St. Elias Range is the highest peak.

The Rockies are composed of deep layers of limestone deposited during the Precambrian and early Paleozoic Eras. During the Mesozoic era, these sedimentary layers were raised and thrust eastward in many places. The result is that the Rockies form a belt 80 to 130 km wide of roughly parallel ranges separated by long north-south valleys. The area has been greatly eroded by glaciers that have carved the peaks to produce *horns*, arm-chair shaped depressions called *cirques*, steep-walled *U-shaped valleys*, *hanging valleys*, and *waterfalls*.

The Rockies are separated from the Purcell, Selkirk, and Columbia Ranges to the west by a great depression known as the *Rocky Mountain Trench*. Rainwater and the melting snows of the mountains collect in this huge valley to form the headwaters of the great rivers of this region — the Kootenay, Columbia, Fraser, and Peace Rivers.

A series of dissected plateaus and scattered mountain ranges, known collectively as The Interior Plateau, separate the Rockies from the Coast Mountains. These interior plateaus generally have a steeper mountain-ous section on their eastern side composed of very old rocks, while the western side is a plateau of younger sediments and lava flows. From the boundary between the U.S.A. and Canada where they are only 80 km wide, they stretch northward to the Arctic where they attain an average width of 320 km.

The southernmost plateau, the Fraser (elevation 1800 m), slopes down to the 1000 m high Netchako plateau. These plateaus have been

Figure 1–17: Features Produced by Alpine Glaciation

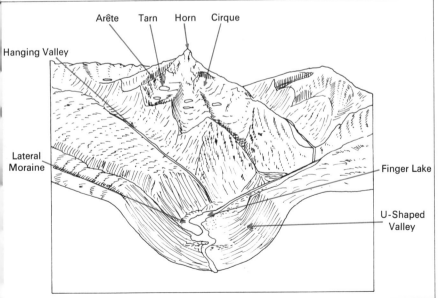

A hanging valley is a tributary valley, normally high above the main valley. Commonly found in a glaciated region, a hanging valley results from the deepening of the main valley by a glacier. A cirque is an armchair-shaped hollow resulting from glacial erosion usually on the upper sides of a valley. An arete is a steep and jagged ridge which forms when cirques erode back to back. A horn results when several adjacent cirques erode into the same mountain. A tarn is a lake occupying the floor of a cirque.

The Physical Environment. S. Inch and W. G. Stone. p. 129. McGraw-Hill Ryerson, 1972

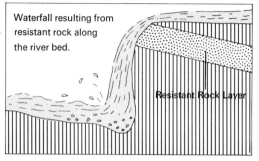

Figure 1–18: *Waterfall*

Waterfalls occur where a river's course is interrupted by an abrupt and steep drop, caused by either an outcrop of resistant rock across a river's course (left) or faulting (right).

deeply eroded and dissected by the Fraser and Thompson Rivers.

The central section of the Interior Plateau is the Stikine Plateau. To the north lies the Yukon Plateau, the largest of the plateaus. Rivers have carved valleys nearly 800 m deep into the surface of this generally rolling plateau. It has several other distinctive features. Great valley glaciers from the high mountains of the St. Elias and Coast Ranges have extended down to this plateau. They have created a series of elongated valleys that are blocked at their lower ends by the terminal moraines. As a result, these valleys have become flooded to create long narrow lakes known as finger lakes.

The Pacific Mountain system that forms the west coast of Canada and the Alaskan Panhandle consists of the Cascade, Coast, and St. Elias Ranges on the mainland and the offshore submerged ranges of the Queen Charlotte Islands and Vancouver Island. Geologically this area is one of great complexity: it consists of rocks ranging in "age" from 600 million years to geologically very recent. The sedimentary and volcanic rocks have experienced repeated periods of folding and faulting as the region was uplifted and then eroded. However, during the Tertiary period about 35 million years ago, massive molten material covered the area. These great upwellings of molten material have now cooled and solidified into great masses of granitic rock known as *batholiths* (Figure 1-19).

At the southern end of the Pacific Mountain System, the Cascade Mountains extend into Canada from the United States on the eastern side of the lower Fraser Valley. This region of rugged mountains, 160 km wide, has mountain peaks towering above 2600 m and covered with active alpine glaciers. Rising abruptly from the sea are the mountains of the Coast Range that extend northward for 1600 km. This mountain

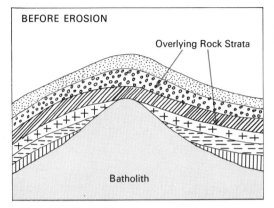

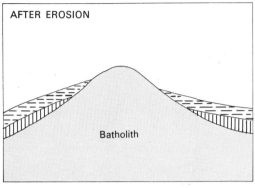

Figure 1–19: Batholith

range, with its 2100 to 4000 m high saw-toothed ridges, collect the moisture from the Westerly Winds blowing in from the Pacific to "feed" the great alpine glaciers and icefields. These glaciers have gouged their way down to the sea and have produced the deep fjords characteristic of the west coast. In the northern regions and in the St. Elias Range, the glaciers flow right down to the sea, where they break off and drift away as icebergs.

Offshore, the Queen Charlotte Islands are the peaks of a submerged range. These islands consist of both sedimentary and volcanic block-like ranges that stand 900 m above the sea. This area receives the heavy precipitation which nourishes the magnificent stands of gigantic trees such as the Douglas fir that attain heights above 100 m. Vancouver Island to the south is also covered with these dense forests, but its elevation is higher, its mountains reaching heights of 2100 m.

WEATHER AND CLIMATE: BRIEF INTRODUCTION

Canada, like all the other countries on the earth, is the floor of a great ocean of air known as the *atmosphere*. The characteristics and motions of the atmosphere have a great influence on both weather and climate, and consequently on the land and peoples. *Weather* refers to the state of the atmosphere over a short period of time — a day, for example. The chief elements of weather are temperature, pressure, wind, humidity, cloud, precipitation, and sunshine. Because the state of the atmosphere is changeable and varies from one place to another, it is necessary to measure and record the weather elements of a given place in order to understand the prevailing weather conditions at that place during a specific period of time. *Climate* is defined as the average weather of a place by calculating weather records over at least a 30-year period.

In Canada, a branch of the federal government known as the Atmospheric Environmental Service has the responsibility for observing, measuring, recording, and analyzing the activities of the atmosphere. A series of recording weather stations are spread throughout the country to enable meteorologists and climatologists to determine the variations in weather and climate across Canada, and to make daily weather forecasts.

The temperature of the air is constantly changing; to measure temperature, meteorologists use special instruments such as the *maximum and minimum thermometers*. The maximum and minimum thermometers are useful not only for recording the highest and lowest temperatures over a 24 h time period, but also for finding out the *mean* or *average daily temperature*. The mean daily temperature is obtained by adding the maximum and minimum temperatures experienced within a 24 h time period, then dividing the total by two. Likewise, the *mean monthly temperature* can be obtained by adding the mean daily temperatures of each day of the month, and then dividing the total by the number of days

Figure 1–20:   Mean Daily Temperature, January (°C)

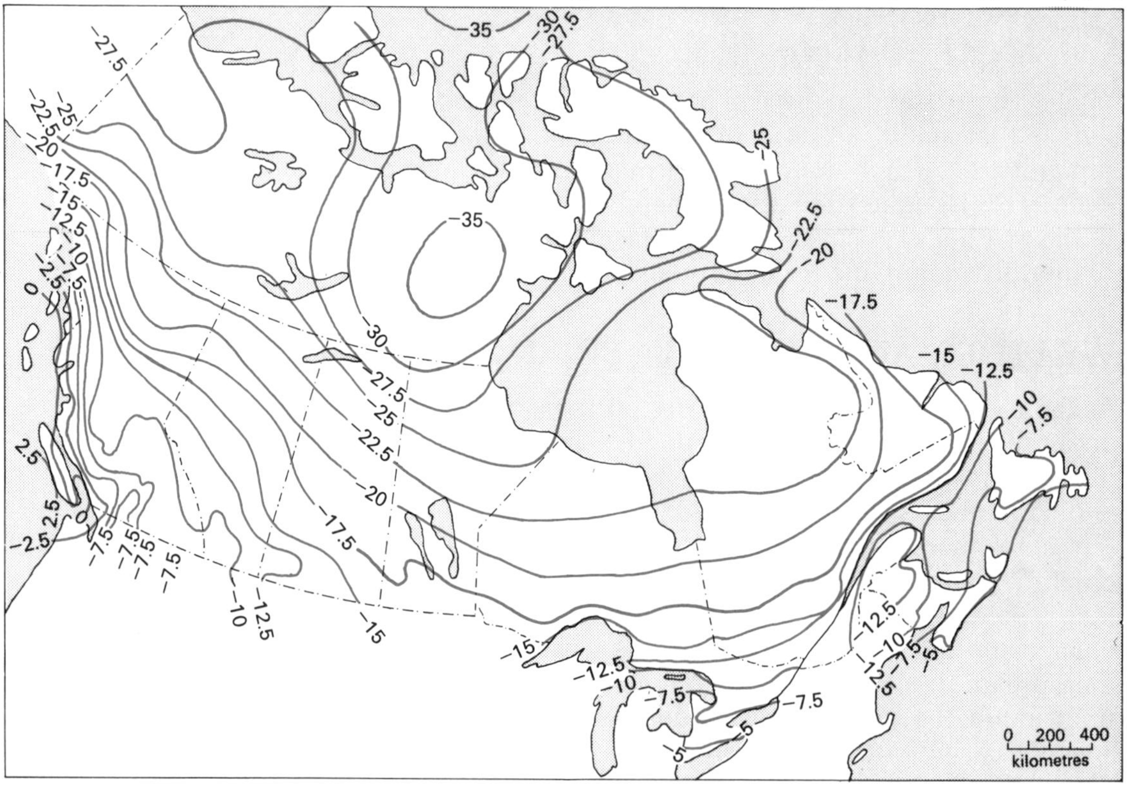

in that month. Similarly, the *mean annual temperature* is calculated by dividing the total of the mean monthly temperatures by 12. On weather maps, temperatures are shown by *isotherms* — lines joining all places with the same temperature (Figures 1-20 and 1-21).

Besides temperature, other elements of the weather and climate are recorded. Various forms of precipitation such as rain, snow, sleet, hail, and fog, associated cloud-types, wind speed and direction, and number of hours of sunshine are also important in analyzing and understanding climate.

Years of careful observation of the temperature and winds of North America have shown that a number of areas known as *source regions* have naturally ideal conditions over which air masses develop distinctive characteristics. *An air mass is defined as a body of air with uniform temperature and moisture characteristics*. Air masses can be grouped according to their origin, characteristics, and distribution. Two types of air masses may be distinguished by temperature — *polar* and *tropical*.

Figure 1–21: *Mean Daily Temperature, July (°C)*

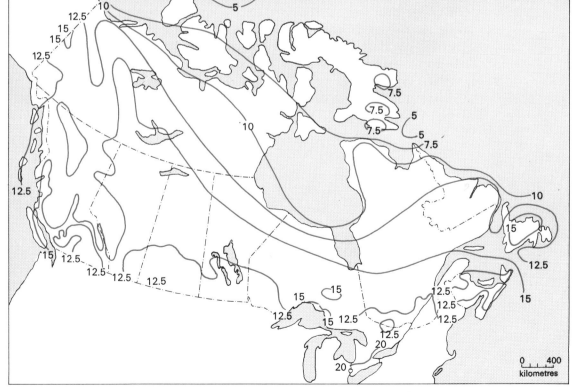

Air masses can be classified by moisture into *maritime* (those that develop over water bodies) and *continental* (those that develop over the interiors of land masses) air masses. The distribution of air masses over the North American continent is shown in Figure 1-22.

The strongly contrasting air masses of North America flow out from their sources in the Arctic and in the tropical latitudes, then collide over the central part of the continent in the westerly-wind belt with dramatic results, producing a *cyclone*. The repeated collisions of these highly different air masses and the resultant development of cyclones, with their low-pressure systems and fronts (warm and cold), dominate the weather pattern of North America.

Cyclones may be located on a weather map by the low-pressure cell at their centre. These low-pressure cells are driven eastward across the continent by the prevailing Westerly Winds. The surface of contact between the tropical and polar air masses is called a *front*. (A cyclone has two fronts: a warm front and a cold front.) Along the edge of the advancing cold air mass known as a *cold front*, warm air is forced upward more violently. As this warm air rises, it expands. This expansion causes the air to cool and in turn brings about the condensation of the water vapour into water droplets in the air. The water vapour condenses on dust particles present in the air; these dust particles are hygroscopic (they can retain water); they act as *condensation nuclei* for the developing raindrops. Once condensation has occurred, the water in the air mass becomes visible as clouds. The tiny droplets of water then coalesce to form a raindrop which eventually falls to the ground under the influence of the force of gravity. Sometimes, the updraughts of air along the cold

Figure 1–22: Air Masses over North America

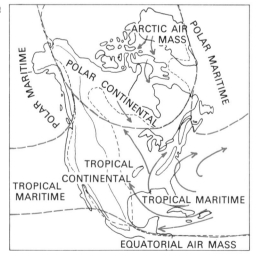

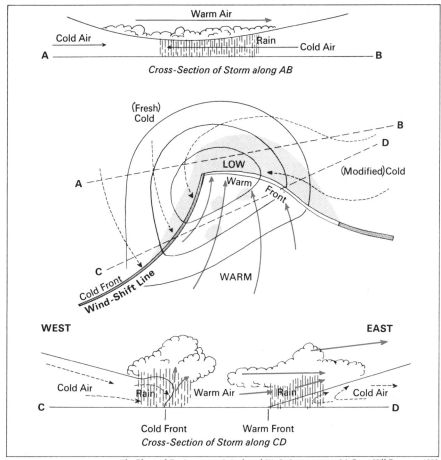

Warm Air

Cold Air | Rain | Cold Air

A ———————————————————————————————— B

Cross-Section of Storm along AB

(Fresh) Cold

B

D

LOW

Warm

A

(Modified) Cold

Front

C

Cold Front
Wind-Shift Line

WARM

WEST

EAST

Cold Air

Rain | Warm Air | Rain | Cold Air

C ———————————————————————————————— D

Cold Front | Warm Front

Cross-Section of Storm along CD

The Physical Environment, S. Inch and W. G. Stone, p. 261. McGraw-Hill Ryerson, 1972

Figure 1–23: A Mid-Latitude Cyclone

front may be extremely vigorous and the water droplet may be hurled upwards to the upper parts of the cloud, cold enough to freeze it into a hailstone. The repeated strong upthrusts of the hailstone within the cloud can cause additional layers of ice to form around it. When it is heavy enough, it falls to the ground as hail. During the summer especially, these cyclonic disturbances are characterized by flashes of lightning and great rumblings of thunder. The storm may be violent, but its area is restricted to the zone of the cold front.

The *warm front* also produces precipitation, but it is distributed over a wider area and is much less violent. The warm air mass glides over the cold air mass as though the cold air was a long ramp. The warm air rises, expands, cools, then produces clouds and eventually rain. These conditions prevail when the sky is overcast for several hours (Figure 1-23).

Mountains can cause precipitation too. When moist air is forced to ascend a mountain, the slope effect is similar to that which takes place along a front. The moist air onshore is forced to rise and in rising it expands and cools. Condensation takes place when the air is sufficiently cooled; clouds form, usually followed by precipitation on the windward slope of the mountains. Precipitation produced in this manner is known as *orographic precipitation* (Figure 1-24).

The third type of precipitation is known as *convectional precipitation* (Figure 1-25). When the land is heated by the sun's rays, the air immediately above the warm land is heated up too. The warm air expands and rises as vertical convectional air currents. In rising, the warm air cools, condensation takes place, creating masses of cloud that release convectional precipitation. This type of precipitation is common in the summer in the interiors of large continental land masses such as in the Canadian Prairies. Southern Ontario also receives convectional rainfall, especially in the hot summer afternoons.

Precipitation is recorded in millimetres in Canada; the annual precipitation across the country is illustrated in Figure 1-26.

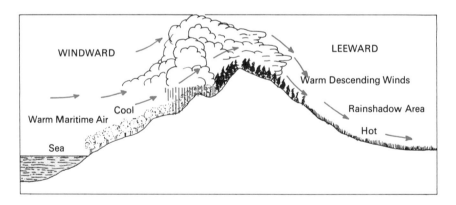

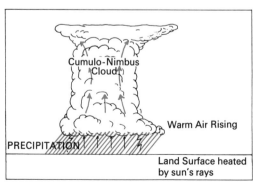

Figure 1–24:   Orographic
Precipitation (above)

Figure 1–25:   Convectional
Precipitation (left)

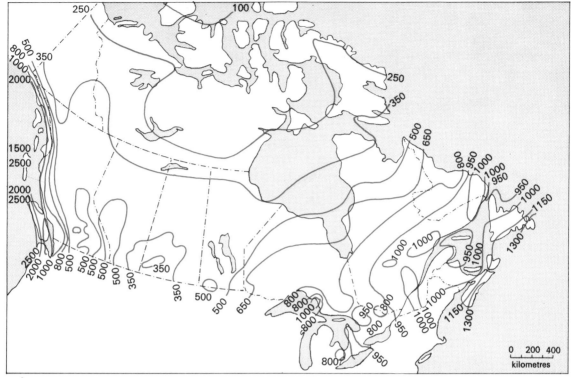

Figure 1–26: Mean Annual Total Precipitation (mm)

FACTORS AFFECTING CLIMATE

The climate at any place is controlled or regulated by a number of factors: latitude, elevation, distance from large bodies of water, prevailing winds, ocean currents, and aspect of land.

LATITUDE Temperature generally decreases from the equator towards the high latitudes because the sun's rays fall on the earth's surface more obliquely the higher the latitude. At the equator, the sun's rays strike the earth's surface at a right angle, hence the more intense heating at the equator than at the higher latitudes (Figure 1-27).

ELEVATION Temperature decreases with elevation at the rate of about 6.5°C/1000 m. This rate of cooling is known as the *normal lapse rate*. Temperature decreases with increasing elevation because the earth's atmosphere is heated mainly by long-wave terrestrial radiation (radiation from the earth's surface). The radiation from the sun that passes through

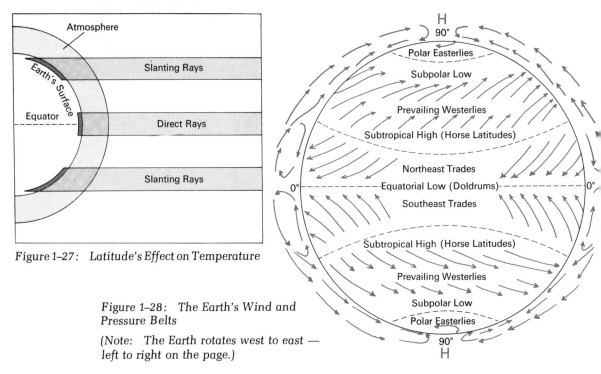

Figure 1–27:   Latitude's Effect on Temperature

Figure 1–28:   The Earth's Wind and Pressure Belts

(Note: The Earth rotates west to east — left to right on the page.)

the atmosphere and strikes the earth's surface is short wave. Also, the air near the earth's surface is denser and contains more water vapour and dust particles that are able to absorb more effectively the heat released by the earth than the thinner, purer air higher up.

DISTANCE FROM LARGE BODIES OF WATER   Land heats up and cools down much more rapidly than water because of their different physical properties. A water body not only absorbs the sun's heat more slowly, but it also retains the heat for a longer period than the land. Large bodies of water thus tend to lag behind the land in the rate of temperature change, especially between the seasons. Water bodies as a result represent a cooling influence in the spring and early summer and a warming influence in the late summer and fall. Large water surfaces thus have a moderating influence on the climate of the neighbouring land masses, preventing them from becoming too cold in the winter or too hot in the summer. By contrast, areas remote from the moderating influence of a water body tend to have extreme climates — hot summers and very cold winters.

PREVAILING WINDS   The horizontal movement of air over the earth's surface is very complex, but Figure 1-28 shows a simplified model of the general circulation of winds in the atmosphere. Winds are named by the direction from which they come. As the general circulation of the wind is induced by the effects of the sun's radiation on the earth, shifts are experienced in the global wind pattern following the apparent movement of the sun north and south of the equator.

Another factor which has to be considered in a discussion of the global wind pattern is the *coriolis force* caused by the earth's rotation which deflects moving objects to their right in the Northern Hemisphere and to their left in the Southern Hemisphere.

OCEAN CURRENTS   Like the general circulation of winds, the pattern of surface currents in the ocean results from the uneven heating of the earth's surface (Figure 1-29). The warm currents originate in the equatorial areas and flow towards the poles — thus helping to carry the warmth of the tropics to the temperate and polar latitudes. The cold currents that originate in the polar latitudes flow towards the equator. These ocean currents give their characteristics to the adjacent land masses by influencing the winds that blow over them. A wind blowing over a warm ocean current will have its temperature raised, while a wind which blows over a cold current will have its temperature lowered. The effect of ocean

Figure 1–29: Ocean Currents

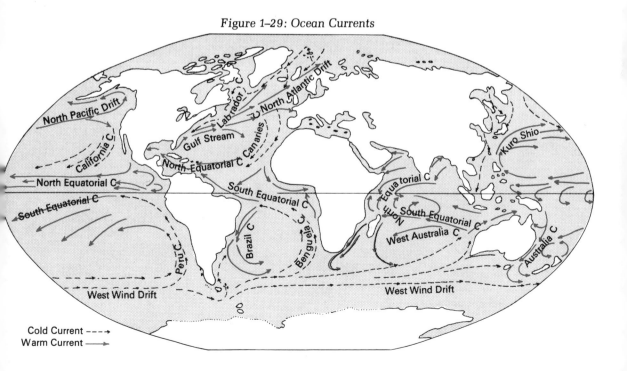

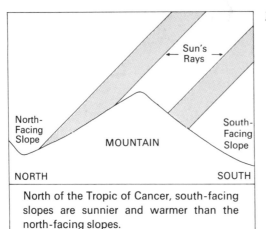

Figure 1–30: Aspect of the Land

North of the Tropic of Cancer, south-facing slopes are sunnier and warmer than the north-facing slopes.

currents on the temperatures of coastal areas is felt particularly when the winds are *onshore*; the effect is minimal when the winds are *offshore*.

ASPECT OF THE LAND   Aspect refers to the direction in which a mountain slope is facing. For example, in the Northern Hemisphere, slopes facing south will be warmer than the slopes facing north; conversely, in the Southern Hemisphere, the north-facing slopes will be warmer than the south-facing slopes (Figure 1-30).

CLIMATE REGIONS OF CANADA

THE WEST COAST CLIMATE REGION

This westernmost climate region of Canada is dominated by the marine influences of the Pacific Ocean. The hythergraphs of Prince Rupert and Vancouver reveal a number of marked characteristics typical of this climate region (Figure 1-35). Temperatures are generally moderate: summer temperatures are warm and above-freezing temperatures are not uncommon during the winters. The seasonal variation is marked more by the rainfall than by the temperature. No month in the year is really dry, but in the summer the high-pressure system over the Pacific Ocean considerably reduces the amount of rain. In the winter, the Westerlies transport warm and moist air from over the warm current in the Pacific; they release this moisture as they ascend the slopes of the mountains. Cyclonic storms produced by the clash of cold Polar and the warmer Pacific air masses cause frontal rain. Additional cloud and rain are

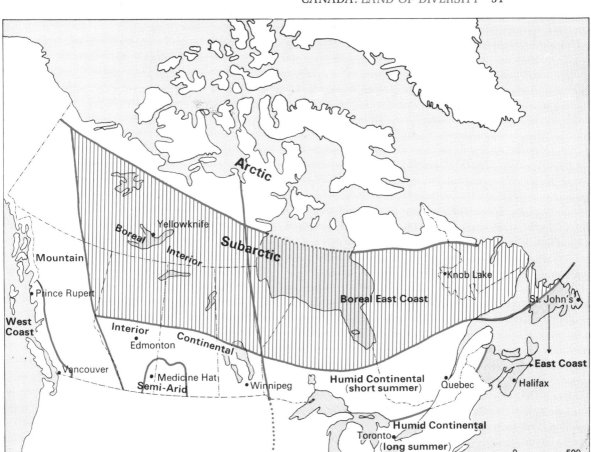

Figure 1–31: *Climate Regions of Canada*

produced when the moist air ascends the slopes of the mountains of the offshore islands and the Coast Range.

The long growing season and abundant rainfall (Figures 1-35 and 1-36) create ideal conditions for the growth of trees such as the Douglas fir, Sitka spruce, western hemlock, and western red cedar. Magnificent specimens of Douglas fir have been known to survive over 1000 years and reach heights of over 100 m. The western red cedars with their light, straight-grained wood provided the raw material for the totem poles, lodges, and ocean-going canoes of the native peoples of the Pacific coast. Further north along the coast the Sitka spruce is more abundant. There are only a limited number of deciduous trees like the leaf maple, black cottonwood, red alder, and Garry oak. One unusual type of tree that

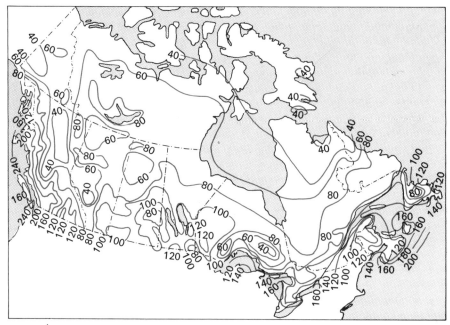

Figure 1–32:   Mean Annual Frost-Free Period (days)

survives here is the arbutus, Canada's only broad-leafed evergreen: it maintains its green leaves for more than one season.

THE MOUNTAIN CLIMATE REGION

The classification of mountain climate does not represent one single homogeneous type of climate. Mountain climates have a number of basic characteristics. The temperature cools with elevation; thus, the mountain peaks may have an Arctic type of climate, the slopes may have Subarctic, while an even warmer type of climate may exist in the sheltered valleys (Figure 1-33).

In the higher elevations the lower temperatures create entirely new environments which are reflected in the tree growth. For example, the huge western red cedars of the coastal areas survive in this harsher environment as stunted trees or shrubs. The most characteristic species of the mountainous uplands are the Englemann spruce, Alpine fir, and the Lodgepole pine.

The second characteristic of mountain climates is that they tend to be wet on the windward side and dry on the leeward. As the moisture-laden winds from over the ocean ascend the windward slopes of the mountain

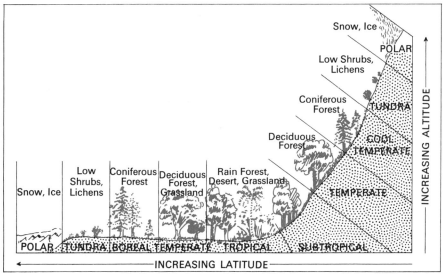

The Physical Environment, S. Inch and W. G. Stone, p. 225. McGraw-Hill Ryerson, 1972

Figure 1–33: *Climate and Vegetation Zones Along a Mountain Slope*

range they deposit their moisture, but when they descend the leeward slopes they are dry and are warmed by compression. On these dry leeward slopes are found the Montane Forests. The smaller Interior Douglas fir, Ponderosa pine, Lodgepole pine, Englemann Spruce, Alpine fir are among the common conifers; some deciduous species also grow here, such as the trembling aspen and white birch. In the very arid areas are found bunch grasses typical of the Prairies.

THE ARCTIC CLIMATE REGION

Figure 1-31 shows that most of Canada can be classified as Arctic or Subarctic. In both these climatic types, the dominant characteristic is obviously the coldness. Arctic and Subarctic are distinguished by the duration and intensity of the cold. The hythergraph of Resolute shows that it has a mean annual temperature of −16.4°C, compared to Toronto's 8.3°C or Vancouver's 10.5°C (Figures 1-35, 1-37, 1-45). The high latitude of Resolute means that the incoming solar radiation is so indirect that it cannot replace the energy radiated back into space. The Arctic areas depend on the global circulation of the atmosphere to transport energy from the warmer tropical latitudes. Resolute is so cold that only three months — June, July, and August — have an average temperature above the freezing point. These summer months are notable for their long hours of sunlight. Winters are severe: the average temperature for December, January, February, and March is less than −30°C.

Have you noticed how different the hythergraph of Resolute is from those of Vancouver and Prince Rupert? Resolute's graph has a vertical pattern, indicating the sharp differences of the summer from the winter temperatures and the almost-non-existent spring and fall. The hythergraph is crowded in the extreme left hand side of the graph, indicating that all months have a low rainfall. Deserts are generally defined as regions with less than 250 mm of annual precipitation. Resolute has only 134 mm. Just because this is a cold desert it does not mean that Arctic precipitation can be ignored. Most of the precipitation comes in the form of snow, which is ten times as deep as an equivalent amount of rain. Fog and blinding snowstorms, known as whiteouts, make visibility extremely poor in the winter.

Vegetation is scarce in the Arctic region because of the low precipitation and the presence of permafrost. The best-known plant in the Arctic region is the lichen; however, a variety of flowers bloom during the short-lived summers.

Lichens on rocks and low flowering plants at Pond Inlet, Northwest Territories, show Arctic vegetation at its most luxuriant development.

National Museums of Canada. Ottawa. Canada

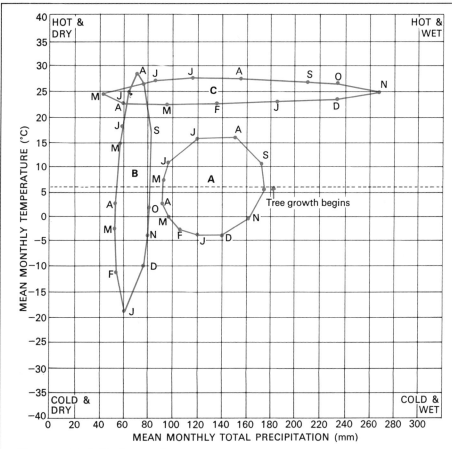

Figure 1–34: A Hythergraph

The hythergraph is a simple graph used for illustrating the characteristics of a climate. The mean monthly temperature (°C) is indicated along the left hand side; the mean monthly precipitation (mm) is indicated along the base. To plot the climate of a place, work one month at a time by finding the point where the temperature and precipitation intersect. Mark this point and identify it with the name of the month. Repeat this process for each of the months, then join the dots in proper sequence to form a twelve-sided figure.

The *location* of this figure on the graph reveals the climatic characteristics of the place that has been plotted. For example, Station A occupies a central location midway between the extremes of temperature and precipitation. The most extreme conditions are indicated in the four corners.

The *shape* of the twelve-sided figure is also important. For example, Station C experiences warm temperatures all year, but the climate is distinguished by a dry season and a wet season. Station B is very hot in summer and very cold in winter showing the typical characteristics of a continental climate. Station A has four distinct seasons, but none of them is very extreme.

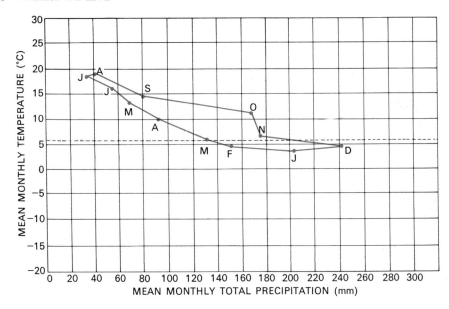

Figure 1–35: Hythergraph for Vancouver
Average temperature: 10.5°C; Total precipitation: 1443 mm

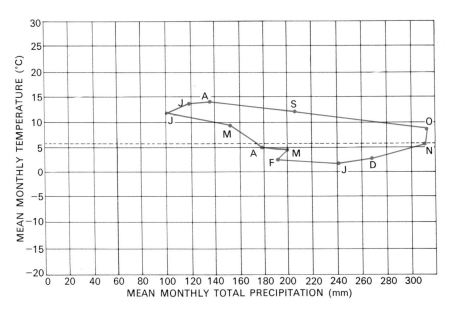

Figure 1–36: Hythergraph for Prince Rupert
Average temperature: 7.7°C; Total precipitation: 2387mm

THE SUBARCTIC CLIMATE REGION

The Subarctic climate is found in a great belt across Canada south of the Arctic Circle. The winters are as severe as the Arctic region, but the monthly average temperatures are not so low. The hythergraphs of Yellowknife in the west and Knob Lake in the east both show that the five months from May to September have an average temperature above freezing (Figures 1-38 and 1-39). Although the July averages are low,

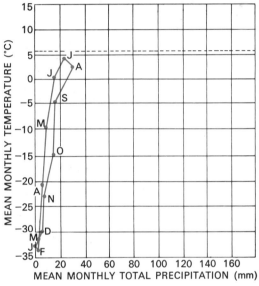

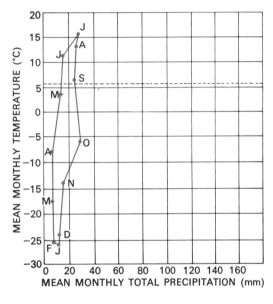

Figure 1–37: Hythergraph for Resolute (above left)
Average temperature: −16.4 °C; Total precipitation: 134 mm

Figure 1–38: Hythergraph for Yellowknife (above right)
Average Temperature: −5.3 °C; Total precipitation: 214 mm

Figure 1–39: Hythergraph for Knob Lake (left)
Average temperature: −4.5 °C; Total precipitation: 699 mm

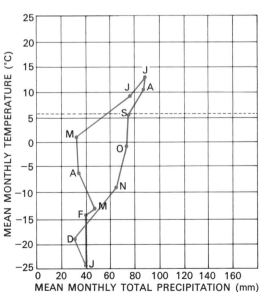

individual days during the summer can, however, become uncomfortably hot. This marked annual range between summer heat and winter cold is a typical characteristic of the Subarctic region.

A comparison of the two hythergraphs reveals that Yellowknife has more of a continental climate than Knob Lake: Yellowknife has hotter summers and colder winters. Yellowknife, with only 214 mm of annual precipitation, is much more arid because of its interior location, far removed from the moderating influence of the sea, and because of the colder air temperatures which decrease the amount of water vapour in the air. Hudson Bay tends to modify the climate of the areas to the east of it. The hythergraph of Knob Lake shows that its temperatures are not so extreme and that it has 699 mm of precipitation annually.

This Subarctic climate supports the great forest of coniferous trees known as the Boreal forest which extends right across the country. In the North this forest meets the tundra at the treeline where the stunted trees fight for survival. Farther south, the climate is warmer and the stands of black and white spruce, jack pine, balsam fir, and tamarack are thicker, but their rate of growth is slow because of the cool temperatures and short growing season.

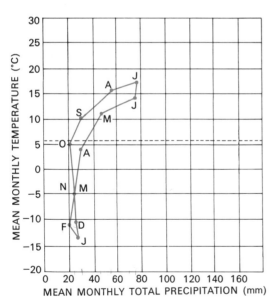

Figure 1–40: Hythergraph for Edmonton

Average temperature: 2.7 °C;
Total precipitation: 448 mm

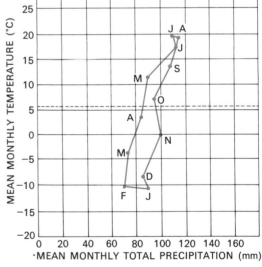

Figure 1–41: Hythergraph for Quebec City

Average temperature: 4.7 °C;
Total precipitation: 1136 mm

THE CONTINENTAL CLIMATE REGION

The Continental climate region lies south of the Subarctic region and stretches across the country from the Rockies to the Atlantic. Although this region seemingly extends over the southern half of the country, the climatic characteristics are not really temperate. The hythergraphs of Edmonton in the West and Quebec City in the East reveal the strong contrasts between the cold winters and the warm summers experienced at these two stations (Figures 1-40 and 1-41). The continental climatic pattern of distinct summer and winter seasons with short transitional spring and fall seasons resembles the pattern of the Subarctic climate. However, temperatures in the Continental type of climate are considerably warmer because of the more southerly location. Both Edmonton and Quebec City have 7 months when the temperature averages above freezing.

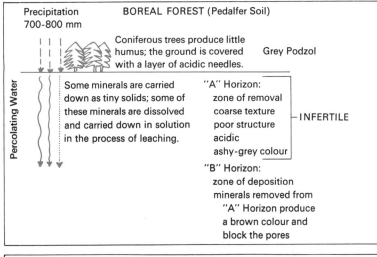

Figure 1–42:
Boreal Forest Soil

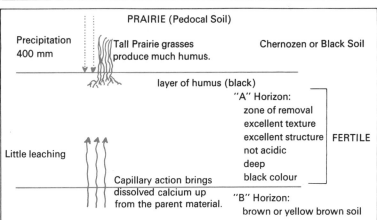

Figure 1–43:
Prairie Soil

The Continental climate region is the scene over which the great battles between the cold Polar air masses and the warm tropical air masses from the Gulf of Mexico take place. Cyclonic storms with their frontal precipitation are driven across the country under the influence of the Westerlies. As in the Subarctic climate region, the western half of the region is more continental in character. Quebec City, in the lee of the Great Lakes, has more moderate temperatures and more than twice as much precipitation.

The longer growing season and warmer summer temperatures of the Continental climate stimulate the growth of the natural vegetation, which consists of trees and tall grasses. In the West where the rainfall is not sufficient to support dense tree growth, trees grow either along the river banks or in isolated areas which receive more than 500 mm of annual precipitation. In the interior portion of the Continental climate area are found the original natural vegetation of tall grasses known as *prairie* (Figure 1-43). In the more humid eastern section, the natural vegetation consists of mixed forest. Here the coniferous trees of the Boreal forest grow in competition with the deciduous species of trees such as the birch, poplar, maples, and elms (Figure 1-42).

THE SEMI-ARID CLIMATE REGION

Compare the hythergraph of Medicine Hat (Figure 1-44) with that of Edmonton (Figure 1-40). You will notice that their temperatures are not very different. The aridity of the area around Medicine Hat gives it its distinctive quality. The aridity is a result of its interior, continental location. Fortunately, much of the rainfall occurs during the early part of the growing season to enable the seeds to germinate and the plant roots to develop. As might be expected, the height of the prairie grasses in the area decreases with lower rainfall.

THE HUMID CONTINENTAL (LONG SUMMER) CLIMATE REGION

This type of climate is restricted to the peninsula of southern Ontario, where the Great Lakes exert a considerable moderating influence. In addition, this most southerly of the climate regions in Canada has the advantage of receiving relatively more direct radiation from the sun. The region is often hot and humid during the summer, cold during the winter. However, the area receives more hours of sunshine than any other part of Canada. The hythergraph of Toronto (Figure 1-45) shows that the distinctive characteristic of this region is that, during eight months of the year,

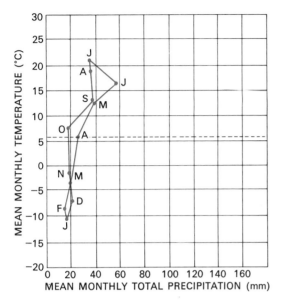

Figure 1–44: Hythergraph for Medicine Hat

Average temperature: 5.7°C;
Total precipitation: 344 mm

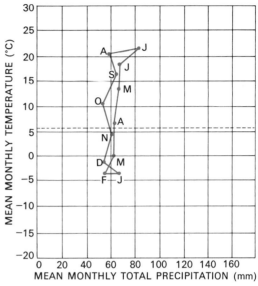

Figure 1–45: Hythergraph for Toronto

Average temperature: 8.3°C;
Total precipitation: 785 mm

the mean monthly temperatures are above freezing. The cyclonic storms that move across the region in a constant succession recharge their clouds with moisture and release this moisture as they move down the St. Lawrence Valley to the east. In the summer, additional rain is received from the convectional thunderstorms.

Originally this region was covered in stands of deciduous forest — maple, oak, elm, beech, basswood, hickory, and walnut. Today very little of this original forest remains, for the trees have been removed to make way for agriculture and cities. The summer heat enables this area to grow crops, such as tobacco and corn, that cannot be grown elsewhere. The mild winters of the Niagara peninsula along the shores of Lake Ontario have proven to be suitable for the production of grapes, peaches, and other tender fruits.

THE EAST COAST CLIMATE REGION

Although the East Coast climate region is located at the same latitude as the Humid Continental region, their climatic characteristics differ. Both regions are influenced by the cyclonic storms which move from west to east across Central Canada, down the St. Lawrence Valley, and over the Maritimes to Newfoundland. On the east coast these disturbances have

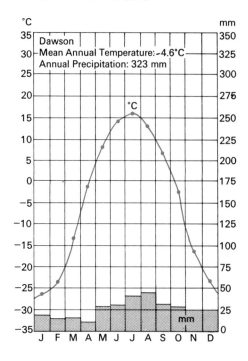

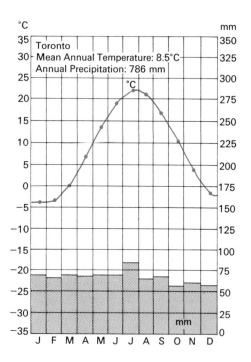

Figure 1–46: Climographs

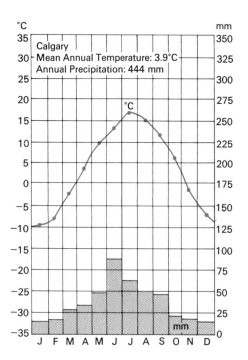

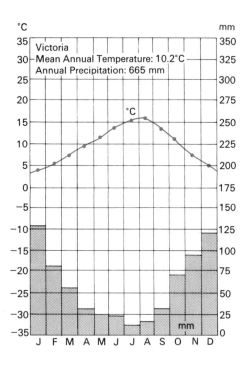

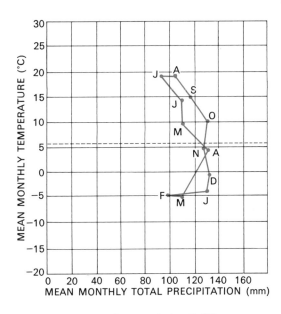

Figure 1–47: *Hythergraph for Halifax*

Average temperature: 7°C;
Total precipitation: 1378 mm

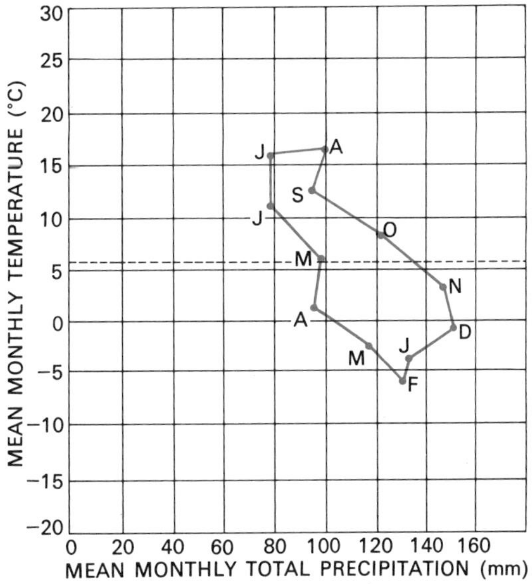

Figure 1–48: *Hythergraph for St. John's*

Average temperature: 5°C;
Total precipitation: 1348 mm

their moisture replenished by the warming influence of the Gulf Stream. The hythergraphs of Halifax and St. John's (Figures 1-47 and 1-48) indicate the humid climate. The nearness to the moderating influence of the ocean ensures that the summers are not too hot or the winters too extreme for their latitude. However, the ocean is responsible for the heavy fogs that may blanket the area for many days each year. Fog occurs over the area where the cold Labrador current meets the warm Gulf Stream.

The Acadian forest so characteristic of the East Coast region consists of red and white spruce, red and white pine, balsam fir, and hemlock as well as deciduous species including sugar maple, yellow birch, and beech.

QUESTIONS

Physical Diversity

1. Describe, using Canadian examples, the three ways mountains are formed.

2. Where are the oldest rocks in Canada located? How old are they? How did they originate? De-

scribe the surface topography of these rocks as they appear today.

3. Explain the following terms:
   igneous rock
   sedimentary rock
   metamorphic rock

peneplanation
folding
faulting
permafrost
batholith

4. Describe the different ways in which glaciers have shaped the landscape of Canada.

Climate

5. Define:
   mean monthly temperature
   mean annual temperature
   air mass
   cold front
   warm front

6. With the aid of fully labelled diagrams, explain the three ways precipitation is caused.

7. Discuss the six factors that control the climate.

8. Why is it necessary to have many years of recorded weather data before it is possible to generalize about the weather of a place?

9. Examine the four climographs in Figure 1-46 and answer the following questions:
   (i) Note the characteristics of the temperature and precipitation at each station.
   (ii) To which climate region do each of the stations belong? Account for the different temperatures and precipitations at each station. Use the factors of climate control in making your explanation.
   (iii) What type of natural vegetation would exist at each of the climate stations?
   (iv) At which station would you prefer to live? Why?
   (v) At which station would you not prefer to live? Why?

10. Examine the maps of the mean annual precipitation and length of the frost-free period across Canada (Figures 1-26 and 1-32). Do you expect agriculture to be extended farther northwards as the world food crisis develops? Discuss some of the problems that will have to be overcome.

RESEARCH

1. In which physiographic region of Canada do you live? Suggest ways in which the physical characteristics of your region have influenced the human activities.

2. Having learned about Canada's physical structure, discuss the major obstacles to development in Canada's North.

3. Why is only a small part of Canada suitable for agriculture?

4. Explain, in terms of its physical and climatic characteristics, why a vast country like Canada has such a small population.

5. Do more research on the major vegetation types in Canada and discuss the effects of climate and soil on the vegetation.

6. Do research on the various ways climate affects transportation during the year in Canada.

2 THE POLITICAL SEPARATION OF NORTH AMERICA

In the previous chapter, North America was described as a continent of mountains, volcanoes, lava flows, and earthquakes. The complex mountain chains of the spectacular Western Cordillera and the smaller Appalachians (both of which have a north-south alignment) are separated by a great interior lowland stretching from the Gulf of Mexico to the Arctic Ocean. Figure 2-1 shows the locations of the mountains, plateaus, highlands, interior lowlands and coastal plains of the North American continent. A common theme thus emerges: nearly all aspects of the physical geography of North America have a distinct north-south trend.

THE FIRST INHABITANTS

Superimposed on this relief was a variety of natural vegetation patterns that reflected the climatic variations within the continent. Into these different environments, so one theory says, the Mongoloid peoples migrated. The precise date of these migrations is unknown, but scholars estimate that sometime between 15 000 and 30 000 years ago the early Mongoloid hunters crossed from Asia into Alaska and, travelling down the eastern slope of the Western Cordillera, dispersed into the vastness of the continent.

Figure 2-2 shows the distribution of the various tribes and their basic foods around the time the first Europeans arrived. Across the northern part of the continent, the peoples spoke Athabaskan or Algonkian. They depended on the caribou to provide food, clothing, tools, and shelter in the inhospitable rock and muskeg (swamps) of the Canadian Shield. In the eastern woodlands, from the Great Lakes to Florida, the women with their digging sticks planted corn, beans, and squash while the men hunted and fished. To the west, where the rainfall was insufficient to

45

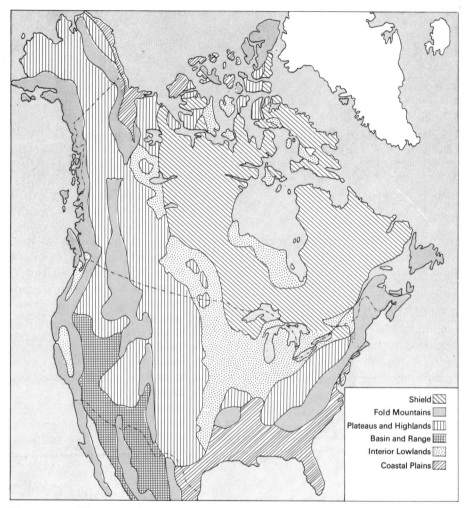

Figure 2–1: Physiographic Regions of North America

support forest growth, were the great plains, an endless ocean of waving grasses. In this environment of subsistence, the Indians followed the herds of buffalo for food and clothing. In the arid southwest corner of the continent, they lived on wild seeds and a variety of corn cultivated around their agricultural villages. However, in the rainy northwest, with its hospitable environment of huge trees and salmon-filled rivers, the people were relatively prosperous. Able to rely on the fish as a reliable staple in their diet, the men were free to spend many hours carving great cedar logs into decorative houses, chests, totem poles, or large ocean-going canoes.

These original peoples thus settled in tribal settlements that coincided with the natural north-south physical regions. However, a political map of North America today will show that the Europeans have divided the continent into two large nations with a border that disects the continent's north-south trends and its natural physical regions. How did this unusual political division take place?

Figure 2–2: Native Peoples of North America

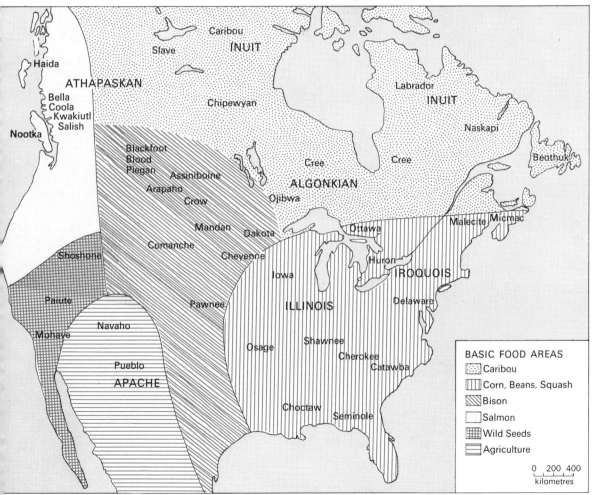

DEVELOPMENT OF THE PRESENT BOUNDARIES

Herjulf and Ericson, the Vikings, are considered the first Europeans to have discovered and explored the northeastern coastal area of North America. Recent research has shown the existence of three Norse settlements: one on the northern tip of Newfoundland, one in Labrador, and the other in the Ungava Peninsula of northern Quebec. The eventual failure of these colonies meant that, despite their heroism, the Norsemen played no part in determining the present political boundaries of North America.

The accidental rediscovery of North America by Christopher Columbus in 1492 started several centuries of further exploration by Europeans. Figure 2-3 provides a summary of the 500 years of conquests of and negotiations over the continent, from the Russians in the

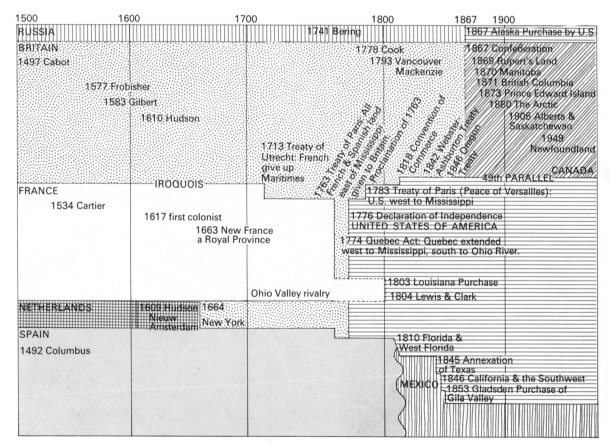

Figure 2–3: *Political Separation of North America*

northwest to the Spanish in the south. The history of North America begins with an era of swashbuckling pirates and self-promoting, profit-motivated "sea dogs" who ventured across the ocean with their crews of "iron men in wooden ships."

Giovanni Caboto, the Genoan navigator, having sailed to Mecca to meet the rich caravans from the Far East, speculated, as did Christoper Columbus, that he could sail west across the Atlantic directly to the riches of the Orient. On May 2, 1497, as John Cabot, he set sail from Bristol, England, with letters patent from Henry VII, "to seek out, discover and find" new lands. After a voyage of fifty-two days in the tiny vessel *Matthew*, Cabot and his crew of eighteen landed on the Atlantic coast of Newfoundland. They returned home, having taken possession of the land in the name of Henry VII. Cabot's reward was £10! The next year the king supplied two ships and 300 men in an unsuccessful attempt to bring back riches from the Orient.

In 1534, Jacques Cartier sailed from France, the first of his three voyages to North America on behalf of King Francis I. These three voyages illustrate why people were willing to risk their fortunes, reputations, health, and even their lives to sail westward from Europe. For example, Cartier's first voyage was to find the Northwest Passage to the Spice Islands. This quest brought him along the coastline of the

"The Departure of John and Sebastian Cabot from Bristol in their First Voyage of Discovery," by Ernest Board, 1497.

Henry VII

National Maritime Museum

The City Art Gallery, Bristol

Maritimes to the Gaspé Peninsula, where he planted a cross on the shore. He kidnapped two Indians before returning to France. His captives told tales of great riches in gold and minerals to be found up the Ottawa River in the Saguenay country. As a result, Cartier returned in 1535 and sailed up the St. Lawrence to Stadacona (now Quebec) and Hochelaga (now Montreal). Just as his first voyage had not yielded the route to the Spice Islands, this second voyage did not produce a wealth of gold and diamonds. It had to be cut short because of the dreadful effects of scurvy among his crew. In May 1541, Cartier again set sail for North America, this time with a fleet of ships full of colonists and with Francois de Roberval as viceroy and commander-in-chief. Sailing up the St. Lawrence, Cartier established a small settlement at Cape Rouge, 14 km north of Quebec. From this base he explored as far as the Lachine Rapids. He sailed home in the spring with a collection of minerals that later turned out to be almost worthless. The next year Roberval and his colonists also returned to France — the disappointment was complete.

Neither John Cabot nor Jacques Cartier achieved their goals of reaching the Orient or acquiring riches. However, in hindsight, we can see

Figure 2–4:   Explorations by Jacques Cartier

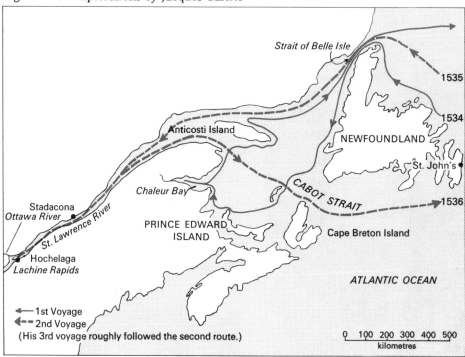

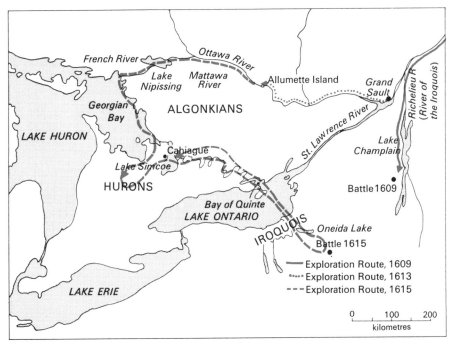

Figure 2–5: *Explorations by Samuel de Champlain*

their accomplishments. Their travels certainly increased the Europeans' knowledge of the geography of the New World and provided grounds for English and French claims of ownership. In addition, they reported an abundance of fish and furs, thereby encouraging others to brave the risks of voyaging to the newly found lands.

The English did not abandon the search for the elusive Northwest Passage from Europe to the Far East. Among the most prominent of them were Sir Martin Frobisher (1535-1594), Sir Humphrey Gilbert (1539-1583), and Henry Hudson (?-1611).

None of these men achieved their goal and two of them perished in the attempt. Nevertheless, they did expand the knowledge of northern waters. Gilbert's colony on Newfoundland provided the English with a base in the New World. Hudson's ill-fated voyage into the bay that bears his name provided the English monarchy with the claim to this area. Many years later England chartered the Hudson's Bay Company to develop the fur trade in the surrounding area known as Rupert's Land.

In 1608 Samuel de Champlain sailed up the St. Lawrence to the present site of Quebec City. There he set his men to constructing a

Jacques Cartier (1491-1557), engraving by P. Gandon, 1934.

Samuel de Champlain, 1607, water colour by De Rinzy.

fortified settlement that was destined to flourish as the colony of New France.

From Quebec, Champlain explored the Ottawa River through Lake Nipissing and the French River to Georgian Bay, where he wintered with the Hurons. In the spring, he canoed via Lake Simcoe and the Trent River system to Lake Ontario and the Iroquois territories of northern New York State. Champlain's alliance with the Hurons against the Iroquois was to play a significant part in the shaping of future events in this area.

In 1663 Louis XIV proclaimed New France to be a royal province. Two years later he sent the capable Jean Talon to be the new colony's intendant; Talon used his genius for administration to good effect. By the time he returned to France seven years later, the colony was much larger and had facilities for worship, education, and health, as well as a sound economic base of agriculture and essential industries to supplement the fur trade.

By the year 1700, the French had successful colonies in the Maritimes and the St. Lawrence Valley, while the British maintained their thirteen colonies along the eastern seaboard, the Island of Newfoundland, and Rupert's Land around Hudson Bay.

THE BRITISH–FRENCH RIVALRY

The history and geography of the next century was dominated by rivalry between the French and the British — rivalry in the power politics of

Europe, rivalry for the fur trade in the New World, and rivalry to explore and claim the wilderness as their own.

In the early 1600s, the French colonies on the St. Lawrence dominated the fur trade. However, when Pierre Radisson and his brother-in-law, Chouard des Groseilliers, became annoyed by the treatment they received at the hands of the French Governor, they decided to deal with the British and bypass the French on the St. Lawrence. To this end, Groseilliers sailed in the British ship *Nonsuch* to Hudson Bay, where he soon acquired a valuable cargo of furs. This cargo excited English merchants; in 1670 Charles II granted them a charter and created "The Governor and Company of Adventurers of England trading into Hudson's Bay," better known today as the Hudson's Bay Company. The English now could compete with the French colonies of the St. Lawrence and the rivalry was on in earnest.

France's first permanent territorial losses in North America resulted from a European war known as the *War of the Spanish Succession* or *Queen Anne's War*. In the terms which were spelled out in the Treaty of Utrecht of 1713, France recognized the British ownership of the Hudson Bay region, Newfoundland, and Acadia (Nova Scotia). However, France

Air view of York Factory, Manitoba, c. 1925.

The Public Archives of Canada

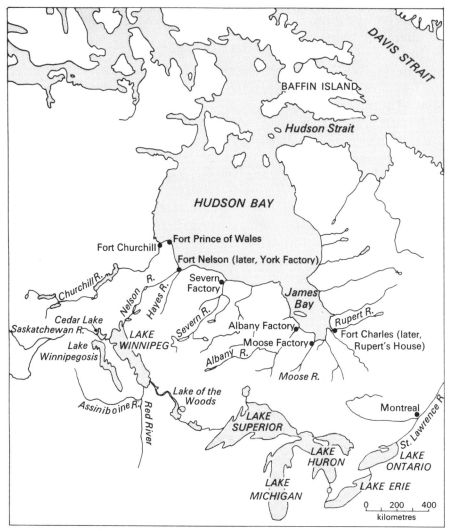

Figure 2–6: Hudson's Bay Company Trading Posts

retained Cape Breton, Prince Edward Island, and the fishing rights along the northern shore of Newfoundland. The political boundary of North America was adjusted as a result of a European war.

The next major adjustment of the boundary came after more military clashes between the two rivals in both the New World and the Old. As early as 1754, the two sides skirmished in an undeclared war for the control of the rich Ohio Valley. Then, two years later in Europe, war was formally declared and the hostilities spread throughout the frontier as the two enemy forces struggled over the forts that marked their land claims. The fighting was long and fierce. Many of the forts changed hands several times during this Seven Years War. The British victories in 1758 led to the long summer's siege of Quebec by James Wolfe's army in 1759, ending with its victory over Louis-Joseph de Montcalm on the Plains of Abraham. The British fleet arrived at Quebec the next spring to deliver the final blow, and in September, New France surrendered. The terms of the surrender were documented in The Treaty of Paris of 1763, wherein France withdrew completely from the mainland of North America and retained only the islands of St. Pierre and Miquelon and its fishing rights in Newfoundland.

THE BRITISH COLONIES IN NORTH AMERICA

With the signing of the Treaty of Paris of 1763, Britain found itself in possession of all the territory east of the Mississippi River from the Arctic to the Gulf of Mexico. (The lands to the west of the Mississippi River and the City of New Orleans had already been transferred from France to Spain by a secret treaty.) In an era when a sailing ship and a good horse were the fastest means of communication, the problems of governing half a continent were enormous. How could a message from the English court or Parliament be delivered to the settlers? How could the pioneers relay their petitions to those in power?

To govern the area, the government of George III issued The Royal Proclamation of 1763. The terms of this document established a number of boundaries and governments within the British territories. The coast of Labrador was annexed to Newfoundland and the colony of Nova Scotia was given power over the area now known as the Maritimes. The bulk of the land, including the former territory of New France, was incorporated into the new colony of Quebec. A significant item in the Proclamation disallowed settlement west of the lands draining to the Atlantic. These western areas were to remain as Indian lands. This last provision annoyed those colonists who were anxious to move west towards the Mississippi.

After eleven years, these plans were amended by the Quebec Act of 1774. By the provisions of this act, Quebec was extended west to the Mississippi and south to the Ohio River. The enlarged Quebec was given control over the fur trade of the interior and the fishing in the Gulf of St. Lawrence. The terms of this new Quebec Act were seen by the British government as a rational way to shape the growth in the new areas. However, to the settlers of the thirteen colonies, the new expanded

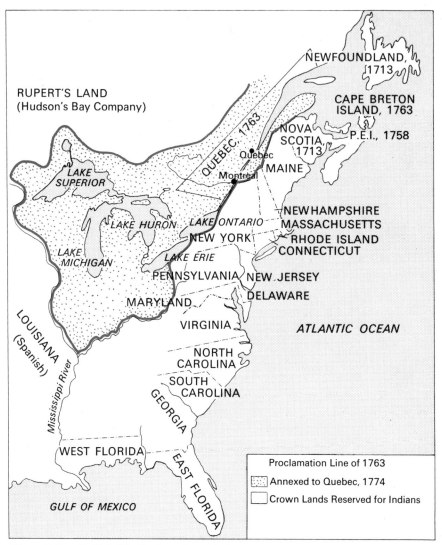

Figure 2–7:   British North America, 1763-75

Quebec was a threat to their hopes of westward settlement and was viewed as just another of the English government's "intolerable Acts." The adjustment of a boundary for administrative purposes provided more fuel for the revolutionary firebrands within the thirteen colonies.

THE AMERICAN REVOLUTIONARY WAR 1775-1783

The difference of opinion between the colonists and the government of King George III grew until a full-scale revolution erupted. The Second

Continental Congress attempted to persuade the northern colonies to join them in the rebellion and, when they refused, troops were sent over-land in the winter of 1775 to attack Montreal and Quebec. However, the attacks were only partly successful and the Revolutionary Forces were compelled to retire when the British fleet arrived in the spring. The Revolutionaries had lost this battle to unite all the colonies of British North America in their cause. Nevertheless, they were more successful in their battles with the British forces in their own colonies and they did win their independence. In 1783 several treaties were signed to officially end the American Revolutionary War.

THE BOUNDARY

The Treaty of 1783, signed by Britain and the new nation of the United States, defined the boundary between the British colonies to the north and the United States to the south. This boundary, from the Bay of Fundy to the Lake of the Woods, followed the major rivers, the 45th parallel and the middle line of the Great Lakes. This boundary followed closely the line of the Iroquois territories. The Iroquois had served to separate the fledgling British colonies on the Atlantic coast from the French colonies of the St. Lawrence. Unfortunately, the map used by the peace negotiators was inaccurate: the discrepancies would give rise to boundary disputes in the years to come.

The dissatisfaction of the Americans with this boundary became evident during the War of 1812. This dispute was both the North Ameri-can branch of the Napoleonic Wars and an attempt by the Americans to annex the western peninsula of Upper Canada. The attacks were concen-trated at Detroit and along the Niagara frontier, but the skill of General Isaac Brock and the Indians under the Shawnee Chief Tecumseh were sufficient to allow the "Canadians" to repulse the invaders. The Treaty of Ghent in 1814 brought peace and a more accurate description of the original 1783 boundary.

The next section of the boundary between the British colonies and the United States was added four years later as an item in the Convention of 1818, which provided for the extension of the boundary from the Lake of the Woods westward along the 49th parallel to the Rockies. The territories to the west of the mountains were to be open to settlement to both British subjects and American citizens for a period of ten years. Certainly these were two very important decisions to have been made by the Convention of 1818 that was primarily designed to settle fishing rights!

Later the boundary of the eastern side of the continent was clarified by the Webster-Ashburton Treaty (1842). It provided for a compromise border wherein the State of Maine separated the Maritimes from the St. Lawrence lowlands.

Ownership of the land to the west of the Rocky Mountains had been left undecided by the Convention of 1818 and, as might have been expected, the problem did not solve itself. By 1846 the Americans were asking that the new boundary be 54° 40'N latitude and had coined the phrase, "Fifty-four Forty or Fight!" The problem was finally resolved when the British and the Americans signed the Oregon Treaty of 1846 that extended the boundary along the 49th parallel.

The purchase of Alaska by the United States from the Russians as well as the Confederation of Canada in 1867 completed the process that had started centuries earlier when areas of North America were claimed by five European powers — Spain, Britain, France, the Netherlands, and Russia. The fibres of their histories had become interwoven to produce the fabric of two independent nations north of the Mexican border. The United States, begun by revolution, added to its lands by means of exploration, annexation, and purchase.

When the American Revolution was virtually complete, the evolution of Canada was just beginning. In 1869, the Hudson's Bay Company transferred Rupert's Land to the new Dominion of Canada. The next year the Province of Manitoba was created out of the great expanse of the Northwest Territories. British Columbia joined in 1871 and Prince Edward Island in 1873. In 1880 the British turned their Arctic properties over to Canada and the nation acquired a new northern boundary. The western boundary was fixed in 1903 when the Alaska boundary dispute was settled to the satisfaction of the Americans by an arbitration board's ruling. The international boundaries of Canada were now complete. The internal boundaries were completed with the creation of Alberta and Saskatchewan in 1905. Then, in 1949, the British colony of Newfoundland voted to join the Canadian Confederation.

QUESTIONS

1. What evidence shows that the physical geography of North America has a distinct north-south trend?

2. Explain why the Norsemen played no part in determining the present political borders of North America.

3. In what ways were the explorations of John Cabot similar to those of

Jacques Cartier? How were they different?

4. Explain why Chouard des Groseilliers' voyage in the *Nonsuch* to Hudson Bay for furs became such an important event in the British-French rivalry for control in the New World.

RESEARCH

1. Compare the different types of housing used by the native peoples. Show how both the building materials and the style of architecture reflected the different environmental regions.

2. Prepare a one-page summary of the life and achievements of any person mentioned in the chapter. Findings can then be exchanged.

3. Examine Fig. 2-3 that shows the political ownership of North America since the year 1500. Then imagine this chart projected for the next 100 years. Do you see any changes in the existing borders? Explain.

4. In the space of about 100 years, the political map of North America was changed by two governmental decrees and by four major wars. Make a summary of all this activity by making a one-page copy of the chart below. Be sure to leave sufficient space to list the territorial changes in point form.

Major War	Name of Document or Treaty	Date	Territorial Changes
Queen Ann's War			
Seven Years War	Royal Proclamation		
	Quebec Act		
Revolutionary War			
War of 1812			

3 | CANADA'S PEOPLES: A CULTURAL MOSAIC

In some ways Canada is a small-scale model of the world. Canada has densely populated areas with large crowded cities, but it also has broad regions of empty space. It is highly industrialized and yet, like a developing nation, it produces and exports raw materials. Side by side exist modern society and the more traditional societies of the native peoples. Its people are a mixture of the nations of Europe, North America, and the other parts of the world. It therefore includes not one but several cultures. And, as we shall see, the great variety of the Canadian peoples is spread unevenly so that each province and territory is different.

The population of Canada is low by world standards: only 21 568 311, according to the census of 1971. According to the preliminary results of the 1976 census, Canada has 22.6 million people. England, all of which could fit inside Ontario three-and-a-half times, has more than twice the number of people Canada has. Our density of population, 2.2 persons per square kilometre, is one of the lowest in the world. Even some countries bordering on the Sahara Desert, such as Morocco, Somalia, and Sudan, have higher densities.

It is true that much of Canada is poor land to live on. Yet even Finland and Sweden, based on rock like our own Shield and without any large productive areas like the Prairies or the St. Lawrence Lowlands, have densities of population over five times as high as ours. Southern Saskatchewan, one of the "bread baskets" of the world, has a rural density of less than two persons per square kilometre. To the people living in the *Golden Horseshoe* of southern Ontario, Canada may seem crowded, but almost everywhere in the northern two-thirds of the country there are too few people to support large-scale economic development. Canada may well be the only country in the world which can afford the luxury of leaving half its area as wilderness.

A festive gathering in Quebec City.

Hutterite settlers near Winnipeg, 1920's.

WHERE THE PEOPLE LIVE

The population of Canada is unevenly spread. Most Canadians live inside a narrow zone some 6000 km long, next to the United States boundary. Figure 3-2 shows that the furthest cities from the border are Edmonton and St. John's, which are 500 km and 1000 km away, respectively. Closeness to the United States is most obvious in southern Ontario

Figure 3–1: Population Distribution in Canada

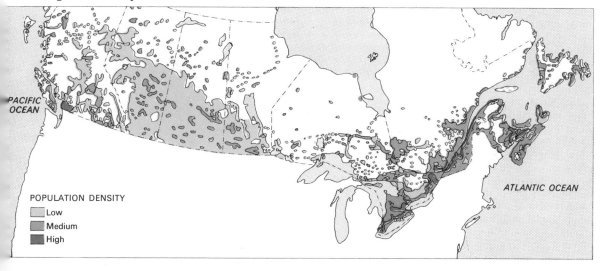

PACIFIC
OCEAN

ATLANTIC OCEAN

POPULATION DENSITY

☐ Low
☐ Medium
☐ High

and southern British Columbia. In both cases, Canadian cities are not only close to the boundary but to nearby American cities (and their television stations) as well.

The populated zone, however, is not continuous. There are clear breaks in northern Ontario, the Rocky Mountains, eastern Quebec, and

Figure 3–2:   Map showing distances between some Canadian and American cities. (Scale: 1 cm = 280 km).

south-central Newfoundland. These gaps between groupings of people help explain why Canada is a nation of regions.

The distribution of people in Canada shows a close fit to physical features. Probably no other country's population is as affected by land-forms and climate as Canada's population is. The low *total* population makes this relationship of geography to population distribution clear. People have had little reason to move out of the warmer and fertile areas into the raw wilderness. In Southern Canada, terrain has been the main physical factor because most people have chosen to live on the flat lands with their rich soils instead of on the hard rock. But in Northern Canada climate has been most important, because climate controls the growing season and creates the permafrost (the permanently frozen soil).

At Lake Superior, the Canadian Shield cuts across the population zone. Even in the few spots of fertile soil, farming is a risky business because of the climate and the distance from markets. On the hard rock, the soil is thin and acidic, while the pockets of soil on lower ground are full of water or muskeg (swamp). Instead of being spread out evenly, people are clustered at the mines or along the railways and highways. Because the Shield comprises half of Canada's total land area, Canada has a population vacuum right in the middle.

To the southeast of the Shield is the main concentration of population — in the fertile lowlands lying between the Shield and the Appalachians. This area is usually called the St. Lawrence–Lower Lakes lowlands; it gradually narrows down towards the northeast until it pinches out along the lower St. Lawrence.

Along the Atlantic Ocean, most of the people live on the coastlines or on the "red soil" lowlands where farming is possible. Thus, thin lines of settlement are located in southeastern Nova Scotia, eastern Newfoundland, and around the Gaspé Peninsula. Prince Edward Island, eastern and southern New Brunswick, and northern Nova Scotia are more evenly populated. Except for Prince Edward Island, the interiors of all the Atlantic Provinces have few inhabitants.

On the western flank of the Shield the Great Plains extend to the west on a broad front, giving Canada a triangle of good farm land, about 1500 km long at its base (the same distance as from England to the Russian border). Except for those in the few cities and towns, the people are scattered fairly evenly over the Prairies. Fewer people live in the south, next to the boundary, because the rainfall of less than 350 mm per year is too little for grain growing. This dry area is called "The Palliser Triangle" because it was first described by the explorer, Captain John Palliser (See Chapter 6).

West of the Prairies, the Rockies and the mountain chains of British

Columbia — the Selkirks, Monashees, and the Coast Mountains — have broken the population zone. Most settlement is clustered along the southern coast and in the warm valleys near the U.S. boundary: the Fraser, the Okanagan, the Columbia, and the Kootenay.

North of the populated zone lies the empty wilderness, "the bush," which includes the Northwest Territories, Labrador, the northern three-quarters of Quebec, and the northern sections of Ontario and of the four western provinces. Most of this area is a hard-rock "barrens." The main factor holding back settlement has not been the rock but rather the harsh climate. The growing season averages less than three months and is in any case undependable; the winters are long and hard; the soils tend to be acidic; evaporation rates are so low that, in summer, bogs or muskegs are widespread and provide homes for billions of insects; besides, permafrost makes building difficult. Canadians may sing about "the true north, strong and free," but few choose to live there!

THE CANADIAN ECUMENE

The great differences in densities of population and in the use of the land show how misleading it can be to use only statistics for the whole area of the country. To help us understand these internal differences, geographers use the word *ecumene*. It is a Greek word which means the "whole inhabited world." When it is used of a country, it means the parts of that country that have unbroken spreads of farms, villages, and cities.

Figure 3-3 shows the Canadian ecumene. It consists of about 10% of the Canadian land, but has over 90% of the people. Within it are the Atlantic shorelines, the St. Lawrence to Lake Huron lowlands, the Prairie triangle, and the southwestern corner of British Columbia. Every city of over 50 000 people (with the exception of Thunder Bay), and almost all of the areas of manufacturing and agriculture, are included in the ecumene.

However, much of the potential wealth of Canada lies outside the ecumene. The mineral ores, the timber, and the tar sands are all close to, but outside of the ecumene. Therefore, the map shows another, larger zone between the ecumene and the Far North. Within this zone, *The Active Frontier*, ground transportation is available. Minerals are mined, purified, and shipped out; and timber is sawed or manufactured into pulp and paper.

The Active Frontier is the area of "the bush," the trapper, the lumberjack, the prospector, and the pulp-mill and mining towns.

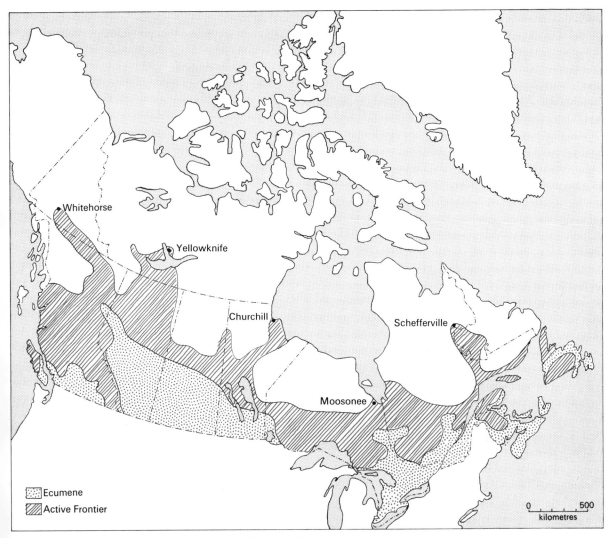

Figure 3–3:   Canadian Ecumene and Active Frontier

The Active Frontier also has the transport "bridges" which tie together the parts of the ecumene: northern Ontario, the southern Rockies, and the Quebec–New Brunswick border country. To the north, the frontier extends along rail and road lines to Whitehorse, Yellowknife, Churchill, Moosonee, and Schefferville.

The ecumene and the Active Frontier together make up the "working" parts of Canada. They comprise about 40% of the total area, but over 99.5% of the population lives in these areas.

The remaining three-fifths of the country, lying north of the Active Frontier, is empty except for government centres, air fields, and Inuit villages. Almost all of these settlements are located on coastlines. The interiors of the Arctic islands have no permanent human settlement.

POPULATION GROWTH IN CANADA

HISTORICAL POPULATION GROWTH   The history of the people of Canada may, for convenience, be said to have had six distinct periods or stages of growth. In the beginning or first stage, the population consisted only of the native peoples who had no idea of a Canada or of an international boundary. They did not feel any kind of continental unity; instead, they were divided into a great number of tribes or nations, such as the Crees, Ojibways, Haidas, Micmacs, and so on. These peoples discovered the water and trail routes along which Canada was explored and organized. We still use the names they chose for many of the rivers and lakes: Miramichi, Ottawa, Timiskaming, Winnipeg, Saskatchewan, Athabasca, and Kootenay.

Figure 3–4:   Linguistic and Tribal Groups, 1000-1600 AD

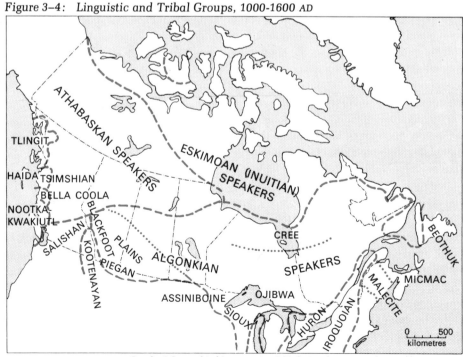

Canada, A Geographical Interpretation. J. Warketin (ed.), p. 23. Methuen Publications, 1969

The second stage may be called the *Early Colonial*. During this period, Europeans first settled in what is now Eastern Canada; the period lasted from about 1600 to 1760. People of various nationalities began to make use of the Newfoundland coast first as temporary and then as permanent bases for fishing. French soldiers and colonists built forts and started farming Acadia and the St. Lawrence Lowlands. British settlers landed in Nova Scotia. This stage ended with the defeat of the French by the British. The 60 000 *habitants* of the St. Lawrence, without much further French immigration, became the ancestors of most of the Francophones (French-speaking people) of Canada.

The third stage, *the American*, lasted from about 1760 to 1812. This was an unusual half-century because most of the new Canadians came not from Europe directly, but from other parts of North America. Just before the American Revolution, New Englanders moved into Nova Scotia to take the place of the French Acadians, who had been driven out. During and after the revolution the Loyalists fled to New Brunswick, Ontario, and the eastern townships of Quebec. Because Lieutenant Governor Simcoe believed that Americans, through their experience, were the people best suited to help settle Ontario, he invited them in. Americans, especially from New England, New York, and Pennsylvania, continued to come to Upper Canada (southern Ontario) until the time of the 1812-1814 war.

After that war American immigration almost ceased. Between 1815 and 1900, the fourth stage, the new settlers came mostly from the British Isles, particularly the poorer peoples of "the Celtic Fringe" — the Scots, the northern and southern Irish. Many of them came to stay in settlements such as the ones near Guelph and St. Thomas. Although groups moved into other provinces too, most of these newcomers came to southern Ontario. Because of this heavy immigration, Ontario replaced Quebec as the leader in both population and industry. During this time of British immigration, the Papineau and MacKenzie rebellions broke out; Quebec and Ontario (Canada East and Canada West) were united and Confederation was achieved. The census of 1871, the first after Confederation, showed a total population of 3 689 000. By 1900 most Canadians were either of British or of French ancestry.

The fifth stage, *The East European*, lasted from 1900 to 1930, the years before the Depression. A new element joined the Canadian population. Thousands of people came from eastern Europe: Ukrainians, Poles, Hungarians, Russians, Germans, and Scandinavians. They joined other thousands from Ontario and the United States in the great rush onto the Prairies and into British Columbia. This surge of newcomers was fol-

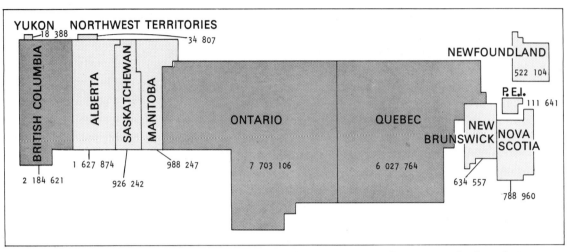

Figure 3–5:   *Canada's Provinces and Territories by Population, 1971*

lowed by 15 years of almost no immigration because of the Depression
and World War II.

Since the end of World War II, Canada has again received many
newcomers. These new Canadians have come from a greater variety of
home countries than ever before: the Dutch in the '40s and '50s; the
Italians ever since World War II; the Americans since the late '60s; the
Portuguese most recently; the refugees from Hungary (1956), Czechoslovakia (1968), and Uganda (1974); smaller numbers from India, Pakistan, Hong Kong, Taiwan, and the West Indies; and a continuing flow
from the British Isles. This has been a different kind of immigration, in
that the newcomers have not come to open up new farmland. For the
most part they are not farmers; they have moved to the booming cities in
southern Ontario, British Columbia, and Alberta.

Each of the six stages of settlement affected a different part of
Canada: the Early Colonial, Quebec; the American, the Maritimes; the
British, Ontario; the East European, the Prairies; the Postwar, the cities.
As a result, the population mix is different in each of the large regions,
even in each of the provinces of Canada.

DIFFERENCES IN THE RATES OF POPULATION GROWTH The
rates of increase in population have been different for each region and
each province. Table 3-1 shows the share that each province has had of
the Canadian total population, at each census taken since 1871. Notice
the steady drop for the Atlantic Provinces. Within one century, the three
Maritimes together (Prince Edward Island, Nova Scotia, New Brunswick)

have gone from 21% to only 7%. As recently as 1901, Nova Scotia had a greater share (8.6%) than all three together have now.

The two central provinces have fared better. Quebec's share declined until 1911, then increased a little by 1941, but has since dropped again. The 1971 percentage for Quebec was about the same as for 1911, roughly 28%. In contrast, notice how sharply Ontario dropped between 1891 and 1911, from 44% to 35% of the total. This decreased share was due to the great numbers of people moving out to the Prairies. Ontario reached its low point in 1951, but has been climbing since then because of the explosive growth of the Toronto region.

Each of the western provinces has had its own pattern of rise and fall. Manitoba was the first to reach its peak, but it has been dropping slowly since 1921. Saskatchewan had a great jump between 1901 and 1911, when most of its farmlands were settled. It was the most populated western province through 1941, but is now the least. Alberta followed the same path as Saskatchewan, but like Ontario has come back since 1951 because the wealth from its oil and gas has attracted businesses and

TABLE 3-1
Each Province's Share of the Total Canadian Population for Each Census, 1871-1976

	1871	1881	1891	1901	1911	1921	1931	1941	1951	1961	1971	1976
Atlantic Provinces												
Newfoundland	—	—	—	—	—	—	—	—	2.6	2.5	2.4	2.4
Prince Edward Island	2.6	2.5	2.3	1.9	1.3	1.0	0.8	0.8	0.7	0.6	0.5	0.4
Nova Scotia	10.5	10.2	9.3	8.6	6.8	6.0	4.9	5.0	4.6	4.0	3.7	3.6
New Brunswick	7.7	7.4	6.7	6.2	4.9	4.4	3.9	4.0	3.7	3.3	2.9	2.9
Central Provinces												
Quebec	32.4	31.5	30.9	30.7	27.8	26.9	27.7	29.0	28.9	28.8	27.9	27.2
Ontario	44.0	44.6	44.0	40.6	35.1	33.4	33.1	32.9	32.8	34.2	35.7	36.0
Western Provinces												
Manitoba	0.7	1.4	3.2	4.8	6.4	6.9	6.7	6.3	5.5	5.1	4.6	4.4
Saskatchewan	0.4	0.6	1.0	1.7	6.8	8.6	8.9	7.8	5.9	5.1	4.3	4.0
Alberta	0.4	0.6	1.0	1.4	5.2	6.7	7.1	6.9	6.7	7.3	7.5	7.9
British Columbia	1.0	1.1	2.0	3.3	5.4	6.0	6.7	7.1	8.3	8.9	10.1	10.6
Territories												
Yukon Territory	—	—	—	0.5	0.1	*	*	*	0.1	0.1	0.1	0.1
Northwest Territories	—	—	—	0.4	0.1	0.1	0.1	0.1	0.1	0.1	0.2	0.2

* Less than 0.05%.

Source: Canada. Census Division. 1971 Census of Canada: Population.
Canada. Census field. 1976 Census of Canada: Population: Preliminary Counts.

people, mainly to its two large cities. British Columbia is the only province that has had an increase in every census.

The Territories north of the 60th parallel have never had any large share of the Canadian population. The North had its highest figure in 1901, the time of the gold rush. Despite a slight increase lately, the Territories still have only half the population of Prince Edward Island, the smallest of the provinces.

ANALYZING POPULATION STATISTICS

THE AGE-SEX PYRAMID   Figure 3-6 shows a population pyramid. This graph shows the number of males and females at each level. Since people die at every age, the expected shape would be a pyramid with the greatest number being in the 0-4 age group. If the base (the youngest years) of the pyramid is wide, it shows that the population has a high birth rate and is probably growing rapidly. If the base is small it means that the birth rate is low and the total number of people is not changing much.

For a long time the Canadian pyramid was that of a young, growing nation, but it is now beginning to look like that of an old nation. The birth rate has been dropping steadily since 1956. It was then 28.0 live births per 1000 people; by 1971 the rate had dropped to 16.8/1000. On the pyramid, the largest age group is the 10-14; the 0-4 age group is the smallest below 25. If this trend keeps on, Canada may become a nation with most of its people in the middle-age and old-age groups. Any gains in population will then result from immigration and the lengthening of the life span.

As the average age of the population becomes older, Canada will face new problems. The total cost of pensions would increase, but not as large a percentage of workers will be around to pay for the pensions. The age of retirement, which is now coming down, could move back up past 65 or 70. Old people would probably want more medical care. Better ways of taking care of the disabled elderly persons will have to be devised. Moreover, living on one pension cheque a month is hardship: persons now often are impoverished by trying to live on such meagre income. The situation for the elderly will most likely grow worse.

Age pyramids vary from province to province. In 1971 the birth rate varied from 14.8/1000 in Quebec to 24.5/1000 in Newfoundland. Highest of all were the Northwest Territories, with 37.0/1000. The birth rate for Canada as a whole according to the 1976 census preliminary results was 15.4/1000. Figure 3-7 shows how the shape of a pyramid differs for the two extreme cases, Quebec and the Northwest Territories. Quebec has

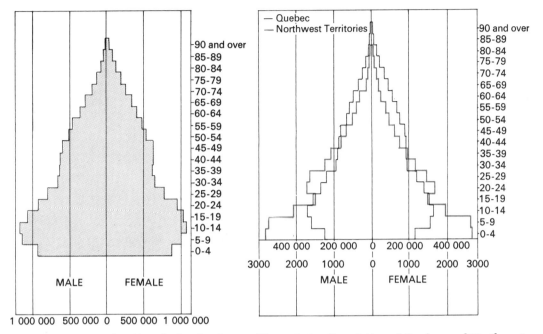

Figure 3-6: *Canada's Population by Age and Sex, 1971*

Figure 3-7: *Population of Quebec and Northwest Territories by Age and Sex, 1971*

a small base, whereas the pyramid of the Northwest Territories is broad-based. (In the Northwest Territories, 43% of the population is under 15 years old; in Quebec it is 29%.) What are some of the implications for Quebec, the Northwest Territories, and Canada arising from these differences in birth rates?

The Canadian age-sex pyramid (Figure 3-6) shows a few more males than females in the younger age groups. This is the normal situation in most countries. However, in Canada the male majority continues until age forty-five. In most countries a female majority is achieved well before this age group. Canada is unusual because the immigrants from other nations include many more young men than young women. After age 45 there is a female majority and the male-female difference increases with time. By age 70, there are five women for every four men, by age 90 more than three to two.

The ratio of male to female is not the same throughout the country. Women tend to live in cities more than men do. As seen in Table 3-2, cities have a female majority, rural areas have a male majority, and villages have an even split of male and female residents. Therefore, a province like Ontario has more women than men, while Prince Edward Island and Saskatchewan have more men than women.

TABLE 3-2
Population By Sex, 1971

	MALE			FEMALE	
	Number (1000s)	%		Number (1000s)	%
Total	10 795			10 773	
Urban	8 105			8 306	
Metropolitan Areas, 500 000 & over	3 383	49.1		3 504	50.9
Urban Areas, 100 000 — 499 999	1 653	49.1		1 705	50.9
Cities, 30 000 — 99 999	954	49.5		977	50.5
Towns, 10 000 — 29 999	871	49.9		878	50.1
Towns, 5000 — 9999	427	50.1		422	49.9
Villages, 2500 — 4999	419	50.0		421	50.0
Villages, 1000 — 2499	402	50.0		399	50.0
Rural	2 691			2 467	
Rural Non-Farm	1 929	51.8		1 809	48.5
Farm	762	53.8		658	46.2

Source: Canada. Census Division. 1971 Census of Canada: Population.

URBAN/RURAL POPULATIONS   At the time of Confederation, most Canadians were called "rural" in the census. They lived on farms or in villages. However, as has happened in all Western nations, people have steadily moved from the countryside to the cities and towns. By 1921, the rural and urban proportions in Canada were equal, but since then Canada has become heavily urbanized. Table 3-3 shows how this trend has continued from 1961 to 1971. By the last census, over 75% of all Canadians lived in urban areas. As a result, the population has become concentrated in a few places rather than spread out.

Almost 32% of all the people in Canada now live in the metropolitan areas which have more than 500 000 people. Of Canada's total population, 25% live in the two giant cities, Montreal and Toronto. It is a paradox that in a country as large as Canada which has so few people, so many of them should live crowded together in a few cities. (The "100 000-499 999" category declined in its percentage of the population between 1961 and 1971 because two cities, Ottawa and Winnipeg, moved into the "over 500 000" category).

Notice too that most of the rural people do not live on farms. Fewer than 7% of all Canadians are farm-dwellers. Most of the people living in the country commute to jobs in the cities, located at some distance away.

The urban, rural, and farm population figures vary greatly from one part of Canada to another. The urban percentages are highest in Ontario (82%), Quebec (81%), British Columbia (76%), and Alberta (74%). They are lowest in Prince Edward Island (38%), the Northwest Territories (48%), and Saskatchewan (53%). The farm percentage is highest on the Prairies: Saskatchewan (25%), Alberta (15%), Manitoba (13%), and lowest in the Northwest Territories (0.07%), the Yukon (0.3%), and Newfoundland (0.86%). Whereas 43% of the population of Newfoundland is called "rural," less than one per cent actually live on a farm. (The many small fishing "outports" are listed as "rural" because they have too few people to be "urban.") The greatest number of farmers are in Ontario (364 000) and Quebec (305 000), but, because of the huge urban totals, the farmers make up only about 5% in each case.

Table 3-4 lists in order of size the largest metropolitan areas of Canada, according to the censuses. Note how many are in Ontario. Of the fourteen with more than 200 000 people, half are in southern Ontario.

On the other hand, only three cities from the Atlantic provinces make the list; the largest city, Halifax, ranks only fourteenth. Prince Edward Island and the territories do not show up at all. The populations in the metropolitan areas of New Brunswick, Newfoundland, and Saskatchewan are all below 150 000.

Almost every country in the world has one city which is clearly its largest; examples are New York, Mexico City, London, Paris, Tokyo,

TABLE 3-3

Urban and Rural percentages of the Total Population, 1961 and 1971

	1961	1971
URBAN	69.6%	76.1%
500 000 or more	25.2	31.9
100 000 — 499 999	18.2	15.6
30 000 — 99 999	9.3	9.0
10 000 — 29 999	5.8	8.1
5000 — 9999	3.3	3.9
2500 — 4999	3.5	3.9
1000 — 2499	4.3	3.7
RURAL	30.4%	23.9%
Non-Farm	19.0	17.3
Farm	11.4	6.6

Source: Canada. Census Division. 1971 Census of Canada: Population.

TABLE 3-4
Metropolitan Areas of Canada, 1971 and 1976

Rank	City	1971	1976
1.	Montreal, Quebec	2 731 211	2 758 780
2.	Toronto, Ontario	2 602 098	2 753 112
3.	Vancouver, British Columbia	1 082 352	1 135 774
4.	Ottawa-Hull, Ontario-Quebec	620 061	668 853
5.	Winnipeg, Manitoba	549 808	570 725
6.	Quebec, Quebec	501 365	543 193
7.	Edmonton, Alberta	496 000	542 845
8.	Hamilton, Ontario	503 122	525 222
9.	Calgary, Alberta	403 343	457 828
10.	Niagara Falls Regional Municipality (includes Niagara Falls, St. Catherines, and Welland), Ontario	285 802	298 129
11.	Waterloo Regional Municipality (includes Kitchener, Waterloo and Cambridge), Ontario	238 576	269 828
12.	London, Ontario	252 981	264 639
13.	Halifax, Nova Scotia	250 579	261 366
14.	Windsor, Ontario	248 718	243 289
15.	Victoria, British Columbia	195 800	212 466
16.	Sudbury, Ontario	157 721	155 013
17.	Regina, Saskatchewan	140 734	148 965
18.	St. John's, Newfoundland	131 814	140 883
19.	Saskatoon, Saskatchewan	126 449	132 291
20.	Chicoutimi-Jonquière, Quebec	126 401	127 181
21.	Thunder Bay, Ontario	114 708	117 988
22.	St. John, New Brunswick	106 744	109 700

Source: Canada. Census Division. 1971 Census of Canada: Population.
Source: Canada. Census field. 1976 Census of Canada: Population: Preliminary Counts.

Moscow, Cairo, and Athens. Canada is different, in that it has two big cities of almost equal size located fairly near each other, with neither one being the national capital.

Usually the big city which becomes most important economically is able to stay on top. For example, once New York and London (England) got the big banks and head offices, no other cities in their countries could catch up to them. In Canada, though, a newer city, Toronto, has caught up with and even passed the older city, Montreal. Most of the large financial institutions (banks, stock exchange) and head offices of giant corporations, which were once mostly in Montreal, have now come to be centred in Toronto. It also has the largest population of Canadian cities.

The fastest-growing cities in Canada are in Alberta, British Columbia, and Ontario. Right now Calgary and Edmonton have the highest rates of increase.

Most of the provinces of Canada have one "big town" which dominates the province. The only exceptions are Saskatchewan and Alberta. In both, two cities of almost equal size are competing for the lead. In each case the capital city is a little ahead. Even in the North, each territory has its one largest town.

ETHNIC ORIGINS

The Canadian population is a mixture of many groups, although 85% of the inhabitants have been born within Canada. Of the others, 8% were born in Europe, 4% in the United Kingdom, 1.4% in the United States, and 1.7% elsewhere.

Table 3-5 shows the ethnic background of our Canadian nation, as well as of the residents of each province. The British are the largest group within Canada, but if we break the British total down into English (23%), Scottish (11%), and Irish (10%), then the French form the largest single ethnic group. The British and French make up almost 75% of all Canadians. It may be surprising to note that the next largest group is the Germans, who have about twice as high a percentage as the Italians or Ukrainians.

TABLE 3-5
Ethnic Background of Canadian Population Percentages, 1971

	Canada TOTAL	%	Nfld. %	P.E.I. %	N.S. %	N.B. %	Que. %	Ont. %	Man. %	Sask. %	Alta. %	B.C. %	Yuk. %	N.W.T. %
British	9 624 120	44.6	93.8	82.7	77.5	57.7	10.6	59.4	41.9	42.1	46.8	57.9	48.6	25.2
French	6 180 120	28.7	3.0	13.7	10.2	37.0	79.0	9.6	8.8	6.1	5.8	4.4	6.7	6.5
German	1 317 195	6.1	0.5	0.9	5.2	1.3	0.9	6.2	12.5	19.4	14.2	9.1	8.5	3.8
Italian	730 820	3.4	0.1	0.1	0.5	0.2	2.8	6.0	1.1	0.3	1.5	2.5	0.9	0.7
Ukrainian	580 660	2.7	*	0.1	0.3	0.1	0.3	2.1	11.6	9.3	8.3	2.8	3.3	1.8
Dutch	425 945	2.0	0.1	1.1	1.9	0.8	0.2	2.7	3.6	2.1	3.6	3.2	2.8	1.0
Scandinavian	384 790	1.8	0.2	0.2	0.5	0.6	0.1	0.8	3.6	6.4	6.0	5.1	5.4	2.6
Polish	316 425	1.5	0.1	0.1	0.4	0.1	0.4	1.9	4.3	2.9	2.7	1.4	1.3	0.8
Native peoples	312 765	1.5	0.4	0.3	0.6	0.6	0.6	0.8	4.4	4.4	2.7	2.4	14.0	53.2
Jewish	296 945	1.4	0.1	*	0.3	0.2	1.9	1.8	2.0	0.2	0.5	0.6	0.2	0.1
Asian	285 540	1.3	0.3	0.3	0.6	0.4	0.7	1.5	1.0	0.8	1.6	3.7	0.8	0.6

* Less than 0.05%.

Source: Canada. Census Division. 1971 Census of Canada: Population.
  Canada. Census field. 1976 Census of Canada: Population: Preliminary Counts.

In terms of Canadian politics, the most important ethnic issue is the use of languages. The federal government has set up an official-languages policy. The government aims to make it possible for both English and French to be used for any government or legal business.

By "Official Language designation," of all Canadians

    67.1% speak English only
    18.0% speak French only
    13.4% speak both English and French
     1.5% speak neither

Most "French only" speakers live in Quebec.

NATIVE PEOPLES

The descendants of Canada's original inhabitants make up only 1.5% of the population of Canada. This indigenous population includes about 250 000 Indians, 18 000 Inuit, and 160 000 Métis. Ontario has the largest

Husband and wife from the Ennadai Lake area in the Northwest Territories.

National Film Board of Canada

Close-up of Cree woman and child at Great Whale River, Quebec.

National Film Board of Canada

number of Indians, the Prairies have the most Métis, and the coasts of the Arctic Ocean and Hudson Bay are the main habitations of the Inuit.

The native peoples have major problems. They have the highest birth rate, but also the highest *infant mortality rate*. (That is, their babies are almost three times as liable to die as are the babies of other Canadians.) They have the *shortest life expectancy*, which means that many of them die young. Many live in areas without hospitals or high schools. Because of the lack of high schools, they leave school early and therefore are at a disadvantage in getting jobs. Native communities often lack the facilities which urban dwellers have come to regard as the necessities of life: hot and cold running water, plumbing, heating, electricity.

The native peoples are spread very thinly over the northern two-thirds of Canada. Because so few white people live there, the native peoples are the majority in the Northwest Territories and the northern parts of the larger provinces. They believe that the North has always been and does now belong to them. This belief has led to many disputes with the federal government over "land claims" and "aboriginal land rights."

At present, more and more are coming to live in grouped settlements.

TABLE 3-6
Native Population, 1971

Province or Territory	Population
Newfoundland (and Labrador)	1 225
Prince Edward Island	315
Nova Scotia	4 475
New Brunswick	3 915
Quebec	32 840
Ontario	62 420
Manitoba	43 035
Saskatchewan	40 470
Alberta	44 540
British Columbia	52 215
Yukon	2 580
Northwest Territories	7 180
	295 215

Note: These figures and the ones in Table 3-5 are from government sources. That they differ shows how hard it can be to get an accurate count of people spread over great areas. Table 3-6 leaves out most of the Inuit.

Source: Canada. Census Division. 1971 Census of Canada: Population.
Canada. Census field. 1976 Census of Canada: Population: Preliminary Counts.

Most of the Inuit live next to the government stations, trading posts, and schools. Some 1200 live at Frobisher Bay alone. Snowmobiles have replaced dog sleds; prefabricated houses have replaced the tents and igloos. The Inuits have formed some thirty cooperatives for arts, crafts, fishing, and so on. Many Indians have migrated into the large cities, but often they keep a kind of home base on their reserves while working in nearby towns.

MELTING POT VERSUS MOSAIC

For a long time the United States boasted that it was a melting pot, where immigrants from all over the world "melted" together to become a new kind of people, Americans. In Canada things have not gone quite the

Mr. Leniavski together with his Polish neighbours clearing land, Prince Albert, Sask., c. 1928.

Ukrainian family harvesting, 1918.

same way. It is true that most immigrants have learned the English or French language and the local customs. However, there has never been one kind of person who could be thought of as the typical Canadian.

Canadians are divided among three very different cultural groups: the English-speaking, the French-speaking, and the native peoples. Immigrants from other lands have tended to "melt" into either the English or the French, but these two groups have remained separate, as have the native peoples too.

Lately, being different has been stressed more than before. The native peoples have been trying even harder than before to keep their languages, cultures, and lands. Because *Francophones* have the same language rights as *Anglophones*, other peoples of European ancestry have asked for recognition of their cultures. This has been especially true of the Ukrainians. We all know, as well, that the Mennonites, the Hutterites, the West Indians, the Italians, and the Asians, have special life styles. As we saw before, each province in Canada is different in its ethnic background.

Therefore, we do not speak of a "melting pot" in Canada. There is too much variety from place to place. Instead, we speak of a mosaic — a picture made by putting together many different-coloured stones. Canada is a country made up of many different kinds of people set next to each other and fitting together to form one nation.

RELIGION

Religion is one of the most important and long-lasting parts of cultural life. Immigrants to a country such as Canada may quickly change the

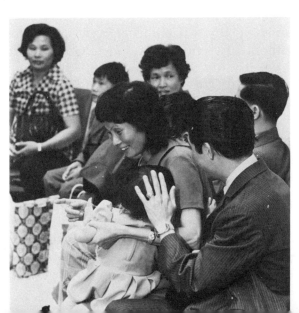

August 25, 1974, at 12:00 at Vancouver International Airport: first arrivals from the People's Republic of China. From left to right in the photograph are: Dang Lai Jun (wife), Dang On May (daughter), Dang Wui Sang (sponsor), Dang Shee Gun (son).

National Film Board of Canada

National Film Board of Canada

National Film Board of Canada

An exterior view of the first Baptist Church in Charlottetown, P.E.I. (above left).

Cook's Creek Ukrainian Catholic Church near Winnipeg, Manitoba (above centre).

An exterior view of St. Anne's Church in Toronto taken from the back (above right).

A small Mennonite Church and graveyard near Kitchener-Waterloo, Ontario (right).

National Film Board of Canada

language they use at home, but they do not easily change their religion. Church membership is usually a more lasting sign of ethnic origin than is language or even the spelling of one's name. Religion is also important in that it affects the way people look at life, at work, and at education.

Table 3-7 shows the percentages of the population who belong to the bigger churches. Canada has almost equal numbers of Catholics (Roman and Ukrainian) and Protestants. The much smaller numbers of Orthodox, Jews, Buddhists, and so on add up to about five per cent of the total. The single largest church is the Roman Catholic.

Of course, the total figures hide the variations between provinces. Over 50% of the Roman Catholics live in one province, Quebec. The Roman Catholic Church is the leading single church in eastern and central Canada, and has a majority in three provinces: Quebec, Prince Edward Island, and New Brunswick. West from Quebec there is an almost steady decline in the Roman Catholic percentage from Ontario (34%) to British Columbia (19%).

The leader in all four western provinces is the United Church, which has about 30% of the people in Saskatchewan and Alberta. The Anglican Church, which was once the established church in Ontario, has its highest percentages at the extreme ends of the country: in Newfoundland, Nova Scotia, British Columbia, and the North. The Presbyterian Church, which is the church of the Scots and the Orange order, has more than 50%

TABLE 3-7
Religious Affiliation of Canadian population, 1971

	Canada TOTAL	%	Nfld. %	P.E.I. %	N.S. %	N.B. %	Que. %	Ont. %	Man. %	Sask. %	Alta. %	·B.C. %	Yuk. %	N.W.T. %
Roman Catholic	9 974 895	46.0	36.5	57.0	36.4	52.3	87.0	33.5	24.5	27.9	24.1	18.7	25.5	41.1
United Church	3 768 805	17.4	19.4	25.0	20.6	13.4	2.9	20.9	26.0	29.5	28.8	24.5	17.0	8.6
Anglican	2 543 175	11.8	27.6	6.2	18.4	10.9	3.0	15.8	12.4	9.4	10.4	17.8	24.4	36.5
Presbyterian	872 335	4.0	0.6	11.8	5.1	2.1	0.9	7.0	3.1	2.2	3.5	4.7	3.8	1.3
Lutheran	715 745	3.3	0.1	0.1	1.5	0.3	0.4	3.5	6.5	9.8	8.2	5.5	5.0	2.1
Baptist	667 245	3.1	0.2	5.7	12.8	14.1	0.6	3.7	1.9	1.6	3.1	3.0	4.8	1.1
Greek Orthodox	316 605	1.5	*	*	0.2	0.1	1.0	1.7	2.6	2.9	2.9	0.9	0.9	0.5
Jewish	276 020	1.3	*	*	0.3	0.1	1.8	1.6	1.9	0.2	0.4	0.4	0.1	0.1
Ukrainian Catholic	227 730	1.1	*	*	0.1	0.1	0.4	0.7	5.8	3.7	2.5	0.5	0.5	0.3
Pentecostal	220 390	1.0	5.5	0.9	0.9	2.7	0.1	1.0	1.0	1.3	1.4	1.6	1.1	2.0
Jehovah's Witnesses	174 810	0.8	0.4	0.4	0.6	0.4	*	*	0.9	1.1	1.1	1.9	3.2	1.5
Mennonite	168 150	0.8	*	*	*	*	*	0.5	6.5	3.1	1.3	1.2	0.3	0.1
Salvation Army	119 665	0.6	7.9	0.3	0.6	*	*	0.6	0.3	0.4	0.3	0.9	0.1	0.1

* Less than 0.05%.
Source: Canada. Census Division. 1971 Census of Canada: Population.

of its numbers in Ontario, but its highest percentage is in Prince Edward Island. The Eastern churches (Orthodox and Ukrainian Catholic) and the Lutherans are proportionately largest on the Prairies, while the Baptists have high figures in Nova Scotia and New Brunswick. Almost all the Jews are in Ontario, Quebec, and Manitoba.

A few provinces stand out as being different from the others. Quebec is unique for its overwhelming Roman Catholic majority. Even the United Church has less than 3% of its members in the province. Newfoundland has a special mix — it has almost half of Canada's Salvation Army, plus a high percentage of Pentecostals and Anglicans. The Northwest Territories are mostly Roman Catholic and Anglican, because of the work of the missionaries of those churches in the last 150 years.

Ontario is interesting in that it probably comes closest to being the "average" Canadian province. Just as on the ethnic table we saw that Ontario has people of every ethnic background, so it has a mix of people of almost every religious belief.

Of the larger urban areas in Canada, the one which is the most homogeneous in religion is Quebec City; it is listed as over 96% Catholic.

INCOME DISTRIBUTION IN CANADA

The Canadian people differ from each other just as much in money as they do in culture. Table 3-8 shows the large difference in the income between urban and rural areas in Canada. The median income drops from a high in the great cities to a low on the farms. Farm-dwellers received only half the income of city-dwellers.

TABLE 3-8
Median Income, 1971

CANADA	$3943	Canada		$3943
Newfoundland	2727	*Urban*	*Population*	4288
Prince Edward Island	2368			
Nova Scotia	3181	Metropolitan Areas	50 000 or over	4580
New Brunswick	2964	Metropolitan Areas	100 000 — 499 999	4364
Quebec	4048	Cities	30 000 — 99 999	4009
Ontario	4426	Towns	10 000 — 29 999	4093
Manitoba	3320	Towns	5 000 — 9 999	3844
Saskatchewan	2725	Villages	4 999 or below	3462
Alberta	3746	RURAL		$2804
British Columbia	4093			
Yukon	6215	Rural, Non-Farm		2975
Northwest Territories	3688	Farm		2389

Source: Canada. Census Division. 1971 Census of Canada: Population.

Table 3-8 also gives us the income spread among the provinces and territories as of 1971. The Yukon ranked highest because of the high wages paid to workers in the North. But notice how much lower the figure was for the Northwest Territories. Within the ecumene, Ontario was clearly the leader, followed by British Columbia and Quebec. Note how much higher the urbanized provinces ranked than the farming and fishing provinces. Considering that Ontario had both the largest population and the highest median income, it is no surprise that so many people in the West and in the Atlantic Provinces feel that Canadian wealth is too strongly concentrated in Ontario.

MIGRATION

So far we have spoken of Canadians as if they were immobile. Actually, they are always moving around, as individuals look for better jobs or for more pleasant places to live. Where the people are moving from and to tells us a lot about the country. Inside Canada are two types of migration: migration from the countryside to the cities and migration from province to province. Most of the new jobs and the new houses are in or around cities, so that even the interprovincial movement ends up being a move to the cities. To these migrations we can add the people coming into Canada from other countries; these people also usually end up moving into the cities. As in Table 3-3, Canada's urban population is rapidly increasing, while the rural population is decreasing steadily.

Table 3-9 gives us an estimate of the gain or loss from migration for each province. Only three provinces gained and most of the movement went to just two of them, British Columbia and Ontario. On the other hand, the net losses for Saskatchewan, Manitoba, and the Maritime Provinces were especially heavy if one compares the losses with the total populations of those provinces. The gain for Ontario was caused by the rapid growth of the industrial cities at the western end of Lake Ontario: Toronto, Hamilton, Kitchener, and St. Catharines. The losses for Saskatchewan and Manitoba were a result of people leaving the rural areas, the farms and the small towns. Nova Scotia suffered from the decline of jobs in the coal-mining and steel-making industries of Cape Breton Island. British Columbia was the "terminal" for people moving towards the Pacific coast. Notice too that there has been very little net movement into the Territories.

By studying Table 3-10 we can see how migration affects the individual provinces. This table tells us: (1) what percentage of the provincial population was born outside Canada and (2) what percentage was born in another province. The first shows where recent immigrants have gone; the second shows where Canadians themselves have moved.

The left-hand column of the table suggests that many of the recent foreign immigrants have gone to Ontario and British Columbia. The bottom half of that column has numbers much higher than the top half. This means that at least in this century most of the people coming from outside Canada have passed by our five eastern provinces in favour of those to the west.

TABLE 3-9
Gain or Loss through Interprovincial Migration

Newfoundland	− 81 000
Prince Edward Island	− 27 000
Nova Scotia	−122 000
New Brunswick	−107 000
Quebec	− 91 000
Ontario	+366 000
Manitoba	−174 000
Saskatchewan	−268 000
Alberta	+ 86 000
British Columbia	+518 000
The Territories	+ 5 000

Source: Canada. Census Division. 1971 Census of Canada: Population.

The high percentage for Ontario is interesting. Because the western provinces were settled after 1890, they could easily obtain a high percentage of foreign-born. Many peoples from eastern Europe came to Canada to settle on the Prairies. But Ontario already had a large population, so that 22% implies that great numbers of newcomers were added onto the locally-born population.

The right-hand column, "born in another province," tells us that the migration inside Canada has tended to be westward. The Yukon and Northwest Territories have the highest percentages because they have very low populations and because few white people were born there. Among the provinces, British Columbia stands out. Many people have moved to the west coast because it is believed to be such a pleasant place to live. The mild climate, the early flowers, the gardens, and the spectacular scenery of the coast, the mountains, and the forests have made British Columbia a popular place for young people to move to and for old people to retire to. Besides, North Americans have an old tradition of moving west.

The high figure for Alberta suggests that many people have moved there because of the rapid growth, based largely on oil. Alberta is also thought of as an exciting place to live because of the Rocky Mountains and the cowboy heritage.

TABLE 3-10
Population Born outside the Province (%), 1971
by Province

	% not born in Canada	% born in another Province
Newfoundland	1.6	3.2
Prince Edward Island	3.4	11.7
Nova Scotia	4.6	11.4
New Brunswick	3.5	11.4
Quebec	7.2	4.3
Ontario	22.1	10.4
Manitoba	15.1	13.7
Saskatchewan	11.9	11.4
Alberta	17.2	21.1
British Columbia	22.9	28.9
Yukon Territory	13.6	55.0
Northwest Territories	6.3	31.6

Source: Canada. Census Division. 1971 Census of Canada: Population.

TABLE 3-11
Population Born outside the Province (%), 1971
By Metropolitan Areas

	% not born in Canada	% born in another Province
Montreal	15.0	5.7
Toronto	34.0	10.4
Halifax	7.3	18.7
Quebec	2.2	2.0
Ottawa	12.5	22.3
Hamilton	28.8	9.0
Winnipeg	20.1	14.5
Calgary	20.5	29.4
Edmonton	18.6	20.9
Vancouver	23.6	27.4
Victoria	24.6	29.8

Source: Canada. Census Division. 1971 Census of Canada: Population.

Notice the very low figures for Newfoundland and Quebec. Clearly, few Canadians move to those two provinces. Most of the migrants head for the cities. Table 3-11 shows the same percentages for most of the major cities of Canada. Notice especially the contrast between Montreal and Toronto. Toronto receives more than twice as many people from outside its province and from foreign countries as does Montreal. Montreal's growth has thus been mostly a Quebec affair, whereas Toronto's has involved all of Canada, and countries overseas.

Among the other cities, we may be surprised to see that Hamilton has the highest proportion of people born outside of Canada. For an immigrant who does not know English or French, it is almost impossible to get an office job. However, he or she can work on construction or in a factory, and Hamilton is one of Canada's main industrial cities.

In contrast, notice how few foreign born live in Quebec City and Halifax. Almost everyone living in Quebec City has been born in the province of Quebec.

The movement of people to the west, noted on Table 3-10, has resulted in high percentages in both columns for the western cities. In Victoria, Vancouver, and Calgary, half or more of the inhabitants were not born there. When you think that most of the young children would have been born there, you can see that in those western cities close to 65% of the adults must have been born someplace else.

CONCLUSION

The Canadian mixture of peoples is uneven. Our country is made up of many regions, provinces, and territories, each of which is itself made up of many cultural units. Much of the world has contributed people and their outlooks on life to Canada. And, although these people have all become Canadians, they have not melted together, but instead have become a mosaic. One part of the mosaic differs as much from another as does one country from the other in some parts of the world.

Taking into account all that has been said in this chapter, two of the provinces stand out as being especially different — Newfoundland and Quebec. Newfoundland has the most self-contained society, with the least number of people from other places, with the most "British" population, a high rural but non-farm settlement, and a unique religious mix. Quebec also has its own special identity of language and religion.

Ontario, in contrast, comes through as the most statistically "average" province. Centrally located, highly urbanized, it attracts people from all parts of Canada and the world. It has an ethnic and religious mix which is much like that of all of Canada.

QUESTIONS

1. Use the following figures from the 1851-1976 census to draw a line graph that shows the growth of the Canadian population from 1851 to 1976.

Census Year	Population Numbers	Province	Population 1976 ($\times 10^3$)	Land Area ($\times 10^3$ km^2)
1851	2 436 297	Nfld.	549	370
1861	3 229 633	P.E.I.	116	6
1871	3 689 257	N.S.	812	53
1881	4 324 810	N.B.	665	72
1891	4 833 239	Que.	6141	1357
1901	5 371 315	Ont.	8132	891
1911	7 206 643	Man.	1006	548
1921	8 787 949	Sask.	908	570
1931	10 376 786	Alta.	1800	664
1941	11 506 655	B.C.	2406	931
1951	14 009 429	Yukon &		
1961	18 238 247	N.W.T.	64	3778
1971	21 568 311			
1976	22 598 016	Canada	22598	9220

2. Using the statistics in Question 1, draw a divided circle graph to show the relative sizes of the populations in the various political units in Canada in 1976. Add a suitable title to this graph.

Note: The formula for the divided circle or "pie" graph is

$$\frac{\text{provincial \%}}{\text{national total (100\%)}} \times 360° = \#° \text{ per province on the graph}$$

3. What are some of the implications for Quebec, the Northwest Territories, and Canada arising from the differences in birth rates?

4. What may be the consequences for Canada of a continued move of the population from rural to urban places?

5. In what ways are the Atlantic Provinces (Newfoundland, Nova Scotia, Prince Edward Island, New Brunswick) affected by the lack of a large city? (In Canada a large city is one with a population of over 400 000.)

6. In what ways does the ethnic distribution in Canada affect the success or failure of the program of bilingualism?

7. To what degree can we consider Ontario to be the most typical Canadian province?

8. Using the statistics in Table 3-8, Median Income by provinces (1976), construct a bar graph to show the differences in median income of the provinces in Canada. Explain the differences.

RESEARCH

1. Using the latest census figures and the median incomes on Table 3-8, calculate about how much of the total income of Canadians is earned in each province and territory. How does this affect Canada?

2. Using Tables 3-3 and 3-8, calculate the income earned in metropolitan areas, cities, towns, villages, and on farms. How do you think these incomes affect wealth, taxes, and political power in Canada?

3. Using Table 3-9 and figures from the 1961 census, calculate the approximate percentages of gain or loss of population through migration for each province. What are the effects of this movement? Is it a good thing? Is there any effective way to slow it down?

4. This chapter tells us that the people of Newfoundland are different in some ways than the people of other provinces. How does this difference show up in other ways — lifestyle, culture, traditions, economy, etc?

5. Which Canadian provinces differ most strongly from the Canadian religious norm? Why?

6. Review Canada's immigration policy and then prepare notes for a debate where you will have to argue either for or against increased immigration for Canada.

4 CANADA'S ECONOMY

Canada's economic history began with the Europeans who voyaged to the Grand Banks to fish off the coast of Newfoundland. They had such a large catch that they continued to return year after year, and thus grew the fishing tradition of the east coast. The same desire for profits motivated the early voyagers to risk their lives in the fur trade of beaver pelts. As settlement moved westward, the lumber firms of Upper Canada sailed their great rafts of timber down the length of Lake Ontario, or loaded locally built sailing vessels with fine squared timber. In the last quarter-century, farmers have prospered from the export of surplus Canadian wheat. In each case, the fishers, trappers, lumberers, and farmers made their money by converting some natural resource into a bulky, low cost, staple item that was transported to a waiting market located outside the country. Canada thus supplied the raw materials that were processed in the factories of Britain, the United States, and continental Europe. In turn, Canada imported the manufactured goods from these countries. Canadians have, as a result, been described as "hewers of wood and drawers of water."

Do you feel this is a fair statement? How much is Canada's rustic image from the pioneer era appropriate for the twentieth century atomic age?

The *Gross National Product* (GNP) is the total value of all goods produced and services rendered during the course of a year. The GNP is a guide to the nation's productivity and economic success. Despite two major world wars (1914-18 and 1939-45), a severe depression, and "galloping inflation," there is no mistaking the trend of the graph in Fig. 4-1.

Figure 4-2 compares the relative importance of various industries in 1929 and in 1970. Are Canadians really "hewers of wood and drawers of water"? Do Canadians still specialize in the so-called primary industries today? Are Canadians dependent on foreign nations for manufactured goods?

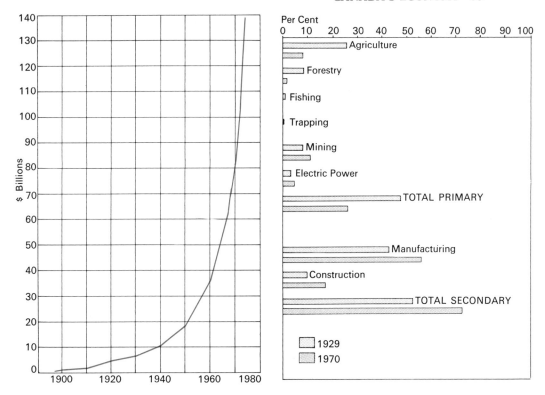

Figure 4–1: *Gross National Product*

Figure 4–2: *Comparison of Commodity-Producing Industries*

These two graphs illustrate that the Canadian economy has not only grown larger but has also undergone great changes. The increasing diversification of Canada's economy over the last forty years is evidence of a developing nation finally maturing.

SECTORS OF THE CANADIAN ECONOMY

The idea of examining the nation's economy may strike many people as being a rather dry topic filled with endless statistics. To simplify this complicated topic, economists usually divide the economy into three distinct sectors: *primary*, *secondary*, and *tertiary*.

PRIMARY SECTOR

The primary economic activities involve the winning of raw materials from the earth: namely, the extraction of minerals from the earth's crust,

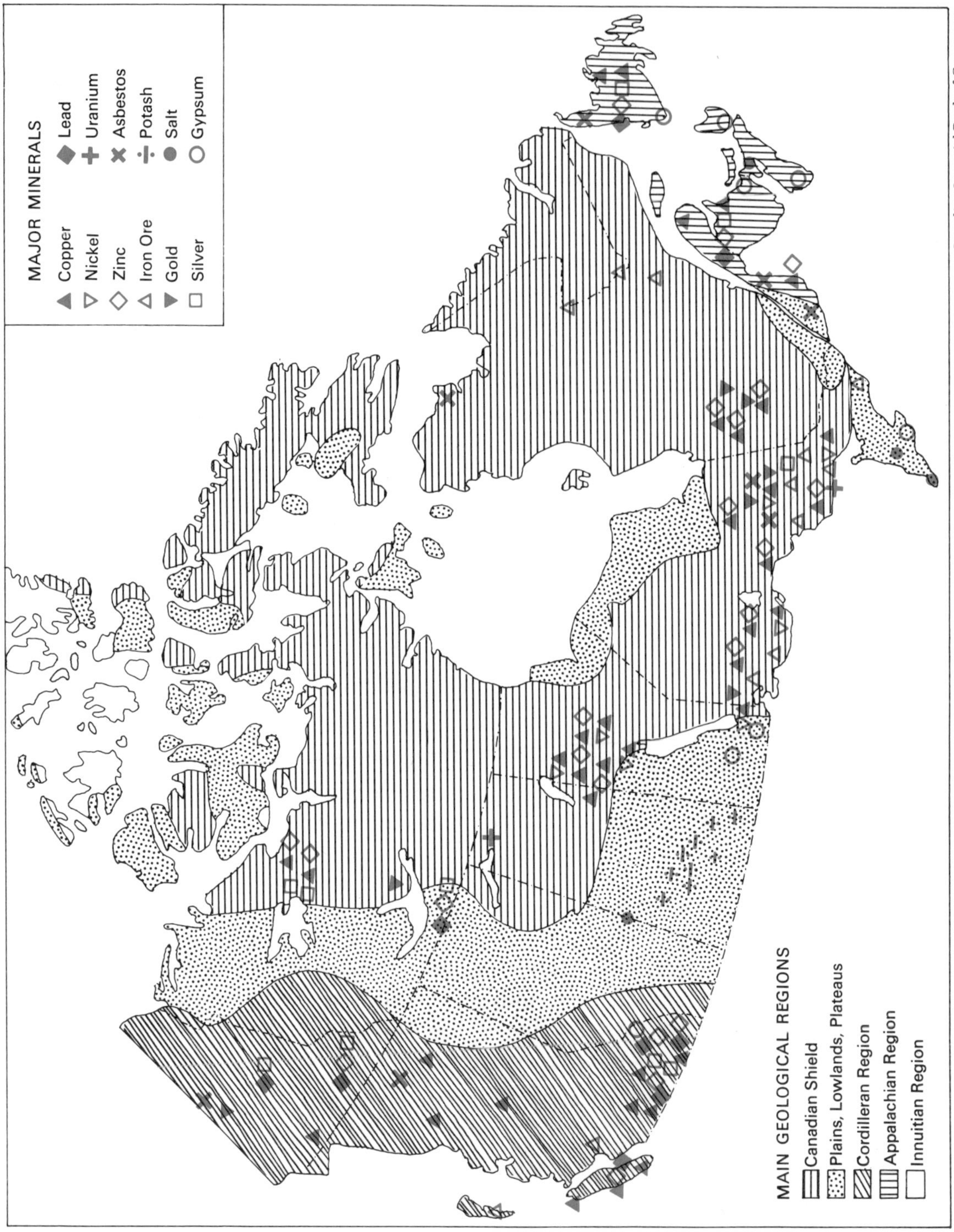

Figure 4–3: Major Mineral-Producing Areas

MAJOR MINERALS

Copper	◣	Lead	◆
Nickel	▽	Uranium	✛
Zinc	◇	Asbestos	✕
Iron Ore	◁	Potash	⫶
Gold	▼	Salt	●
Silver	☐	Gypsum	○

MAIN GEOLOGICAL REGIONS

Canadian Shield
Plains, Lowlands, Plateaus
Cordilleran Region
Appalachian Region
Innuitian Region

Canadian Imperial Bank of Commerce

the raising of crops and livestock, the cutting of forests, the catching of fish, and the hunting and trapping of animals. In the early stages of Canada's economic history, the primary sector was important; by 1970, however, the primary sector accounted for less than 25% of the total net value of the commodity-producing industries.

Mining. The Canadian mining industry has expanded in an unprecedented manner during this century. For example, in 1900 the value of mineral production was $65 million, but, by the mid-1970s, this figure had topped $11 billion. Canada now produces over 60 different minerals from nearly 300 operating mines. Canada ranks third after the United States and the U.S.S.R. among the mineral producers of the world. Underground mines, open pits, and drill holes yield a variety of minerals that are grouped into four categories: *metallics, non-metallics, mineral fuels*, and *structural materials*. Since the domestic market for minerals in Canada is limited, over 80% of the country's total mineral production is exported. As a result Canada leads the world in mineral exports: 60% of Canada's mineral export is in the form of crude minerals, while the remaining 40% is processed prior to export.

The most valuable are the metallic minerals which occur in the hard crystalline rock of the Canadian Shield and parts of the Western Cordillera. Here the mining companies have to cope with the problems not only of discovering the ore and developing the mine, but also of finding a suitable transportation system to move the ore to a smelter and finally the metals to the customer. Often a number of metal ores are found in the same rocks, so that they have to be separated during the smelting process. Nickel is an example of an ore that is not easily extracted from the rock; even so, Canada is the world's leading producer of nickel. Canada produces 10% of the world's supply of copper from 30 different mines that supply the smelters at Copper Cliff and Falconbridge in Ontario, Noranda and Murdochville in Quebec, and Flin Flon in Manitoba. Nickel, copper, and iron ore are the big three of the metallics but zinc, lead, and silver are also important. The locations of the major mines in Canada are shown in Figure 4-3.

Because so much of Canada's minerals are exported, the Canadian mining industry is particularly sensitive to changes in the international market for minerals. When the international demand is high, the prices of minerals rise and the mines work overtime. When the demand in foreign markets declines and international prices drop, the mining companies must either stockpile minerals and operate at a loss or close the mines. In many mining towns where the mine is the major employer, the closing of the mine means the closing of the town.

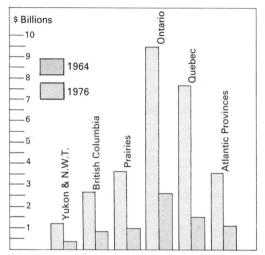

Figure 4–4: Value of Mineral Production, by Region

Statistics Canada. Cat. no. 26-202

One of the minerals that has experienced a cycle of boom and bust is uranium. The value of uranium mined in Canada grew from almost nothing during the 1950s to $269 million in 1959 as new mines were developed to supply the military needs of the United States. However, by the 1960s, the market was saturated with stockpiled uranium and, by 1964, the value of uranium mined had decreased to $74 million. Then, in the 1970s, the development of nuclear power stations created a new demand for uranium. In 1971, the government formed a Crown Company, Uranium Canada Limited (UCAN), to control the sales from the government stockpile. Today in the Elliot Lake area of Ontario, Denison Mines Limited and Rio Algoma Mines Limited mine quartz-pebble conglomerates for uranium; in Saskatchewan, Eldorado Nuclear Limited produces uranium for pitchblende; Gulf Minerals Canada is developing its new mine at Rabbit Lake.

The non-metallic minerals mined in Canada have a total value of about 18% of the total value of metallic minerals. Nevertheless, these minerals are important to the economy; some of them even form the basis for an entire industry. The non-metallic minerals in order of value are asbestos, potash, salt, titanium dioxide, sulphur, and gypsum.

The construction industry, which forms such an important part of the country's economy and prosperity, depends on the pits and quarries to supply cement, sand, gravel, stone, and clay. Because these items tend to be bulky, low-value items, they are generally mined close to the place of use in order to cut down on the high cost of transportation.

The article which follows examines the current situation of the

Canadian mining industry as well as the future of this important industry in the country's economy.

The Canadian Mining Industry

The mining industry continues to play an important part in the development of the Canadian economy. Were it not for this basic resource industry, Canada's export earnings would be much lower, there would be significantly less new investment spending and there would be slower growth in the Canadian standard of living. In 1976, mineral production in Canada (excluding coal, oil, and gas) was valued at $7.4 billion, the equivalent of four per cent of the total output of goods and services as measured by the value of Canada's Gross National Product. The mining industry also directly and indirectly provided employment for about nine per cent of Canada's total employed labour force and spent nearly $1.2 billion on new capital investment, or about four per cent of total new Canadian non-residential business capital expenditures.

Between 1966 and 1976 the total volume of mineral production rose by

almost 30 per cent, while its value rose by over 160 per cent. The main reasons for the advance were the increases in the value of the production of nickel, iron ore, copper, and zinc. There were also substantial increases in the value of gold, silver, and lead production. Together these major metallic minerals accounted for 95 per cent of the total value of metallic mineral production and 67 per cent of the value of total mineral production in 1976. Other metallic minerals produced in significant quantities were uranium, molybdenum, platinum and cobalt.

Of the non-metallic minerals, the most important to Canada are asbes-

Figure 4–6: *Major Minerals — Value of Production*   Statistics Canada

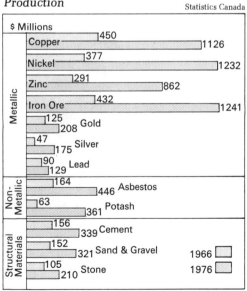

Figure 4–5: *Mineral-Production Index*   Statistics Canada

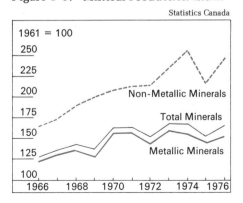

tos and potash, but sizable quantities of sulphur, titanium dioxide, salt, sodium sulphate, gypsum, peat moss, and quartz are also produced. The value of potash production has risen sixfold, while those of titanium dioxide, salt, sulphur, sodium sulphate, and peat have also increased considerably. Of the structural materials, while the most important are cement, sand and gravel, and stone, there is also substantial output of clay products and lime. The volume and value of the production of structural materials has risen more slowly than that of the metallic and non-metallic minerals because they are more readily available and their market is almost entirely domestic.

Minerals: Exports and Imports

A large proportion of Canada's mineral production is exported, mainly to the United States, Japan and Europe.

In terms of value, the United States provided a market for 56 per cent of Canada's exports in 1976, compared with 61 per cent in 1966. The United Kingdom's share declined to ten per cent in 1976 compared with 15 per cent ten years earlier, while Japan's share rose from five per cent in 1966 to eight per cent in 1976. Other significant buyers of Canadian minerals are Norway, Belgium-Luxembourg, West Germany, the Netherlands, France, and Italy.

Canada in 1976 was the world leader in the volume of production of nickel, zinc, potash, silver, and asbestos, and the second largest producer of molybdenum and uranium. With such a dominant position in their production Canada must benefit from the expansion in world demand for these metals.

Our exports do not consist solely of crude minerals, i.e. ores, concentrated ores, and scrap. A large proportion are fabricated and are in a form, e.g.

Figure 4–7: Imports and Exports of Minerals, by Percentage, 1976

Statistics Canada

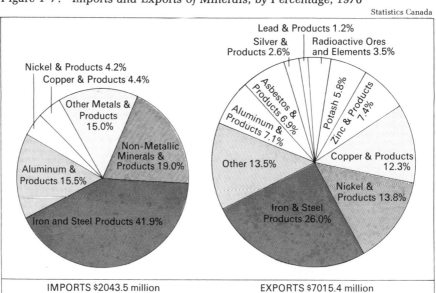

IMPORTS $2043.5 million   EXPORTS $7015.4 million

Crude and Fabricated Mineral Exports ($ billions), 1966-76

	Crude	Fabricated	Total	Fabricated as % of total
1966	1.19	1.39	2.58	54
1967	1.34	1.54	2.88	53
1968	1.58	1.81	3.39	53
1969	1.48	1.72	3.20	54
1970	1.81	2.30	4.11	56
1971	1.69	2.00	3.69	54
1972	1.69	2.03	3.72	55
1973	2.39	2.54	4.93	52
1974	2.88	3.37	6.25	54
1975	2.72	3.10	5.82	53
1976	3.18	3.87	7.05	55

ingots, castings, bars, rails, plates, alloys, wire, pipe, brake linings, and fire-brick, in which they can be used in the manufacture of finished products. Indeed, these fabricated mineral products have amounted to about half the value of Canada's total mineral exports during the past ten years. (See table.)

From 1966 to 1973, the world economy expanded at a fairly rapid rate, and the standard of living in the industrialized countries improved markedly. The increased demand for consumer goods and for the industrial machinery and equipment required to produce them greatly stimulated the need for minerals. Canada as the world's third largest producer of minerals, after the United States and the Soviet Union, reaped the advantages of the steadily growing market. However, during the following two years the world economy stagnated and demand for minerals fell drastically, causing some mines to lay off workers and others to close down. With the world economic recovery, which began in 1976, the outlook appeared to be more encouraging.

The value of exports of crude minerals and their basic fabricated products has nearly tripled during the decade rising from $2.6 billion in 1966 to $7.0 billion in 1976. The most important groups in 1976 were iron, nickel, and copper and their respective semifabricated products. Other leading groups were zinc, aluminum, and asbestos, and their respective semifabricated products.

For a country rich in mineral resources and a large exporter of minerals and mineral products, Canada imports substantial amounts of these minerals, though largely in fabricated form. In 1976, the value of Canada's imports was about $2.0 billion or about 30 per cent of the value of Canada's total crude and fabricated mineral exports. Iron and steel imports alone amounted to $800 million. Most mineral imports come from the United States, although significant quantities are also imported from Japan, West Germany, the United Kingdom, Norway and Australia.

The future of the Canadian mining

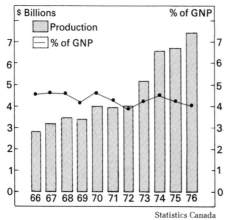

Statistics Canada

Figure 4–8: Value of Mineral
Production as a Percentage of GNP,
1966-76

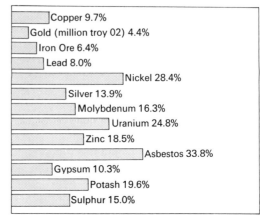

U.S. Dept. of the Interior. Commodity Data Summaries 1975

Figure 4–9:   Canada's Share of World
Production (selected minerals), 1966-76

industry will continue to depend on both external and internal factors. Since the industry relies so much on exports, the state of the economies of our main customers will largely determine the volume and value of our mineral production. To the extent that serious recessions in the world can be avoided, the demand for minerals should grow substantially into the 1980s. If the Canadian mining industry can remain competitive, it can expect to retain a major share of this growing market. Major internal factors which will shape mining companies' future plans and profitability include the costs of exploration and development of new mines, rising production costs, the level of taxation, as well as other governmental policies and regulations.

Continued demand for Canadian minerals will require sustained exploration for new sources of minerals. The relatively rich deposits now being mined will eventually be exhausted. Poorer-grade deposits which have already been discovered are more

expensive to mine per unit of mineral extracted, while the search for and development of deposits in the far north are much more costly than similar operations in the less remote areas. According to some estimates, Canada has sufficient existing known reserves of its major minerals to provide enough production to satisfy domestic and export demands for many years. However, if Canada is to maintain its position as a major world mineral producer, exploration will have to be done on a continuing basis. It must also be borne in mind that a lead time of up to ten years is required before a new mine can be brought into production.

New methods of exploration will be used in the future and searches will generally be carried out to lower depths than at present. This means that airborne geophysical surveys and geochemical surveys of surface materials will decline in relative importance, except perhaps in remoter areas where shallow orebodies may still remain undiscovered. One fact is cer-

CANADA'S ECONOMY 97

tain — exploration will become more costly as the search goes further and deeper. Costs of exploration, of capital equipment and transportation continue to rise rapidly. The increased requirements of protecting the environment will also raise costs considerably. In the case of long-term mining projects, forecasting costs up to ten years ahead will become more hazardous. Another continuing problem is likely to be that of regulatory change and government involvement at all levels.

In the past, Canadian mining has risen to meet the challenges it has faced and, in overcoming them, has developed into one of the strongest mining industries in the world. In the future, however, competition may well become even more intense. Rich deposits are being found in many other countries and where these are located in developing nations, the incentives to exploit them are frequently considerable. Certainly no monopoly in minerals exists for Canada and, if we are to remain a competitive world producer resolution of internal conflicts is an important and necessary priority.

Source: Adapted from the Canadian Imperial Bank of Commerce Commercial Letter, Issue No. 2, 1975, "The Canadian Mining Industry."

The International Nickel Company of Canada, Limited

Gulf Oil Canada Limited

Iron Ore Company of Canada

A load-haul-dump machine, with its five metre bucket loaded with approximately six tonnes of broken ore, is shown moving along the haulage way toward an ore pass at one of Inco's mines at Sudbury, Ontario (above left).

Gulf Minerals Canada, Limited, Rabbit Lake, 1974: an open pit uranium mine. The mill produces yellowcake uranium oxide for German power plants (above right).

An iron-ore mine at Labrador City (bottom right).

Agriculture. Agriculture has traditionally been Canada's most important primary activity. Generations of Canadians have been fortunate to enjoy the benefits of abundant, high quality food at relatively low cost. Agriculture in Canada today accounts for approximately 30% of all primary activity in the country. At a time when population explosion and crop failures have combined to create food shortages and widespread malnutrition in the world, Canada is exceptional in having a food surplus. Since Canadians consume only 69% of the nation's agricultural output, the remaining 31% is available for export. Considering Canada's northern latitude, inhospitable climate, and rugged landscape, it is surprising that the country is self-sufficient in food supply. Since less than 8% of the country's land area is considered to be useful farmland, the explanation of the high level of agricultural productivity must lie within our human and cultural resources rather than in our physical geography.

The 69 million hectares of agricultural land in Canada are being worked by a dwindling number of farmers: less than 7% of the Canadian labour force is employed on these lands. Yet, at the turn of the century, over 80% of the population worked on the farms and ranches. This century has seen a revolution in agricultural techniques. Individual

A dairy farm in the Atlantic Provinces.

A machine harvesting grapes on an Ontario farm.

International Harvester   International Harvester

The increasing use of agricultural machinery in Canada has resulted in a dwindling number of farmers. Machinery is now used in several phases of farm work — ploughing, harvesting, etc.

farms have grown larger and the number of workers to care for them has grown smaller as agricultural machinery has been developed. The subsistence farm and the family-operated mixed farm that raised both livestock and cash crops have in many cases been replaced by scientific, specialized operations. As a result the yield per hectare has been increased so that now fewer farmers produce more food than ever before (See photographs above).

Current agricultural techniques have also brought about additional responsibilities for the farmer. Not only must farmers master the latest scientific techniques, but they must also be able to invest heavily in machinery, equipment, and buildings. Agricultural land, the farmer's basic raw material, has also increased in cost: many farmers find that they must farm larger areas to make the high cost of their equipment a worthwhile investment. As a result, most farmers are in debt; therefore, they depend on the productivity of their farms to pay off their debts and to provide them with a living.

Although more than 80% of Canada's farm land is located in Western Canada, farming is done in all provinces, even in a few isolated spots of the Yukon Territory and the Northwest Territories. Five major types of agricultural practices can be distinguished within the country: dairying, livestock rearing (excluding dairying), grain cultivation, grain growing in combination with livestock rearing, and the cultivation of specialty crops. Dairying is popular in Ontario and Quebec. Together these two provinces contain the highest number of the country's dairy farms. Of the Atlantic provinces, 40% of the farms in Nova Scotia are classified as dairy farms. Alberta and Ontario lead the way in livestock rearing, followed by Quebec and Saskatchewan. Grain cultivation emphasizing crops such as wheat, rapeseed, oats, barley, and flax is dominant in the Prairie provinces of Saskatchewan, Alberta, and Manitoba; these three provinces also contain the largest number of farms involved in a combination of grain growing and livestock rearing. In the cultivation of specialty crops (fruits, vegetables, potatoes, tobacco, and so on), Ontario comes first, followed by Quebec and British Columbia.

Wheat. Among the crops grown in Canada, wheat is by far the most valuable. This crop is cultivated in every province except Newfoundland, but it is the specialty of the Prairie provinces. In fact, the economic development of the Prairie provinces and of the country as a whole has been very closely tied to wheat farming. Of the Prairie provinces, Saskatchewan, as is evident from Table 4-1, is the largest grain producer. In the past 10 years, that province has produced over 60% of the total amount of wheat grown in the country, and this wheat has provided one-half of the province's farm cash income.

The total farm cash receipts from grain in Canada is derived particularly from wheat, as Figure 4-10 illustrates. In addition, just under 80% of

TABLE 4-1
Wheat: Area, Production, and Gross Farm Value (1973)

	Area (1000 ha)	Total Tonnes	Gross Farm Value ($1000s)
P.E.I.	3.2	7 212	846
Nova Scotia	1.2	2 412	280
New Brunswick	1.6	2 438	278
Quebec	17.8	27 707	3 709
Ontario (winter)	151.5	376 165	63 099
Ontario (spring)	4.8	9 143	1 543
Manitoba	1252.4	2 031 680	331 100
Saskatchewan	6544.8	10 031 420	1 725 000
Alberta	1979.6	3 403 064	538 480
British Columbia	46.5	76 188	13 500
Total	10 003.4	15 976 430	2 654 826

Source: *Canada Year Book 1975.*

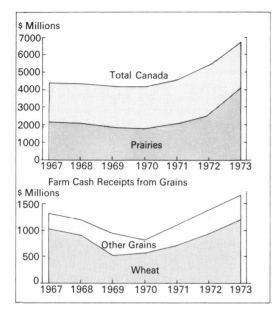

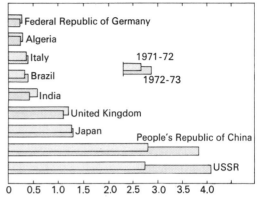

Figure 4–10: *Farm Cash Receipts (left)*
Statistics Canada

Figure 4–11: *Wheat Exports (above)*
Statistics Canada

Canada's wheat crop is exported. Thus, wheat is an important foreign-exchange earner for the country. The surplus wheat of the Prairies is shipped to European markets from the ports of Churchill or Thunder Bay, or to the Far East from Vancouver.

Exports of Canada's bulk wheat, as shown in Figure 4-11, have been increasing. In 1972-73, the U.S.S.R. was the leading customer; the People's Republic of China was the second-leading customer. Other leading purchasers of Canadian wheat are Japan, the United Kingdom, India, Brazil, Italy, Algeria, and The Federal Republic of Germany.

In Canada, two types of wheat — *winter wheat* and *spring wheat* — are cultivated. Where winter temperatures are mild, and there is sufficient snow cover, wheat is planted in the fall. This winter wheat germinates and establishes a deep root system before the snow falls. When temperatures warm up in the spring, the plant develops. In this way, the plants escape the damage caused by the summer heat. In Canada, this winter wheat crop is important in the peninsula of Southern Ontario between Lake Erie and Lake Huron. The grain is suitable for milling into high-quality pastry flour. The cultivation of winter wheat gives flexibility to farming: if the crop fails, the field can still be ploughed and planted in the spring. Besides, any surplus or damaged grain can be used as feed for livestock. (However, in recent years, corn has become more popular as a feed grain.)

On the Prairies, where the extreme cold temperatures of the winter make the cultivation of winter wheat impossible, the success of the grain trade is based on the production of spring wheat. The first Prairie settlers who tried to grow the European types of wheat soon discovered that their crops were being destroyed by the fall frosts before they could fully ripen. The development of new, quick-ripening types of wheat has been a major part of the success story in wheat cultivation in Western Canada. In 1842, a wheat that originated in Eastern Europe was developed in Ontario and called *Red Fife*. This wheat grew well in the West and produced an excellent grain for milling and baking but it too suffered from frost damage.

Experiments involving the crossing of different types of wheat were then carried out to try to produce new hybrids. In 1911, a variety called *Marquis* was introduced. It proved capable of maturing before the fall frosts. Within a few years, this variety was grown throughout the Prairies. By the 1930s a hardier and faster-ripening variety of wheat, called *Thatcher,* with excellent milling qualities had been developed.

Wheat, besides being extremely susceptible to damage by frosts, is also subjected to attacks by grasshoppers and other insects and various plant diseases such as rust. Stem rust is a kind of fungus that can drastically reduce the value of a field of wheat to the point that it is not economical to harvest the crop. As the *Thatcher* variety of wheat was not rust-resistant, researchers had to develop a new super variety that not only ripened quickly and possessed excellent milling and baking qualities but was also rust-resistant. This newest variety of wheat possessing all the above qualities is called *Manitou.*

The amount of wheat produced in Canada in any year is determined by a number of factors. One factor, climate, is always important in determining the yield, but another significant factor is the demand for grain on the world market. In 1970, when Canada had a considerable surplus of wheat, the federal government introduced another factor: a program known as LIFT (Lower Inventories for Tomorrow), designed to discourage the production of wheat. Since Canada exports 80% of the wheat crop, the world demand for wheat and the price it fetches on the international market are of great importance to the Canadian wheat farmer.

Canada's wheat crop is marketed by the Canadian Wheat Board which controls all interprovincial and export sales. The marketing program of the Wheat Board includes the delivery of the kinds, grades, and qualities of the grain which are in demand by the customers. Delivery of the grain takes place in two stages. First, the wheat farmer delivers the grain to the nearest county elevator; the amount is subject to a quota system whereby the Wheat Board controls the kind and grade of grain delivered, which in turn depends on the demand in the market.

Secondly, from the county elevators the grain is transported to the large terminals at Thunder Bay, Churchill, and Vancouver by railway according to tariffs determined by the terms of the National Transportation Act. The Canadian wheat farmer receives an initial payment from the Wheat Board when the wheat crop is delivered; this payment is based on the price fixed before the start of a crop year. The final payment is only made when the Board has sold all the grain after the end of the crop year. If the selling price of wheat in the world market falls below the price established, the deficit is not borne by the wheat farmers but by the federal treasury.

Fishing. The catching of fish for profit is the oldest economic activity practised in North America by the European settlers. Canadian waters have yielded a supply of fish for over 400 years — fish that is eaten fresh, dried, salted, canned, or frozen. In Canada the natural conditions for both marine and fresh water fishing are excellent; the techniques to harvest the resource have been developed. Canada's ocean "storehouses" yield over $700 million worth of fish each year. About 66% of the catch is exported, mainly to the U.S.A. and Europe.

The domestic market for fish products in Canada is limited because of its small population. Because of this situation, Canada's fishing industry has to compete with other countries — the U.S.A., Japan, and the U.S.S.R. But Canada has the advantages of being close to the rich fishing grounds off the northeast coast of North America, and of being the next-door neighbour of the world's biggest fish importer — the U.S.A.

In Canada, British Columbia is the leading province in *value* of fish caught, followed by Nova Scotia and Newfoundland. However, these three provinces must be listed in the reverse order when ranking them in terms of the *amount* of fish caught (Table 4-2). The fish from the Pacific Ocean sell at a much higher price per kilogram than fish from the Atlantic. The salmon catch alone is worth over $100 million each year; halibut, the second most valuable catch, is also a high-value fish. Herring was so important to the people who fished the Pacific that overfishing occurred in the 1960s: the federal government had to restrict the catch to allow the fish stocks to be replenished. On the Atlantic coast the lobster is the most valuable species; nearly 18 million kilograms of this delicacy are harvested annually. Scallops are another valuable shellfish. Cod, flounder, sole, redfish, haddock, pollock, whiting, hakes, and herring are the most common fish "harvested" from the Atlantic Ocean.

TABLE 4-2
Landings and Value of Sea Products,
by Province 1972 and 1973

Province or Territory	Quantity (1000s kg)		Value ($1000s)	
	1972	1973	1972	1973
Newfoundland	295 135	306 270	100 599	144 780
Prince Edward Island	25 780	28 501	19 964	22 322
Nova Scotia	286 855	279 054	142 102	175 685
New Brunswick	162 144	129 897	86 380	89 988
Quebec	83 210	70 717	25 938	35 478
Ontario	19 589	24 059	16 238	20 752
Manitoba	11 103	10 250		
Saskatchewan	4 865	3 818	15 449	16 590
Alberta	2 202	2 091		
Northwest Territories	1 602	1 470		
British Columbia and Yukon	153 084	176 332	159 178	285 052
Total	1 045 566	1 032 463	545 587	772 086
Sea Fish	1 001 708	987 566		
Inland Fish	42 908	44 897		

Source: *Canada Year Book 1975.*

In recent years, however, both the Pacific and Atlantic fish stocks have suffered from overfishing because the fishing nations of the world competed for this cheap source of protein food. In 1964 the Canadian Government established a "12-mile" (19.2 km) fishing zone along Canada's coastline that was reserved for Canadians who fished commercially. The federal government also signed treaties with other nations to try to protect the marine fisheries.

Dwindling stocks of fish indicate that agreements made between individual nations have not been adequate. A plan must be developed by the nations who fish these areas to practise conservation. Only by all sides agreeing to limit their catch can enough fish be available to feed future generations. This logical move seems to be thwarted as individual nations follow their own short-term interests and refuse to join in an international agreement to regulate the use of the sea. Hence, in 1977 both Canada and the United States declared the establishment of a "200-mile" (322 km) limit with no guarantee that their regulations will be respected by the other fishing nations.

The *inland* or fresh water fisheries are concentrated in the Great Lakes area, where Ontario produces about 50% of the annual $16 million

Crewmen assist the landing of a net full of fish aboard this
modern stern trawler.

A net full of scallops has just been raised over the side of a
scallop-dragger. Shellfish such as these are an important part
of Nova Scotia's fisheries.

catch. The whitefish is the most valuable fish caught here, followed by yellow pickerel, pike, trout, and bass. The problems of fishing in the freshwater lakes do not arise from failure to reach an international agreement, but from the lamprey eel and pollution. The lamprey eel has destroyed the stock of valuable lake trout; however, recent efforts to control the eels seem to be effective. The pollution problems have resulted from untreated sewage from municipal sewage systems and industrial wastes like mercury that render the fish dangerous for human consumption. The solution to this problem will require more time. Both the Canadian and American governments are attempting to improve the water quality and restock the lakes with fish.

Fishing zones: Canada's biggest issue with U.S.

By John Picton

The talk in the ante rooms at the U.S. State Department these days is about fishing zones. For four weeks, with barely a two-hour daily break for lunch, the talkers have been attempting to negotiate fishing boundaries between Canada and the United States.

These negotiators . . . for both sides argue principle and international law, debate historic fishing practice, pursue intricate detail on fish stocks and map co-ordinates and catch quotas.

But neither side is prepared to give up a single degree of latitude or longitude in its claims of ocean title — and for reasons these representatives are not even discussing.

For although their subject is fishing

Figure 4–12: *Canada's Fishing Zones*

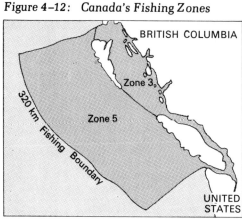

grounds, there is a simultaneous dispute between the two countries . . . over maritime boundaries, with all that implies for future underwater mineral development.

Both debates involve national sovereignty and jurisdiction, subjects that have become hypersensitive in political circles in recent years. . . .

The result is that the fishing talks, at least psychologically, are being viewed by the participants as all-encompassing.

Combined, these issues represent the most contentious ones outstanding between Canada and the United States.

When the long-established land boundary was negotiated, maritime boundaries were hardly looked at by negotiators who did not see the need for, or the potential of, having offshore areas of demarcation.

It has taken the depletion of fish stocks and a dramatic decline in intrinsic fuel reserves to emphasize the need for such boundaries.

Canada put an edge to this need when, on Jan. 1 this year, it extended the country's fisheries management zone to 200 miles[1] from the previous 12 miles.[2]

The United States will extend its fishing territory to 200 miles[1] on March 1; maritime nations in the European Economic Community have already done so.

On the East Coast, Canada's new zone extends from a point midway between Canada and Greenland (which is Danish territory) to a point in the Gulf of Maine at the entrance to the Bay of Fundy, bringing an additional 502,000 square miles[3] of ocean under Canadian jurisdiction.

On the West Coast, the extended area encompasses a 128,000-square-mile[4] rectangle stretching from the tip of Vancouver Island to a point north of the Queen Charlotte Islands.

When a 200-mile[1] fishing zone is added in the Arctic, that will add another 420,000 square miles[5] of sea — although there is no commercial fishing in that area at the present time.

Announcing last year that it was extending its fisheries limits, Canada said it was making the move "in light of the crisis situation pertaining in the fisheries off Canada's coasts".

It was a move for which Canadian fishermen — particularly on the East Coast — had for long fought, given the decline in their catch in recent years due to over-fishing.

Lately, it has been estimated, foreign countries have been operating about 800 fishing vessels off Canada's East Coast, compared with the 200 being operated by Canadian companies.

The fishing industry has been providing about 70,000 jobs in the Atlantic region, an area where the unemployment rate has been higher than 15 per cent.

Yet, so bad has the over-fishing become that processing plants in Newfoundland, able to handle a billion pounds of fish a year, have been reported working at 40 per cent of capacity.

Under a series of bilateral agreements that have been negotiated, the Soviet Union, Norway, Spain, Portugal and Poland are being given quotas within the 200-mile[1] fishing limit based on catches that are said to be "surplus to Canada's needs."

Fishing boats from these countries, which will have to be licenced by

Canadian authorities, will lose their licences if they are caught violating Canada's new and extensive regulations. . . .

In addition, trawlers can be impounded for varying periods, and a captain can face penalties of up to two years in jail and a fine of up to $25,000.

Some spokesmen for the fishing industry in Atlantic Canada, who had been advocating a complete ban on foreign fishing within a 200-mile[1] limit, are suspicious of the quota system. They also are uneasy that an agreement has not yet been negotiated with the French islands of St. Pierre and Miquelon, south of Newfoundland.

They do not want to adopt a median line approach toward St. Pierre and Miquelon because then these French possessions would control much of the rich fishing grounds in the area, out of proportion to the size of the islands.

East Coast fishermen also are uneasy about talk in Ottawa of proposed co-operative fishing ventures.

Canadian Fisheries Minister Romeo LeBlanc has said any such ventures must be temporary, of benefit to Canadian industry and fishermen, aimed at catching fish that otherwise would not be caught by Canadians, and must teach Canadians new techniques.

However, there still was a storm of protest in Newfoundland when a joint venture with West German interests was announced to catch 6,000 metric tons of cod from Hamilton Bank off Labrador.

The bank area has seldom been fished by Canadians because of ice problems there and because of the availability of fish closer to home.

Ottawa's rationale in allowing the venture was to encourage larger fishing vessels to try the area, that it would harvest fish that Canadians normally would not catch, and that it would teach Canadians how to fish under the difficult conditions there.

Objections to the scheme highlighted the expectations that East Coast fishermen had of the 200-mile[1] declaration.

They were incensed because the Fisheries Department had withheld all quotas from some offshore areas where fish stocks were considered to have been seriously depleted.

"Most governments are unwilling to accept a limitation of their fishing effort until a resource is severely depleted for fear that other nations will reap the benefit of their forebearance," a report written for the Canadian-American Committee said a few years ago.

It left unsaid that the same conditions can apply to a nation's own fishermen.

For the West Coast, Canadian and U.S. officials are attempting to negotiate a separate salmon treaty while trying to agree on a comprehensive fishing agreement.

This separate treaty would replace the existing Fraser River Treaty which came into effect in 1937. Under it, pink and sockeye salmon stocks from the Fraser River are divided equally between Canada and the United States although the entire river system is in British Columbia.

Each country is required to provide matching funds to conserve and manage the salmon stocks. But Canada maintains it is getting a raw deal because, after all, the fish originate in Canadian waters and because the treaty has cost Canada a great deal in indirect costs — such as in pollution control and in forfeiting the possibility of developing hydro-electric projects in the Fraser River system.

It has been established that it would be uneconomic to build fish ladders around proposed dams.

In turn, the United States is reluctant to give up what it considers historical fishing rights.

Figures relating to the benefits explain why.

Between the signing of the treaty in 1937 and June, 1973, the Canadian and U.S. governments each contributed $8.3-million toward the direct cost of operating the fishery. During that period, U.S. fishermen harvested pink and sockeye salmon of Fraser origin worth $150-million.

And, ever since it was discovered in the 1950s that Alaskan net fishermen, working close to the U.S. coast, were catching significant numbers of salmon bound for northern British Columbia, there has been a simmering dispute over the means of reducing the capture by nationals of one country of salmon spawned in the other country.

Then there is the Other Dispute, the one over latest boundaries, with their effects on offshore exploration for oil and natural gas.

Here, the most problematical area of discussion, the one that suggests the most immediate potential for riches, given offshore oil and gas, is how to divide the waters off the East coast in the Gulf of Maine.

However, the Beaufort Sea holds the promise of hydrocarbon discoveries. Other contentious areas: the Strait of Juan de Fuca and Dixon Entrance in Hecate Strait. . . .

Put simplistically, Canada favors a line out to sea from existing land boundaries that would be equidistant between Canada and U.S. territory.

The Canadian proposal would give Canada jurisdiction over about a third of Georges Bank, a rich fishing ground.

The United States says the bank is a natural prolongation of U.S. territory and, therefore, claims the whole area.

In 1969, in a dispute between West Germany, Denmark and the Netherlands involving lateral boundaries, the World Court said that such agreements must be based on "equitable principles," taking into account the unity of mineral deposits, the contours of an underwater shelf and the proportion of a disputed area awarded to each party.

The court added that, with regard to the contours of a shelf, it did not want a median line to divide an area that was a "natural prolongation" of only one nation, saying that there should be a "balancing up of all such considerations."

Based on this and earlier rulings, a group of commentators opined that such decisions enable nations "to rationalize a limitless number of circumstances so that the seemingly clear median-line principle is considerably weakened".

But there are precedents for a median-line concept of partition.

The Anglo-Norwegian division of the North Sea follows a line of equidistance, ignoring a trench close to the Norwegian coast.

Likewise, an agreement separating the seabed between the Canadian Arctic archipelago and Greenland also follows the median-line principle and disregards an undersea trench (which would have given a larger share of the seabed to Denmark).

Canada began issuing exploration

permits for drilling on Georges Bank in 1964 — that part of the bank that would be Canadian under Canada's proposed boundary line. It was not until 1969 that the United States objected, in a diplomatic note.

Why did it take five years for such a reaction? Perhaps it was the result of work carried out on the bank by the U.S. Geological Survey in 1968 which, perhaps, suggests that the bank holds good oil and gas potential.

And Canadian and U.S. officials have such considerations very much in mind when they supposedly are talking about fishing zones.

---

[1] 320 km   [2] 19.2 km   [3] 1 299 678 km^2 [4] 331 392 km^2 [5] 1 087 380 km^2

Source: *The Globe and Mail*, Toronto (February 17, 1977).

Forestry. The early pioneers who worked hard to clear the forest and create land that could be farmed would be surprised to discover that less than 20% of Canada today remains as commercially valuable and economically accessible woodland. Where the settlers often viewed the forest as an obstacle to be eliminated, Canadians today regard the forest as one of their most valuable assets and among their greatest renewable resources. In 1971, 259 000 workers earned $2091 million cutting and processing timber. In the same year, Canada exported $3140 million worth of wood, wood products, and paper. Canada, the world's largest newsprint producer, produces nearly 40% of the world's newsprint. In

A lumber dockyard at Port Moody, B.C.

addition, the pulp and paper industry is the country's leading industry in employment, in salaries and wages paid, and in value added by manufacture (Table 4-3).

Canada's forests contain about 140 recognized tree species, of which

TABLE 4-3
The Pulp-and-Paper Industry in Canada, 1973

Shipments		
Value	$ 3.7 billion (e)	
Volume	18.8 million tonnes	
Exports		
Value	$ 2.6 billion	
Volume	14.6 million tonnes	
Number employed in the industry		
Mills and offices	80 000	
Forests	60 000	
Wages and salaries paid	$ 1.3 billion	
Shipments		
Newsprint	43.6%	8 192 t
Groundwood Printing Papers	2.3%	428 t
Book and Writing Papers	3.8%	717 t
Kraft Papers	3.1%	572 t
Tissue and Special Papers	1.6%	308 t
Containerboard	7.5%	1 413 t
Boxboard	3.1%	589 t
Wood Pulp	35.0%	6 590 t
Total	100.0%	18 809 t
Where products used		
In Canada	22.5%	4 229 t
Exported	77.5%	14 580 t
United States	53.1%	9 985 t
Western Europe	7.6%	1 438 t
United Kingdom	5.7%	1 077 t
Latin America	3.9%	724 t
Japan	3.6%	683 t
All others	3.6%	673 t
Total	100.0%	18 810 t

(e): estimate
Note: The statistics on shipments and exports are for companies participating in the Canadian Pulp and Paper Association statistical exchange, and account for some 98% of the Canadian industry.
Source: Canadian Pulp and Paper Association Bulletin, 1976.

Douglas firs in Cathedral Grove, Victoria Island.

British Columbia Government Photograph

31 are *coniferous* or *softwood* trees. About 65% of the coniferous trees are commercially marketable.

The distribution of forest land and the volume of softwoods and hardwoods (or deciduous trees) in the various provinces and territories across Canada is shown in Table 4-4. In terms of standing timber, the most numerous forest trees in Canada are the spruces, pines, huge firs, poplars, hemlocks, birches, cedars, Douglas fir, maples, and larches. Spruce, which accounts for about 35% of Canada's timber volume, is found across Canada from the Atlantic to the Pacific coast. Pines (of which the 2 most important species are the jack pine and lodgepole pine) make up 10% of standing timber in Canada; their range extends from

TABLE 4-4
1973 National Forest Inventory

	Forest Land (km²)	Volume in Million Cubic Metres		
		Softwood	Hardwood	Total
Newfoundland	127 444	220	35	255
Prince Edward Island	2 504	4	2	6
Nova Scotia	44 425	178	76	254
New Brunswick	63 084	415	164	579
Quebec	695 786	2 744	947	3 691
Ontario	432 063	2 586	1 649	4 235
Manitoba	135 420	345	101	446
Saskatchewan	128 148	293	198	491
Alberta	307 294	952	569	1 521
British Columbia	544 710	7 369	204	7 573
Yukon	232 270	—	—	—
Northwest Territories	546 903	—	—	—
Canada	3 260 048	15 105	3 946	19 051

Source: *Canada Year Book 1975*.

Nova Scotia to Alberta, British Columbia, and the Yukon Territory. Among the firs, the balsam fir is the most popular commercially and it grows from Newfoundland westward across the country to the Prairies. The Douglas fir is British Columbia's most well-known tree species and it has helped the province earn the worldwide reputation for timber.

In Canada, about 90% of the forests are at the moment publicly owned crown land. The trees are, however, harvested by private companies that either purchase the timber rights or acquire a tree-farm license; a license allows them to cut the timber and then replant the forest for future use. The demand for wood and by-products of the forest industry is growing and it has been estimated that it will increase by 300% by the year 2000. Reforestation and conservation are therefore essential and the success or failure of the regeneration of the forests will determine whether these forests are a renewable or a non-renewable resource.

Among the hazards facing the forests of Canada are fires, diseases, and insects. Records show that in the ten-year period between 1962 and 1971, Canada had an average of 7662 fires per year; the total value of the damage and fire-fighting cost was over $25 million each year. Only 27% of these fires were caused by lightning; the remaining 73% were caused by careless individuals.

Of the tree diseases, the Dutch elm disease has in recent years caused considerable concern, especially in Ontario and Quebec. The disease which attacks elm trees is caused by fungus carried by beetles. Fortunately, methods to control and eliminate the spread of the disease have been successful. In New Brunswick, the budworm problem has also been effectively brought under control by spraying insecticides on about 2 million hectares of forest land.

SECONDARY SECTOR

Secondary economic activities are the processing of the primary activities into more useful and, hence, more valuable form. If the items produced are stationary, the work is classified as *construction*; if the products are mobile, the activity is classified as *manufacturing*. In 1970 the secondary sector of the Canadian economy accounted for approximately 74% of the total value of all industry in Canada, with manufacturing accounting for 56% and construction 18%.

In order to better understand the nature of Canadian manufacturing, let us examine each of the prerequisites for the development of manufacturing industries:

The Development of Manufacturing Industries
Requires the Presence of Certain Prerequisites:

A Natural Resources ——————————————	1. Raw Materials 2. Power
B Human Resources ——————————————	3. Labour 4. Market
C Stage of Economic Development ———————	5. Transportation 6. Capital

A. NATURAL RESOURCES

1. Raw Materials. These basic items are provided either by the primary industries of Canada or by importing materials such as ores, metals, rubber, and tropical foods, which this country does not produce. The absolute necessity of having a steady supply of raw materials forces Canadian manufacturing industries to have alternative sources of supply and to maintain stockpiles. These measures ensure that industries can operate throughout the year, even during the winter when conditions often cause the movement of raw materials to come to a standstill. Some large manufacturing concerns in Canada produce their own raw materials, process them, then distribute them to their customers. This is known as *vertical integration,* of which two examples are the Noranda Mines Limited and The Steel Company of Canada Limited (better known as Stelco).

2. Power. Canada's earliest energy requirements were met by using human and animal muscle power. Then brute strength gave way to engineering skills and to the use of rushing waters to drive mills, saw timber, grind grain, and process cloth. For decades, Canadian children complained about the drudgery of keeping the woodbox full — wood to feed the open fireplace, the Franklin stove, and the Quebec heater. By contrast, today's children enjoy the convenience of simply adjusting a thermostat, leaving ample time for leisure and relaxation. They are the beneficiaries of a revolution in energy production. People have learned to harness the energy contained in fossil fuels and to transmit this energy, in the form of electricity, over long distances. In order to maintain this high standard of comfort in Canada, over nine tonnes of coal (or equivalent energy) are required per year for every man, woman, and child in the country. At this rate, Canadians are the highest per capita consumers of

The Noranda Group:

a group of 61 companies under Noranda Mines Limited operating mines, smelters, refineries and manufacturing plants as well as forest product operations. The organization is 92% Canadian owned and is Canada's tenth-largest Canadian owned corporation.

Mining: The Noranda Group and its associated companies operate 26 mines.

Noranda (Geco, Bell Copper, Boss Mountain)
Gaspé
Brenda
Brunswick
Central Canada Potash
Kerr (Joutel, Icon/Sullivan)
Mattagami Lake (Mattagami, Mattabi)
Orchan
Pamour Porcupine
Placer (Endako, Craigmont, Gilbraltar)

Ores Treated:
Copper, zinc, lead, silver, gold, molybdenum, potash

Smelting and Refining:
Horne
Gaspé Copper
Canadian Copper Refiners
Canadian Electrolytic Zinc
Brunswick Smelting
Noranda Aluminum (U.S.)

Smelting and Refining Products:
Copper, zinc, lead, silver, gold, cadmium. The 23 products produced in Noranda's smelting and refining facilities are sold by Noranda Sales Corporation Ltd. from Toronto and London, England, to customers in 45 countries.

Fabricating: 57 manufacturing plants (47 in Canada)

Canada Wire and Cable Noranda Metal Industries	Copper: Wire and high-voltage power cables, 17 000 wire and cable products, copper pipe, tube, sheet, strip.
Canada Wire and Cable Noranda Aluminum Norandex	Aluminum: Doors, windows, siding aluminum wire, rod, and cable.
Bridon — American Wire Rope Industries	Wire Rope
Canplas Industries Grandview Industries	Plastics: Synthetic rope, plastic moulding, PVC plastic pipe.
Quebec Iron Foundries	Grinding Media
Belledune Fertilizer St. Lawrence Fertilizer	Fertilizer

Source: Noranda Annual Report 1975.

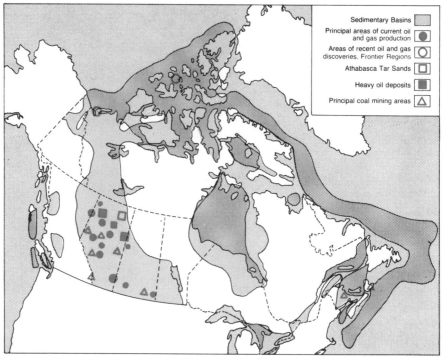

Figure 4–13: *Canada's Fossil-Fuel Resources*

Imperial Oil Limited

energy in the world, followed closely by the U.S.A.; in fact, North Americans consume energy at four times the world average. Our appetite is insatiable and the demand grows all the time.

How is this ever-increasing demand for energy to be met? Can the growth charts of domestic energy consumption curve upward indefinitely?

Physicists tell us that people can neither create nor destroy energy, they can merely alter its form. It is believed that seven "sources" of energy exist in our solar system. Two of these sources are *external* to our planet and five of them are *internal* — that is, found on the planet itself.

The two external sources of energy are:

  (i) *solar energy,* which is radiated into space from the explosions on the sun, and

  (ii) *gravitational energy,* which exists as the attraction between masses.

The five internal sources of energy are:

  (i) *fossil fuels* preserved within wood, coal, and petroleum

(ii) *nuclear energy,* which involves the breakdown of radioactive elements

(iii) *latent heat of crystallization,* or the exchange of heat associated with changes in crystal structure

(iv) *chemical energy,* which is familiar to anyone who has struck a match

(v) *geothermal energy,* which refers to the presence of heat inside the earth's crust.

In the 7000 years of recorded civilization, people have directed their technology almost exclusively to the development of energy from fossil fuels. The distribution of Canada's fossil fuel resources are shown in Figure 4-13.

Petroleum. Canada's petroleum resources are derived from the remains of ancient marine animals and plants that have been changed into natural gas and crude oil by the processes of heat, chemical reactions, and bacterial and radioactive activities. The pressures from these actions force the oil and gas through the tiny spaces in porous rock until they become trapped by a geologic structure.

A petroleum corporation must obtain a government licence to explore and develop. It then conducts a careful geological survey of the area by using aerial photographs, magnetometers, gravity measurements, and seismographs; this ground work by geologists helps to pinpoint the most likely locations of oil deposits. At this stage the corporation must decide if it will gamble millions of dollars to sink a test hole (see "The costs of energy"). They are not always successful, as the "Diary of a dry hole" illustrates.

The costs of energy

The cheapest producible energy in the world today is the oil from the vast pools of the Middle East. In those pools, wells produce at rates 50 to 100 times as great as the Canadian average. With wells so prolific, fewer have to be drilled. For this and other reasons, the investment in facilities needed to produce a barrel* of oil per day is very low, about $300.

Canadian oil costs more to produce than that, unfortunately. In the existing fields of the Prairies, it needs between $2,000 and $3,000 of capital investment to add another barrel-per-day of oil production. New oil from the Prairies, because it will come from small fields that are widely scattered, will require investments of between $5,000 and $10,000 per additional daily barrel. Oil from the frontiers — the Arctic and the Atlantic — will require investments of from $10,000 to $20,000. Oil from the tar sands and heavy-oil deposits of Alberta will require investments of $15,000 to $25,000 per daily barrel of production. Energy from gasified coal will require investments of $20,000 to $30,000 per daily barrel equivalent. And from hydroelectric or nuclear sources, the investment required will be the equivalent of $25,000 to $50,000 per daily barrel.

The implication is clear: the days of low-cost energy are gone.

* 1 barrel ≐ 0.16m³
Source: Imperial Oil Limited.

Diary of a dry hole

Last December Imperial announced that a well drilled from its artificial island in the Beaufort Sea was abandoned at 8,883 feet[1] when the drill encountered formation pressures that made further drilling unsafe. The announcement marked the end of a project that had taken four years and 10 months to complete, and cost approximately $9 million.

The result was a disappointment, but the project proved that artificial islands are a practical — if expensive — means of drilling in the Beaufort Sea. Imperial has already built a second island at much less cost, using techniques suggested by the experience gained in building the original island, and found indications of gas-bearing sands in a well drilled from it. Other islands will be built and other wells drilled in the search for the petroleum reserves that are believed to lie in the sedimentary rocks under the Beaufort Sea.

A time-table for Immerk, as the island is known, and its well demonstrates the long lead times that are necessary for petroleum exploration, the amount of planning that must go into such projects, and the costs. The result is a measure of risk.

February, 1969 — Research begins on feasible ways to drill into the bed of the Beaufort Sea, which is covered with shifting ice for nine months of the year.

June, 1971 — Preliminary report of the Arctic Petroleum Operators' Association indicates the feasibility of artificial islands for offshore drilling. Imperial is a participant in this research.

July, 1971 — Engineering work on the design of the artificial island begins.

October, 1971 — Specifications for the dredging and other equipment needs are approved.

January, 1972 — Final approval for this project is given by Imperial, and contracts for the supply of the dredging equipment are let, at a commitment of $6,600,000.

June, 1972 — All equipment for the project is assembled at Hay River, N.W.T., for barging down the Mackenzie River to the island site.

June, 1972 — Field work for an environmental impact study begins. The study will continue for 15 weeks, and cost Imperial $130,000.

June, 1972 — Construction begins.

September, 1972 — Construction halts for the season. In 39 working days, 118,000 cubic yards[2] of material has been placed, creating an island 3.4 acres[3] in extent, rising at its highest point to eight feet[4] above sea level. The work crews leave, and the island is left to the rigors of an Arctic winter. The cost for the year reaches $3,100,000.

July, 1973 — Work resumes. During the summer, an additional 210,000 cubic yards[5] of dredged material is put in place, increasing the island's extent to 6.3 acres[6] and raising its overall level to 15 feet.[7] The island slopes are protected by a combination of filter cloth, chain-link fencing and submarine netting, and a dock is built. Cost for this work: $1,900,000.

August, 1973 — The drilling rig begins to arrive from Hooper Island for assembly.

August to September, 1973 — The drilling rig is assembled.

September 7, 1973 — The well is spudded and the rig begins drilling. Planned depth is 15,000 feet.[8]

December 22, 1973 — The well is abandoned at 8,883 feet[9] and the rig released. Approximate total cost for the project: $9,000,000.

[1] 2700 m   [2] 90 152 m³   [3] 1.4 ha   [4] 2.4 m   [5] 160 440 m³   [6] 2.5 ha
[7] 4.5 m   [8] 4560 m   [9] 2665 m   Source: Imperial Oil Limited.

Figure 4–14: *Exploring for Oil by Sound Waves*
  Sound waves from small controlled explosions near the surface travel downward, strike underlying layers of rock and are reflected back to the surface where they are recorded by the seismograph.

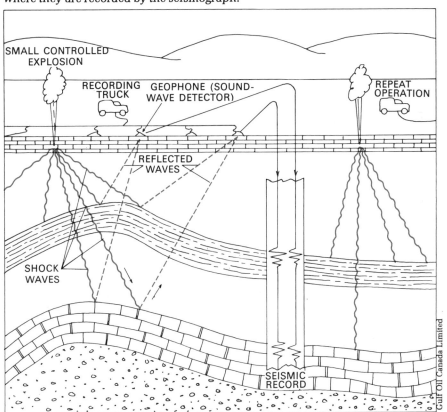

Gulf Oil Canada Limited
Photo by Ron. W. Sculthorp

Surveying an oil field in the Arctic (above).

Seismic operations in the Arctic (left).

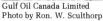

Gulf Oil Canada Limited
Photo by Ron. W. Sculthorp

Even when the well is successful and the crude oil or natural gas is piped to the surface, there is still the problem of transporting it to the refinery which is invariably located at the market for the refined petroleum. Canada's petroleum supply is located in the West, while most of the demand for petroleum comes from the East. The oil demands of the Atlantic provinces and Quebec have for a long time been met by importing petroleum from foreign sources such as Venezuela or the Middle East; importing oil was an advantage to Eastern Canada when foreign crude oil was cheaper than Canadian crude oil. However, as foreign crude has in recent years become more expensive and the supplies less assured, the need to extend the oil-pipeline network from the West to the East has become obvious. In Western Canada, the reverse situation is true, since it has an oil surplus. The amount of oil surplus to Canadian needs and eligible for export, mainly to the United States, is regulated by the National Energy Board.

The Need for Conservation. Petroleum is a non-renewable resource: once it has been used, it is gone forever. Over the last few decades, petroleum consumption in Canada has been increasing; as more oil is produced, more is being demanded for use in industry, transportation, and homes. Although Canada has vast reserves of petroleum, it still faces a possible energy shortage in the not-too-distant future. (About 65% of Canada's primary energy demand is supplied by oil and natural gas.) Estimates of the amount of petroleum which remains in Canada range from 145 to 270 billion barrels (23 to 43 billion cubic metres) of crude oil.

Some experts have said that as much as 150 billion barrels (24 billion cubic metres) of oil lie beneath the Canadian Prairies, and another 100 billion barrels (16 billion cubic metres) are locked up in the Arctic Islands. These estimates do not include the 300 billion barrels (48 billion cubic metres) which could be extracted from the Athabasca Tar Sands (sand saturated with oil) of northeast Alberta. However, all these resources are remote from Eastern Canada — the major oil consumer in the country. Several problems have still to be overcome before the mining of oil in Western Canada can be considered an economic operation. By the mid-1980s, oil experts foresee that Canada will be consuming much more oil than it can produce. They estimate that the oil shortage could be as much as one million barrels a day (160 000 m³/day). This imminent crisis will certainly cause changes in the Canadian energy picture.

The Effects of the Energy Crisis on Oil

1. *Increased Costs.* The price of any item offered for sale on a free market is determined by the supply and the demand. When a growing number of customers compete for a dwindling amount of petroleum, the price is bound to go up. The price for Canadian crude oil, for example, rose from $3.00 a barrel in 1973 to $11.00 a barrel in 1976.
2. *Increasing Government Involvement.* In a highly technological society dependent on vast amounts of energy to power its primary and secondary industries, people turn to their government to ensure a steady flow of energy at a fair price. As a result, both the federal and provincial governments in Canada have become more and more involved with the petroleum industry, controlling it by means of regulations on prices and export volumes and taxes on its sales and profits. Unfortunately, the various governments do not share a common opinion of how the oil industry should be regulated. Under the terms of the British North America Act (B.N.A.), the producing provinces such as Alberta and Saskatchewan are the owners of the oil resources they produce and, of course, they wish to take full advantage of their assets. On the other hand, the importing provinces wish to obtain the petroleum as cheaply as possible. However, the federal government has control over the movement of oil across interprovincial or international boundaries. A permanent solution to this problem will therefore require a formula that is acceptable to eleven different governments.
3. *Increasing Development of New Sources.* The Canadian petroleum industry, faced with sharply increased prices for foreign crude oil and the gradual depletion of the wells currently in production, is search-

ing for new supplies. The oil sites are becoming more and more remote: the search for oil is concentrated in the Arctic and on the continental shelf off the east coast.

4. *Increasing Distance between the Source of Supply and the Market.* As the new oil resources of the Arctic are being developed, the problem of transporting them to the markets in Central Canada becomes more pressing. The problem is obvious and finding solutions for it requires a great deal of research, negotiation, and applied wisdom. Is it technically possible to build a pipeline that will not break in the extreme temperatures or upset the delicate ecological balance of the Arctic environment? A study by the Mackenzie Valley Pipeline Research Limited in 1969 reported that the engineering know-how was available and that pipelines could be constructed without irreparable damage to the environment.

The Arctic Pipeline Problem. The development of new oil resources to supply energy for domestic and industrial use often raises a series of questions. Who should build and finance the construction of pipelines? The Canadian Arctic Gas Pipeline Limited proposes a joint Canadian – United States project at a cost of $5500 million to bring natural gas from the Mackenzie Delta southward to Canadian customers, and Alaska North Slope natural gas southward to the American consumers. Other American interests distrust the Canadian control involved in a joint operation, and favour an all-U.S. route through Alaska. Conversely, some Canadians support the Maple Leaf Project sponsored by the Alberta Gas Trunk Line Company, which would build a smaller diameter, all-Canadian, pipeline.

Which route should be given perference? The all-American route would provide the Americans with complete control at the risk of an ecological disaster should an oil spill occur from the shipwreck of one of the supertankers along the west coast. The Mackenzie Valley route is favoured by some experts because it is a natural transportation corridor, but other experts have reservations about the impact of such a pipeline on the environment. Still others favour the replacement of the pipeline with a railway with its advantages of two-way traffic. Other investigators are prepared to support a 5000 km route from the Arctic to southern Canada and the U.S. via the Arctic Islands and across the open bodies of water, then southward along the shores of Hudson Bay.

All these problems and the proposed solutions, options, and variations must be carefully studied by the National Energy Board before the Canadian government will grant a permit for construction to begin. The

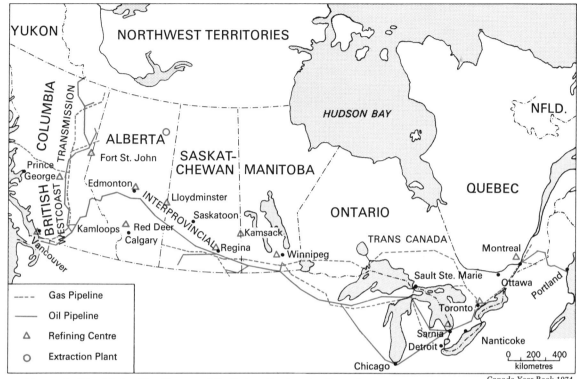

Figure 4–15: *Major Pipelines and Refining Centres in Canada*

Canada Year Book 1974

process of evaluating all the evidence began in 1975 with the appointment of the Berger Commission, based at Yellowknife. Simultaneously the Department of Indian and Northern Affairs began reviewing applications for a negotiated right of way through the Yukon and the Northwest Territories.

In May 1977 when the first volume of the Berger Commission's findings was published, Justice Berger recommended a ten-year delay in the building of a gas pipeline down the Mackenzie Valley, but he totally rejected any plans of building a pipeline from Alaska across the North to the Mackenzie Delta. According to Justice Berger, the building of a pipeline linking the delta and the Alaska reserves would irreparably damage the natural environment for the wildlife in that part of Canada's north. The following articles summarize the impact of such a pipeline and the concern expressed for the protection of northern wildlife.

The growing importance of petroleum and the variations in the flow of this vital supply of energy in Canada between 1947 and 1985 are summarized in Figure 4-16.

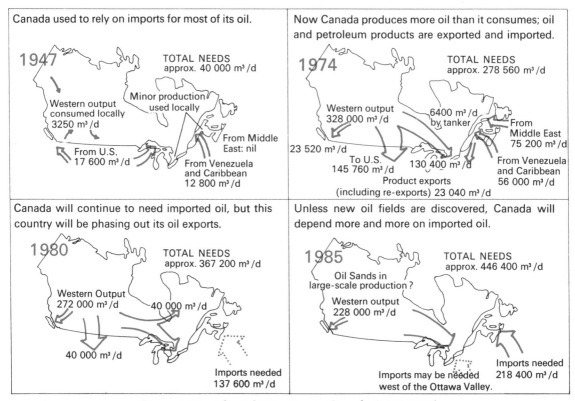

Canada used to rely on imports for most of its oil.

1947
TOTAL NEEDS
approx. 40 000 m³/d

Western output
consumed locally
3250 m³/d

Minor production
used locally

From U.S.
17 600 m³/d

From Middle
East: nil

From Venezuela
and Caribbean
12 800 m³/d

Now Canada produces more oil than it consumes; oil and petroleum products are exported and imported.

1974
TOTAL NEEDS
approx. 278 560 m³/d

Western output
328 000 m³/d

6400 m³/d
by tanker

From
Middle East
75 200 m³/d

23 520 m³/d

To U.S.
145 760 m³/d

130 400 m³/d

From Venezuela
and Caribbean
56 000 m³/d

Product exports
(including re-exports) 23 040 m³/d

Canada will continue to need imported oil, but this country will be phasing out its oil exports.

1980
TOTAL NEEDS
approx. 367 200 m³/d

Western Output
272 000 m³/d

40 000 m³/d

40 000 m³/d

Imports needed
137 600 m³/d

Unless new oil fields are discovered, Canada will depend more and more on imported oil.

1985
TOTAL NEEDS
approx. 446 400 m³/d

Oil Sands in
large-scale production?

Western output
228 000 m³/d

Imports may be needed
west of the Ottawa Valley.

Imports needed
218 400 m³/d

Figure 4-16:   The Oil Situation in Canada (1947-1985).

Impact of a pipeline

No pipeline, ever, across the Northern Yukon. Postponement of any pipeline down the Mackenzie Valley for 10 years.

These are the recommendations of the Berger Inquiry. Unless they are overborne by the economic findings of the National Energy Board, which has still to report, they would seem to put an end to the Arctic Gas proposal for a joint United States-Canada pipeline to carry both Alaskan and Canadian natural gas to the South. They would also seem to advance the case of the Alcan Project, which would parallel the Alaska Highway route. Indeed, Mr. Justice Thomas Berger gives aid to this case:

"Some of the concerns about wildlife, wilderness, and engineering and construction that led me to reject the corridor across the Northern Yukon do not appear to apply in the case of the Alaska Highway route. It is a route with an established infrastructure. In my view, the construction of a pipeline along this route would not threaten any substantial populations of any species in the Yukon or in Alaska. But I am in no position to endorse such a route: an assessment of social and economic impact must still be made, and native claims have not been settled."

Mr. Berger opposes either a coastal or interior route across Northern Yukon to bring Prudhoe Bay gas into the proposed Arctic Gas system. This is the range of the last great caribou herds in North America — some 110,000 animals — and of migratory waterfowl. It is a "unique ecosystem" which has so far survived because of its "inaccessibility". Enormous damage would result from a Northern Yukon coast pipeline and the proposed interior route "would have a devastating impact on Old Crow, the only community in the Northern Yukon".

Mr. Berger goes beyond recommending against any pipeline in the area now: "If we are to protect the wilderness, the caribou, birds and other wildlife, we must designate the Northern Yukon, north of the Porcupine River, as a National Wilderness Park. Oil and gas exploration, pipeline construction and industrial activity must be prohibited within the park. The native people must continue to have the right to hunt, fish and trap within the park. The park must indeed be the means for protecting their renewable resource base."

The Mackenzie Delta and the Beaufort Sea, Mr. Berger also finds too environmentally delicate for much further exploration until more protective techniques are developed. He rejects an opinion on the Government-approved Dome drilling in the Beaufort Sea, but urges "careful consideration be given to the timing and extent of the drilling and development that may take place thereafter".

The commissioner's concern for a pipeline along the Mackenzie Valley is less for the environment — though that exists — than for the native peoples. The purpose of a pipeline, he suggests, is not to solve northern economic problems but to take gas to the developed South. "The social costs of building a pipeline now will be enormous, and no remedial programs are likely to ameliorate them."

The native peoples want a settlement of their land claims before a pipeline is built. They want a settlement that will permit them to keep and develop their own way of life, in part at least based on living off the land and not exclusively on the southern system of work for wages. That is Mr. Berger's view: "In my opinion, a period of 10 years will be required in the Mackenzie Valley and Western Arctic to settle native claims, and to establish the new institutions and new programs that a settlement will entail. No pipeline should be built until these things have been achieved."

Mr. Berger's report — what was presented yesterday is the first volume of two — will be of immense value in acquainting Canadians with their North and with the aspirations of the native peoples who view it not as a frontier but as their home. It is a unique and precious piece of work.

It is not the last word. If Mr. Berger's recommendations are followed southern Canada — where the welfare of millions not thousands must be considered — would not have early access to northern natural gas. It will be the job of the National Energy Board to assess the immediacy of the southern need for this energy and the effect a failure to develop it would have on an already troubled economy.

Would we ever get the Beaufort Sea and Mackenzie Delta gas if it were not piggybacked on Alaskan gas in a single pipeline? Would we be driven to import foreign oil to replace the gas, at a cost of billions of dollars every year, and serious damage to our international balance of payments? Mr. Berger says we can have our own Canadian pipeline when and in the way we choose. But will economics say that we can? Will the development which the native peoples say they want come without the stimulus of the pipeline?

Laying an oil pipeline.

Gulf Oil Canada Limited   Photo by Ron. W. Sculthorp

Nobody knows. At this stage we have only a part of even Mr. Berger's facts. It is not a time for decisions.

Source: *The Globe and Mail*, Toronto (May 10, 1977).

Protection of northern wildlife is a special concern of report

As the pipeline hearings came to an end, Mr. Justice Thomas Berger increasingly talked of the birds, fish, whales and caribou of the North. He seemed to take a special interest in the wildlife, as if he felt they weren't adequately represented by the assorted pressure groups fighting tooth and nail over the pros and cons of a gas pipeline.

He described the caribou migration as "an awesome sight." He worried publicly about the plight of white

whales in the Mackenzie River estuary, about the millions of birds that use the Mackenzie Valley. "Canada is the guardian for mankind of these species," he once said in an interview in Yellowknife.

He proposes a national wilderness park smack in the path of one of the prime routes of the gas pipeline, in the Northern Yukon, north of the Porcupine River. For the white whales of the Beaufort Sea, 5,000 of them, he calls for a sanctuary in West Mackenzie Bay, where the water is warm for calving. "If the herd is driven from its calving area," the judge said, "it will die out. Unlike the bird sanctuary, the whale sanctuary will be an area in which oil and gas exploration and development would be forbidden at any time of the year."

Judge Berger describes the wilderness as a non-renewable resource, just like the non-renewable resources of coal, oil, gas and minerals. "Wilderness implies to all of us a remote landscape and the presence of wildlife," the report says. "I think there are three kinds of wilderness species. The first are species that, because of their intolerance of man or their need for large areas of land, can survive only in the wilderness. Such are caribou, wolf and grizzly bear. . . .

"Second are the species that conjure up visions of wilderness for every Canadian, although they are often seen in other areas, too. I do not believe there can be a Canadian anywhere who does not think of wilderness on hearing the call of a loon or of migrating geese.

"Third are the rare and endangered species that do not inherently require a wilderness habitat, but, because they are tolerant of man, have been driven close to extinction. The peregrine falcon, trumpeter swan and whooping crane are well-known examples of species that are abundant . . . only in wilderness areas. Our concern is that the process of adaptation and evolution through the millenia of each of these species should not be ended. We cannot allow the extinction of these species."

Source: *The Globe and Mail,* Toronto (May 11, 1977).

Coal.   Another important source of energy in the world is coal. In Canada, 10% of the energy demand is currently supplied by coal. Canadians are fortunate to have areas where conditions were suitable for the accumulation of coal from organic matter. (Of all of Canada's coal reserves, 98% are located in Saskatchewan, Alberta, and British Columbia.)

Over millions of years the pressures of the overlying sediments have compressed the partially decomposed organic matter and created various types of coal. *Lignite* or brown coal is the youngest and softest type of coal; it has a lower carbon and energy content than the other coals. This very soft coal is useful as a fuel in thermal-electric stations. *Bituminous* coal is of double importance since it is not only a useful fuel but is also suitable for conversion into coke, a major requirement of the iron and steel industry. The coal is made into coke by heating it in an oven to get rid of the coal gas. *Anthracite* coal has been created by even greater pressures and as a result it is very hard, producing great quantities of heat with little ash.

Coal powered the steam engines of the Industrial Revolution in Canada. Since 1947, however, when oil was struck at Leduc, Alberta, the rival petroleum has displaced coal in many instances; but recently, the worldwide demand for power has sparked a renewed interest in Canadian coal reserves. In Cape Breton, new shafts are being sunk to supply the local steel mills in Sydney. In the West, the large-scale open-pit operation is being developed at Sparwood, and the coal is being carried by CP Rail trains to the ports of Roberts Bank south of Vancouver, where it is exported to Japan. Coal is a heavy, bulky substance, so it is costly to transport. The steel mills and thermal-electric plants of Ontario find it cheaper to import coal from Pennsylvania and West Virginia via Lake Erie and the Welland Canal rather than use the native Canadian coal.

Electric Power. Electricity has proven to be a very convenient method of supplying energy to our industrialized society. Canada now has the second highest per capita production of electricity in the world. Originally the power stations were operated by private industries for their own needs and the surplus power was sold to nearby communities. Today so many people "live better electrically" that government agencies are hard-pressed to meet the requirements.

Hydroelectricity. About 75% of Canada's electrical energy is generated by the action of running water. This form of energy is a renewable resource, but unfortunately the necessary conditions are not found everywhere. Currently about 23% of Canada's primary energy needs is supplied by hydroelectricity (Figure 4-17).

Thermal Electricity. These stations use the heat energy of fossil fuels to convert water to steam, then use the steam pressure to turn the turbines that power the generators (Figure 4-18).

Nuclear Electricity. Nuclear stations are a variation of the thermal plants. Instead of fossil fuels, they use heat generated by a controlled nuclear-fission reactor to create the steam. Canada has developed the CANDU reactor, a type that uses natural uranium, rather than the more expensive enriched uranium as a fuel, and heavy water as a medium to slow the passage of the neutrons in the atomic reactor. The heat absorbed by the heavy water is used to convert ordinary water into steam for powering the turbines and generators. Unlike the other two techniques, the nuclear plants produce a radioactive waste that must be carefully removed and stored (Figure 4-18).

These three types of generating stations feed their electricity into the power grid or network of distribution towers. The demand for electricity

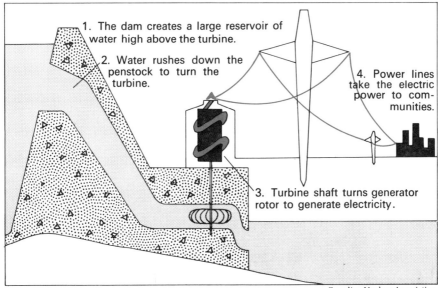

Figure 4–17:   *How Water Power Produces Electricity*

Canadian Nuclear Association

Figure 4–18:   *Comparison of Conventional and Nuclear Power Plants*

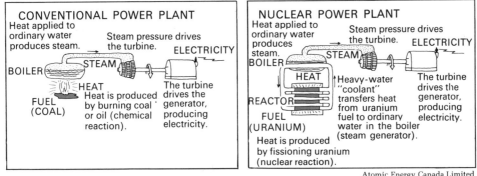

Atomic Energy Canada Limited

fluctuates throughout a 24 h time period, but the available power can be directed to the area of need across the continent. Since electricity is so convenient, requiring no storage facilities, and generating no waste for the user, it has proven to be very desirable. As a result, the demand has grown at the rate of 7% per year. The maintenance of this rate of expansion requires massive capital investment to develop the more remote hydroelectric sites and to build thermal and nuclear plants where fuel, water, and demand coincide. The Ontario Hydro Electric Commission

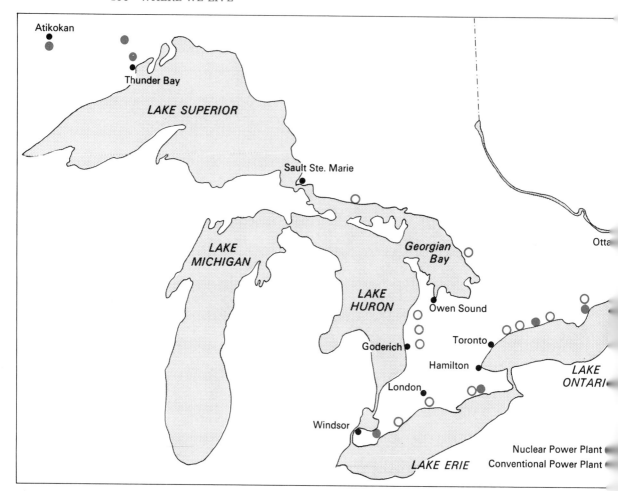

Figure 4–19:   Forecast of Nuclear-Power Plants Required to Meet the Demand for Electricity

alone will require $40 billion to finance its expansion between 1975 and 1986 (Figure 4-19).

Energy in the Future. An abundance of relatively inexpensive energy of all types has produced the high standard of living enjoyed by the citizens of the industrialized part of the world. It has also brought some unwanted by-products in the form of air and water pollution. Now society faces a decision. In evaluating the recent energy crisis, it is obvious that the generation of all forms of power cannot continue to grow as it has in the past. What course will people choose to follow? Will Canadians continue to consume non-renewable power resources at an ever-increasing rate, or pursue a policy of energy conservation? Will international, political, economic, and military forces attempt to gain control of the precious reserves of petroleum and coal for their own use, or will we all cooperate at an international level to develop alternative sources of energy? The answers to these questions will determine how much energy will be available to future generations.

Nuclear Power in Canada

Nuclear power is assuming a place of increasing importance among the sources on which Canadians rely for their supplies of energy. This is particularly so in Ontario, where most of the present nuclear generating capacity in Canada is concentrated. Ontario has tapped most of its hydraulic resources and is virtually without coal and oil, but has large supplies of uranium.

In January 1974 some 17 per cent of Ontario's electricity was supplied by nuclear plants. This will increase to 28 per cent by 1980, and reach 59 per cent by 1990. For Canada as a whole, it has been forecast that by 1990 one-quarter of the electricity supply will come from nuclear stations and 10 years later the proportion will be 44 per cent.

The showpiece of the Canadian nuclear power programme is Pickering Generating Station, just east of Toronto. Canada's first fully-commercial, utility-owned nuclear plant, Pickering consists of four units, each with a capacity of 500,000 kilowatts. Since the four units came into service (1971-73), they have set records for production and performance unmatched by any other nuclear station in the world.

Ontario Hydro

The station is located on Lake Ontario, east of Toronto. The site is dominated by the large vacuum building closest to the lake on the south. Four reactor buildings are joined to the vacuum building by a pressure relief duct. The turbine hall, auxiliary bay, and administration and service buildings are north of the reactor buildings. The station first fed power to the grid on April 4, 1971, and was fully operational by May 1973. Total installed capacity is 2 160 000 kW. Construction has begun on the twinning of the station. The first unit of Pickering B is scheduled to enter service in 1981, and the station is slated to be complete by 1983.

In Ontario are two other operating nuclear power plants. NPD (Nuclear Power Demonstration), at Rolphton, on the Ottawa River, is Canada's first nuclear power station, with a capacity of 25,000 kilowatts. NPD was completed and went into operation in 1962. On Lake Huron, near Kincardine, is the 200,000 kilowatt Douglas Point station, which first produced power in January 1967.

Benefiting still further from the experience gained at NPD, Douglas Point and Pickering will be a series of big nuclear power stations to be brought into service in Ontario in the decade, 1975-1985. The first of these is the Bruce Generating Station, on Lake Huron, where four 750,000 kilowatt units are scheduled to start up successively between 1975 and 1978. Next will come a duplicate of Pickering, adjacent to the present plant.

Quebec has one nuclear power station, a 250,000 kilowatt prototype at Gentilly, near Trois Rivières. A second station, a 600,000 kilowatt commercial plant, is under construction at the same site. Scheduled for first operation in 1979, the latter is expected to be the forerunner of a programme that could result in 40 per cent or more of Quebec's electricity coming from nuclear stations by the turn of the century.

Next to introduce nuclear power will be the Atlantic provinces, with the first station to be located in New Brunswick. A possible sequence after that could be Manitoba, British Columbia and the other two prairie provinces. How soon and how much will depend on a number of factors, among them the extent of regional electricity demand and the availability and costs of other energy sources.

Source: Atomic Energy of Canada Limited.

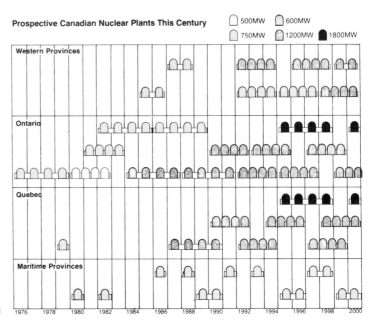

Prospective Canadian Nuclear Plants This Century

Figure 4-20: *Power Plants to Be Built in Canada by 1993*

Atomic Energy Canada Limited

What is CANDU?

In power stations using coal, oil or gas, the fuel is burnt in a furnace. The heat produced is used to convert water into steam to run the turbine-generators and so produce electricity. The supply of these fuels is limited and their cost is rising rapidly.

In a nuclear power station, the heat is produced by the splitting of atoms inside the uranium fuel. This heat then goes to a boiler where water is turned into steam. From this point on, a nuclear plant is like any other thermal generating station.

Canada is well endowed with deposits of uranium, and with the developments taking place in the nuclear industry, is assured of adequate capability to meet its electrical needs well into the distant future.

The steam generating system employed in Canada's nuclear power stations is a distinctive Canadian development conceived in the laboratories of AECL [Atomic Energy of Canada Limited], and brought to maturity in a co-operative effort by AECL, electrical utilities and private industry. The system is known as CANDU, which stands for CANada Deuterium Uranium, signifying that the concept is Canadian, that it uses deuterium oxide, or heavy water, as the moderator and that the fuel is natural uranium.

The CANDU fuel cycle is simple, and since natural uranium is used, no enrichment facilities are required. The fuel is fabricated into relatively short bundles that are comparatively light in weight and easy to handle. The design of the fuel bundle is simple, permitting mass production techniques with inherently low fabrication costs.

The use of heavy water as both moderator and coolant, coupled with the careful design and selection of the core materials, results in a high utilization of the natural uranium fuel. For the same unit of power produced the CANDU reactor requires only about one-half as much uranium as a reactor that burns enriched fuel.

Figure 4–21: The CANDU System   Atomic Energy Canada Limited

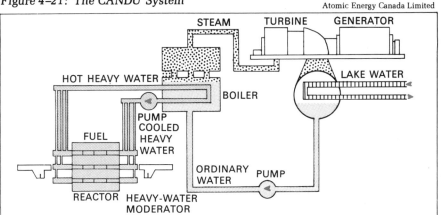

Heavy water has the highest "moderating ratio" of any material used as a moderator (water, graphite etc.). Moderating ratio is a term used to indicate the effectiveness of a substance in slowing down the neutrons needed to sustain the fission process without absorbing them.

Deuterium, an isotope of hydrogen, is compounded with oxygen to form heavy water (D_2O). It occurs naturally in ordinary water at a concentration of about one part in 7000. Thus a large volume of water must be processed in a highly complicated manner in order to extract the liquid. Two plants are in operation in Canada producing heavy water, and others are under construction, in order to meet the needs of the CANDU programme.

Source: Atomic Energy of Canada Limited.

B. HUMAN RESOURCES

Labour and market are the two prerequisities of manufacturing that are supplied by the people. Some industrial nations, such as Japan, emphasize these human resources to make up for their lack of natural resources. Canada, which has an abundance of natural resources and a relatively small population, has fewer producers and fewer consumers than other industrialized countries in the world.

3. Labour The increase in the size of the Canadian labour force is presented in Figure 4-22. This graph includes both the skilled and un-

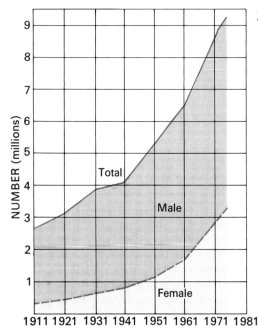

Figure 4–22: *Canadian Labour Force*

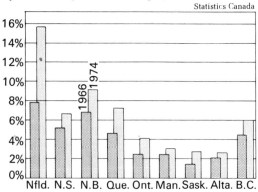

Figure 4–23: *Unemployment Rates in Canada, by Province (annual averages)*

Note: Unemployment rate for Prince Edward Island is not provided because of the high sampling variability resulting from the small size of the sample.

skilled section of the labour force. The ever-increasing growth in the number of female workers in Canada in recent years is obvious. The training of citizens with management or production skills has been a longstanding Canadian goal; this goal partially explains our high investment in education. In those areas of Canada, however, that have not been able to provide this training, both the proportion of unskilled workers and level of unemployment are relatively higher (Figure 4-23).

4. Market. The size of the market for manufactured goods is determined by the total number of potential customers and by the amount of money they have to spend. In turn, their disposable income is determined by their earning power, as revealed in Figure 4-24. Because of the large number of female workers in the Canadian labour force, the "Total Family Income" would be a much more realistic guide in the measurement of purchasing power. In 1971 the average Canadian family income was $10 112. According to the preliminary results of the 1976 census, the average family income in Canada for 1975 was $16 263 (Table 4-5). Deviations from this average are not so related to regional differences within Canada as they are to the size of the community. Generally,

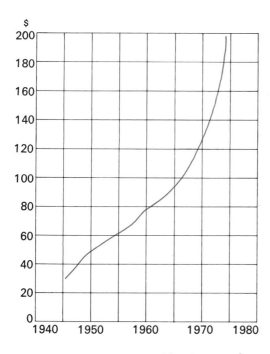

Figure 4-24: *Average Weekly Wages and Salaries in Canada*

TABLE 4-5
Average Family Incomes, 1975

Province	Average Income
Ontario	$17 780
British Columbia	17 283
Alberta	16 838
Saskatchewan	15 711
Quebec	14 929
Manitoba	14 759
New Brunswick	13 403
Nova Scotia	13 182
Newfoundland	12 853
Prince Edward Island	12 078
Canada	16 263

Source: Statistics Canada.

employment opportunities and higher rates of remuneration tend to be found in the larger urban centres.

Despite the high incomes and the willingness of Canadians to spend their money, the total demand for some goods is still not large enough to make it worthwhile for a Canadian manufacturer to manufacture the products. Instead, the items are imported. Conversely, other manufacturers try to lower the cost of their manufactured articles by producing them in volume, then exporting the surplus.

Two other important factors must be considered when examining the prerequisities of manufacturing: transportation and capital. The availability of transportation and capital is directly related to the economic development of the nation. Developing nations, by a simple definition, are those that lack the capital and transportation systems necessary to develop their own resources.

C. STAGE OF ECONOMIC DEVELOPMENT

5. Transportation. Canada, with its vast area and scattered population, has difficulty in providing adequate transportation facilities. In terms of population numbers, however, Canada possesses one of the best transportation networks in the world. Two major transcontinental railways (Canadian National and CP Rail) link the East with the West. The Trans-Canada Highway, the longest road in the world, also runs from east to west. Canada boasts one of the most impressive inland waterway systems along the St. Lawrence and Great Lakes. The two major airlines — Air Canada and CP Air — facilitate speedy movement of people across the country. Each of these modes of transportation has its own advantages and disadvantages. Trucks are the most feasible over short distances; rail is efficient over longer distances; and ships are excellent for transporting bulky and low-value goods over very long distances. Transportation by air is the most costly and thus is restricted to high-value, low-bulk items.

Because of its huge size, Canada's transportation network is a long way from being completed. Canada has thousands of kilometres of poorly surfaced, unpaved roads; also extensive areas have no roads at all. The building of the east-west transcontinental railway following Confederation marked the first step in binding the new nation into an economic unity. Because of various economic and political considerations, the once great fleet of Canadian ocean-going ships is much reduced, and the operation of airlines is carefully controlled by the federal government, which operates Air Canada.

In the 1975-76 federal government budget, seven cents of every dollar was assigned to transportation. Obviously, this spending reflects that our transportation system still needs to be developed. (See Chapter 11 for more on transportation.)

6. Capital. Capital is undoubtedly the most essential prerequisite for manufacturing. Capital is the material wealth (money, machines, and so on) needed to produce goods and services. In a simple society a foot-powered potter's wheel represents the potter's only capital investment. In our complex industrial society, the creation of mass-produced clay products requires the operation of a large, machine-filled factory.

Entrepreneurs can finance the building and equipping of a modern factory in a number of ways. If they have good credit, they can borrow money by issuing a kind of promissory note called a *bond*. The bond requires the borrower to pay interest at a fixed rate from the day the bond is issued until it is redeemed. The principal is to be payed by a stated date.

Another way in which funds can be acquired is by selling part ownership or shares in a venture. These shares may be of several types. *Preferred shares* assure the holders of the first claim on the assets of the company and the first claim to the profits — but at a fixed rate. *Common shares* provide the holders with part ownership of the corporation and a chance to share the profits remaining after payments to bondholders and the holders of preferred stock. If the company is very successful, the common shareholders will receive healthy dividends and profits on the sale of their stock. If conditions are poor, they may receive nothing.

Some companies are well known and considered to be safe investments. As such, their shares are sometimes referred to as "blue chip" stocks. Other companies may be unknown or may be seeking capital to finance a completely new product. Money invested in this type of corporation is known as *venture capital*. Canadians have a reputation of being very cautious about investing their funds in venture schemes, preferring to put their money into insurance policies, bank accounts, trust certificates, and other savings plans. Nevertheless, the stock exchanges in Montreal, Toronto, and Vancouver handle thousands of stocks and shares transactions every day.

GOVERNMENT INVOLVEMENT IN THE FINANCING OF CANADIAN INDUSTRY

In Canada the federal and provincial governments are involved in the financing of industrial development. They provide low-cost loans, forgivable loans (that do not need to be repaid), and cash grants to encourage industry to locate or expand. The government can also assist by adjusting the rates of taxation on profits or by allowing the manufacturers to make sizable claims for the depreciation of their buildings and machinery. In some instances, the government becomes a shareholder; as such, it participates in the operations of the company. Certain enterprises are considered to be so important for the nation's development that the government may completely finance and operate them through crown corporations. Examples of crown corporations are Atomic Energy of Canada Limited and the Canadian Broadcasting Corporation. Altogether, 16% of the 1975-76 federal budget was devoted to economic development.

FOREIGN INVESTMENT IN CANADA

As a developing nation, Canada has more opportunities for industrial growth than funds to finance them. As a result, individuals from foreign countries and multinational corporations invest heavily in Canada. The entire matter of foreign investment has come under close examination in Canada in recent years. Foreign ownership has both positive and negative aspects (Table 4-6).

On the positive side, the foreign investors provide capital for the growth of industry and venture capital for the development of promising enterprises. Consequently, Canadians benefit from the increased employment opportunities and the improved standard of living.

The negative aspect of foreign investment is that the profits belong to the foreign owners; these profits are often reinvested by buying up other Canadian companies. If a large number of industries are allowed to be operated by foreign owners for their own benefit, Canadians will stand to lose their autonomy. Many people, who strongly oppose foreign ownership, claim that it leads to a "branch plant" economy and a type of economic colonialism.

MANUFACTURING IN CANADA

Canadian manufacturers must constantly adjust their operations to the stresses and strains of the changing world. Factories such as those that produce components, as in the electronics industry, require a great deal of labour skilled in intricate handwork. These industries have found that they cannot pay the high wage rates prevailing in Canada and still compete with foreign producers who have lower labour costs. In the face of such a situation, the manufacturer is forced either to go out of business

TABLE 4-6
Long-Term Foreign Investment in Canada, 1970 and 1974 ($ millions)

Type of Investment	Estimated distribution of ownership						Total investments of non-residents	
	United States		United Kingdom		Other countries			
	1970	1974	1970	1974	1970	1974	1970	1974
Government securities	6 635	8 518	306	371	997	2530	7 938	11 419
Public utilities	1 601	2 266	472	405	211	200	2 284	2 871
Manufacturing	10 405	13 996	1006	1279	905	1433	12 316	16 708
Petroleum and natural gas	6 179	8 001	613	958	802	1153	7 594	10 112
Other mining and smelting	3 163	4 095	250	364	452	663	3 865	5 122
Merchandising	1 375	1 995	312	382	170	261	1 857	2 638
Financial	2 848	4 320	803	1255	704	905	4 355	6 480
Other enterprises	764	1 117	89	158	86	141	939	1 416
Miscellaneous investments	1 944	2 382	170	220	775	905	2 889	3 447
Total Investments	34 914	46 690	4021	5332	5102	8191	44 037	60 213

Source: Canada Year Book 1975.

TABLE 4-7
Percentage Distribution of the Employed, by Industrial Group, 1965-74

Year	Total employed (1000s)	Agriculture	Other primary industries	Manu-facturing	Construction	Transportation, communication and other utilities	Trade	Finance insurance and real estate	Service*
1965	6 862	8.7	3.4	23.8	6.7	9.0	16.7	4.1	27.6
1966	7 152	7.6	3.1	24.4	7.0	8.7	16.5	4.2	28.5
1967	7 379	7.6	3.0	23.8	6.4	8.9	16.6	4.2	29.5
1968	7 537	7.2	2.9	23.3	6.2	8.9	16.7	4.3	30.4
1969	7 780	6.9	2.8	23.4	6.2	8.9	16.6	4.5	30.7
1970	7 879	6.5	2.8	22.7	6.0	8.8	16.8	4.6	31.9
1971	8 079	6.3	2.8	22.2	6.1	8.7	16.5	4.8	32.7
1972	8 329	5.8	2.6	22.3	6.0	8.8	16.9	4.6	33.0
1973	8 759	5.3	2.6	22.5	6.3	8.8	17.1	4.7	32.7
1974	9 137	5.2	2.6	22.2	6.5	8.6	17.2	4.9	32.8

* Includes public administration and defence.
Source: Canada Year Book 1975.

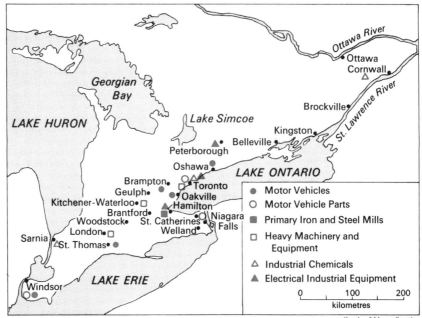

Figure 4–25:   Main Manufacturing Centres in Ontario

Bank of Nova Scotia

or to have the manufacturing transferred to the low-labour-cost foreign factories, with only the final assembly being done in the Canadian plant.

Raw materials, power, market, labour, transportation, and capital are the prerequisites of the successful development of manufacturing industries. As Canada has grown as a nation, secondary industry has also grown. We now depend less on foreign countries for our manufactured goods.

The concentration of manufacturing in the Great Lakes – St. Lawrence Lowland reflects the interaction of the six prerequisites. Sometimes, however, a manufacturer will continue in business long after the original conditions that stimulated the industry have changed. For example, in southern Ontario, an abundance of black walnut trees were once ideal for the making of fine furniture. Today, these trees have been cleared and the few remaining walnut trees are valued at nearly $5000 each. Yet the furniture factories continue in business and bring in the wood they require from other areas. This is an example of *industrial momentum*.

The future for Canadian manufacturing is bright. In a world experiencing a population explosion where the competition for raw materials is bound to become fierce, Canada is relatively rich in natural resources.

TABLE 4-8

The 12 Leading Manufacturing Industries of Canada (1973)

Industry	Establishments	Employees	Value of Factory Shipments ($1000s)
Motor vehicle manufacturers	21	46 811	$ 4 715 829
Pulp and paper mills	146	80 085	3 790 939
Slaughtering and meat processors	473	30 937	3 288 521
Petroleum refining	42	14 843	2 975 852
Sawmills and planing mills	1 519	62 424	2 558 546
Iron and steel mills	45	53 008	2 317 520
Motor vehicle parts and accessories	229	52 831	2 304 562
Dairy products industry	646	30 338	1 715 903
Miscellaneous machinery and equipment manufacturers	794	53 444	1 602 915
Smelting and refining	28	32 186	1 143 419
Miscellaneous food processors	262	19 159	1 045 610
Metal stamping and pressing industry	520	25 099	1 034 865
Totals, 40 leading industries	16 000	1 102 618	46 459 200
Total, all manufacturing in Canada	31 143	1 772 109	66 776 992

Source: Quick Canadian Facts 1976-77

Our nation occupies half a continent and possesses large supplies of forests, water, food, and energy sources, such as petroleum, coal, hydroelectricity, and uranium (for nuclear power development). The domestic and world market for Canadian-made products is guaranteed to some extent in the future — providing the customers can afford the Canadian prices! The steadily improving level of education should enable Canadians in the work force to improve their level of efficiency and technological knowledge. With each passing year, great strides are made in improving the nation's transportation systems.

In the past, Canada has been a colony, an emerging country and a developing nation, but the future should see Canada with a fully developed economy generating sufficient reserves of capital for developing its own resources and for investing in the economies of other nations.

TERTIARY SECTOR

Raw materials, as mentioned, are the preserve of the primary sector of the economy, while the processing of these raw materials belongs to the secondary sector. The rendering of services in the economy of a country is classified under the *tertiary sector*. Modern society calls for numerous and varied types of services in order to function smoothly. Our widespread national and international financial interests are all tied by communication services to the head offices of business and government. Transportation services literally "make the wheels go around," carrying raw materials to factories and the finished goods to market. The services of advertising agencies create interest in the goods produced by industry; the retail-sales people conduct the transactions. Government at three levels collects taxes to pay for a growing list of public-administration services including defence, health, education, and recreation. These services are just a few of the major ones of the tertiary sector, which is expanding in Canada at a faster rate than the other two sectors. As is evident in Table 4-7, most occupations today are to be found in the field of service rather than of production.

CANADIAN TRADE

Canada, like many other modern nations in the world, is not completely self-sufficient. Foodstuffs, raw materials, and manufactured foods that cannot be obtained locally have to be imported. The money to pay for these foreign items must be earned by selling surplus Canadian goods to foreign nations. Canada is therefore deeply involved in foreign trade whose total value in 1974 amounted to more than $63 billion. Between 1969 and 1974, the total *value* of Canada's foreign trade had more than doubled (Table 4-9).

In terms of the *volume* of world trade, Canada is sixth. The U.S.A. is first, followed by West Germany, Great Britain, Japan, and France. That Canada is able to command an important position in world trade is

TABLE 4-9
Foreign Trade of Canada, 1969-74 ($ millions)

Year	Exports	Imports	Total trade	Balance of trade
1969	14 871	14 130	29 001	741
1970	16 820	13 952	30 772	2 868
1971	17 820	15 618	33 438	2 202
1972	20 140	18 669	38 809	1 471
1973	25 301	23 303	48 604	1 998
1974	32 052	31 579	63 631	474

Figures may not add, owing to rounding.
Source: *Canada Year Book 1975.*

TABLE 4-10
Commodity Exports, 1970-74 ($ millions)

Commodity	1970	1972	1974
Wheat	687	927	2 041
Animals and other edible products	1 181	1 428	1 783
Metal ores and concentrates	1 522	1 397	2 372
Crude petroleum	649	1 008	3 408
Natural gas	206	307	494
Other crude inedible materials	707	848	1 490
Lumber	664	1 174	1 289
Pulp	785	820	1 861
Newsprint	1 110	1 158	1 722
Fabricated metals	1 995	1 716	2 944
Other fabricated inedible materials	1 311	1 700	2 774
Motor vehicles and parts	3 499	4 718	5 579
Other machinery and equipment	1 665	2 014	2 809
Other domestic exports	418	445	726
Re-exports	419	479	760
Total exports	16 820	20 140	32 052

Source: *Canada 1976*, Statistics Canada.

TABLE 4-11
Commodity Imports, 1970-74 ($ millions)

Commodity	1970	1972	1974
Food	974	1 216	2 165
Animals and other edible products	141	185	349
Metal ores and concentrates	244	239	394
Crude petroleum	415	681	2 646
Other crude inedible materials	513	620	1 031
Fabricated textiles	426	588	817
Chemical products	712	830	1 537
Fabricated metals	663	819	1 862
Other fabricated materials	1 084	1 342	2 260
Motor vehicles and parts	3 252	4 934	6 995
Other machinery and equipment	3 992	5 183	8 411
Other imports	1 536	2 032	3 112
Total imports	13 952	18 669	31 579

Source: *Canada 1976*, Statistics Canada.

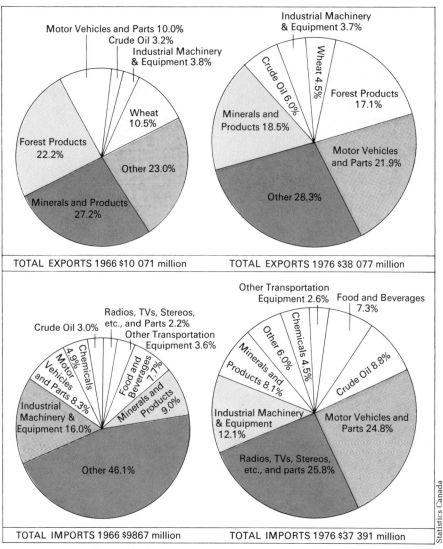

Figure 4–26: Value and Share of Exports and Imports by Major Group

largely attributed to its vast natural resources — mineral, agricultural, and forestry — even though Canada has a very small population. Thus great quantities of raw materials are available for export purposes, enabling Canada to earn the money to pay for imported goods. Examine the list of Canada's commodity exports (Table 4-10). You will see that, besides raw materials, Canada exports many manufactured items (motor vehicle parts, fabricated metals) as well.

Look at the list of the commodity imports (Table 4-11). Notice that manufactured items and food also figure importantly among Canada's imports. Why is this so? First, Canada's domestic market, as mentioned, already is too small to make the production of certain manufactured items economically feasible; second, being a northern country, Canada has to import special products, such as fruits and vegetables, to ensure a year-round supply for its population.

Every country attempts to sell at least as much as it buys to maintain a *balance of trade*. Some nations are fortunate because they always show a trade surplus, since they export more than they import. Other nations have difficulties because their peoples import more goods than they export. When the money spent on imports exceeds the money received from exports, a nation is said to have a balance-of-trade deficit. That nation, like people who spend more than they have, is in debt. Canada, however, is fortunate to have — most of the time — a favourable balance of trade.

Some governments try to dissuade their citizens from purchasing foreign goods, particularly if comparable or alternative items are produced locally. The device they use is a tariff, a type of tax that is added to foreign goods when they are imported. Various international agreements exist, such as the General Agreement on Tarriffs and Trade (GATT), which provide for special lower rates between certain countries. Canada's lowest tariff, the British Preferential Tariff, exists between members of the Commonwealth.

Among Canada's trading partners, the United States is the most important partner. In fact, the economies of the two nations are so intertwined that trade with the U.S. accounts for over 70% of our total. (For more on U.S.A.-Canada trade see Chapter 12). Japan and Great Britain are our two other major trading partners. Germany is fourth on both the import and the export list. The dollar value of trade with any other country is not large, but from time to time Canada makes large sales of wheat to China and the Soviet Union, as already noted in an earlier section of this chapter.

Now that you have examined the list of major export and import items that Canada has to offer to the world, reconsider the image of Canada that was introduced in the first paragraph of this chapter. Is it valid? Are Canadians really "hewers of wood and drawers of water"?

QUESTIONS

1. Define the following terms:
   (i) Gross National Product (GNP)
   (ii) Primary sector of the economy
   (iii) Secondary sector of the economy
   (iv) Tertiary sector of the economy
   (v) Vertical integration
   (vi) Preferred stock (shares)
   (vii) Common stock (shares)
   (viii) Venture capital
   (ix) Industrial momentum
   (x) Balance of trade

2. What are the major prerequisites for the development of manufacturing industry? Which of these items does Canada have in abundance and which items does Canada lack? How is this shortage overcome? Are there any alternative methods that might be used?

3. What are the advantages and disadvantages of Canada's economy being closely linked to that of the United States?

RESEARCH

1. Prepare an essay on one of the following topics:
   (i) The Future of Canada's Primary Economic Activites
   (ii) Foreign Ownership of Canadian Industry
   (iii) Canada and the Energy Crisis

2. Discuss the future prospects of the Canadian mining industry.

3. Prepare an "Energy Crisis" scrapbook of newspaper clippings and magazine articles that discuss the extent of the problem or offer suitable solutions.

4. Conduct an environmental hearing on the Mackenzie Valley pipeline. Present arguments on behalf of:
   1. the native people
   2. the Canadian petroleum industry
   3. a concerned environmentalist
   4. the citizens in your community.

5. Do research to find out more about:
   (i) General Agreement on Tariffs and Trade (GATT)
   (ii) the British Preferential Tariff.

6. Read closely the Article on "Fishing Zones: Canada's biggest issue with the U.S.," and discuss the following:
   (i) "In view of the declining fish stocks, should Canada continue to grant quotas to foreign vessels to fish off its east coast?"
   (ii) Should the historical fishing rights on the Fraser River, established in 1937 between Canada and the U.S., be upheld? Do you think Canada should share its natural resources with another country?

7. Do research to find out what is being done to preserve the forests in Canada to make them a continuing renewable resource.

PART TWO: REGIONAL DIVERSITIES

5 BRITISH COLUMBIA: RESOURCE MANAGEMENT

British Columbia's economy is essentially based on the province's natural resources. The successful management of these resources (minerals, agriculture, fishing, and forestry) by the people is studied in this chapter.

> The serenity of the climate, the innumerable pleasing landscapes, and the abundant fertility that abundant nature puts forth, require only to be enriched by the industry of man . . . to render it the most lovely country that can be imagined.
>
> — Capt. George Vancouver

Captain George Vancouver, while charting the British Columbia region in the early 1790s, was impressed with the landscape of the province and accurately assessed its potential for the future. British Columbia has a varied landscape. It is isolated from the rest of Canada by rugged mountains which reach heights of 3600 m. But it also has low-lying river deltas where towns have sprung up and where agriculture flourishes. It has coastal areas adjacent to the Pacific Ocean where rain falls almost daily; it has inland areas with near-desert conditions. This remarkable variety in physical features and climate has provided a great challenge to the people of British Columbia. Through intelligent use of the natural resources of this complex landscape — minerals in the mountains, fish in the ocean, agriculture in the lowlands, and a wealth of forests, the people of British Columbia have accepted the challenge to the "industry of man."

PHYSICAL FEATURES

Between the western border of Alberta and the Pacific Ocean, two major physiographic regions, the *Cordillera* and the *Great Plains* are found.

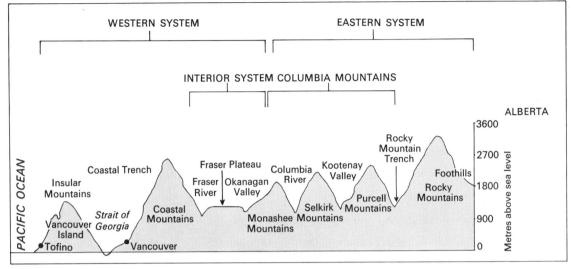

Figure 5-1:   Cross-Section of Southern British Columbia

The Cordilleran complex consists of two broad mountain regions on either side of a central upland; it is part of a continuous mountain system that extends down the Pacific coast to the tip of South America. These mountains occupy over 90% of the province of British Columbia, while the Great Plains in the northeastern corner make up the other 10%. As a result, the cross-section of British Columbia has many contrasts.

CLIMATE

One of the major attractions of the British Columbia coast is its climate. Central and Eastern Canadians may still be shovelling snow when the residents of Vancouver and Victoria are tending their tulips.

The most significant factor in the climate of British Columbia is its closeness to the Pacific Ocean. As a result, the coast of British Columbia receives the heaviest rainfall in all of Canada. Moisture is picked up over the relatively warm North Pacific ocean current and is carried inland by the westerly winds. This moist air mass is forced up by the coastal mountains and by each succeeding mountain range. The air cools and condenses into great banks of cloud that release orographic rainfall on the windward or west-facing side of the mountains. The coastal areas receive as much as 2540 mm annually, while the mountain areas behind Vancouver receive 2030 mm of precipitation. In the interior of the province, the annual precipitation is about 560 mm.

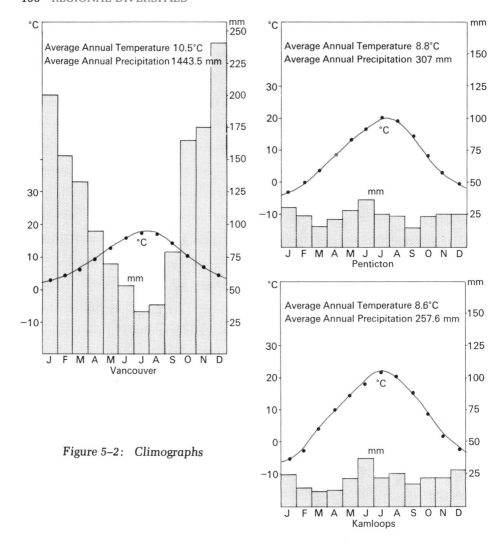

Figure 5-2: Climographs

The aridity or dryness on the leeward (rainshadow) side of the mountain ranges increases in the same direction, west to east. The descending air on the leeward side is heated by compression, the moisture evaporates, and thus reduces the total precipitation for the interior valleys. Penticton and Creston, behind the Monashee and Selkirk Mountains, record only 410 mm of rain annually; Victoria, while close to Vancouver but on the leeward side of the Coastal Range, has a yearly total of less than 770 mm. The net result for the province is alternating wet and dry climates from west to east.

Furthermore, few areas of Canada experience British Columbia's

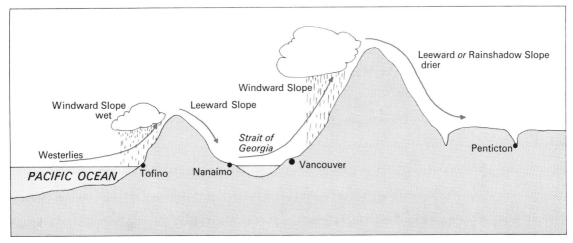

Figure 5-3: *Orographic Rainfall and Rainshadow Area*

variations in temperature. The maritime influence gives Victoria and Vancouver cool summers and mild winters: temperatures seldom dip below the freezing point. Kamloops, on the other hand, experiences continental extremes, with summer temperatures often reaching 37°C and winters often dropping to −27°C. To further emphasize the contrasts, consider that, while the coastal areas enjoy 200 to 240 frost-free days each year, the frost-free period diminishes to approximately 140 days in the Okanagan Valley and to less than 80 in the Peace River district. These variations in the frost-free season account for the differences in agricultural productivity across the province. This factor, combined with the shortage of flat land, prevents British Columbia from attaining self-sufficiency in food production. The climate does, however, promote the growth of trees, which form an important part of the provincial economy.

AGRICULTURE

Over 90% of British Columbia's total land area is unsuitable for agriculture. In fact, very few flat areas are large enough to permit large-scale growing and harvesting. Most of the valuable soils are confined to the lower Fraser Valley and the southern mountain valleys where grasslands predominate. The brown, dark brown, and black soils of these grassland areas lend themselves to intensive cultivation; under irrigation, they produce excellent yields of vegetable and fruit crops.

Food-crop production is restricted to the Fraser Delta, the interior plateau, some of the mountain valleys, and the Peace River district. The

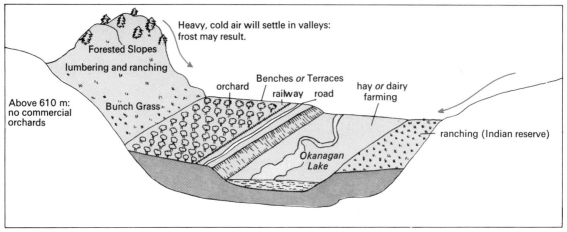

Figure 5-4: Land Use in the Okanagan Valley

wide differences in climate and terrain cause each area to produce certain specialized crops.

FRASER DELTA   The most productive agricultural area of the province is the Fraser Delta. Almost half of the farming in British Columbia is carried on here to take advantage of the rich alluvial soil, mild climate, flat land, and a large accessible market — a factor especially important for perishable products. It is a choice area for dairy farming, poultry farming, and the growing of fruits and vegetables.

Unfortunately, farmers in the Fraser Delta have to compete for land with urban and industrial developers. As the size of Vancouver increases, for instance, it takes up more farm land. Excellent delta farmland has been reallocated to meet the needs of industry and housing, thus creating a shortage of agricultural products in the Vancouver area and increasing prices. At present, Vancouver gets almost as much produce from Vancouver Island as it does from its neighbouring farmlands.

THE OKANAGAN VALLEY   Those excellent British Columbia apples you may have had for lunch probably came from the 111 km length of the Okanagan Valley where irrigation, fertile soils, and a long, hot growing season have combined to create a region second only to Ontario in commercial fruit production. The apple industry centres around Vernon, the chief exporting centre, while Kelowna and Penticton act as shipping centres for pears, plums, peaches, cherries, and apricots. An increase in domestic wine production has recently led to the inclusion of grapes as a significant item of the food-processing industry.

However, prosperity does not prevail everywhere in the Okanagan Valley. In many places the soil and the mountains prohibit the growth of a continuous belt of orchards necessary for the pollination of the fruit trees. Nor is water always in adequate supply during the hot, dry summer months. The area around Vernon, for example, uses the largest irrigation system in the province. The seasonal nature of the fruit industry results in heavy unemployment in winter and a shortage of labour in summer; this situation, combined with the ever-present danger of insects, blight, or a poor-crop year, can make agriculture in the Okanagan Valley a risky business.

FRASER PLATEAU The grazing of cattle and sheep is the major agricultural practice in the drier southern Fraser Plateau, which is well dissected by numerous river valleys. The Gang Ranch in the Chilcotin area covers roughly one million hectares and is possibly the world's largest. The pastures on the plateau itself support approximately 125 000 cattle and 18 000 sheep. In late October, the 322 km road to Quesnel and Williams Lake is the scene of one of North America's last remaining regular cattle drives.

PEACE RIVER DISTRICT Short summers with long daylight hours are common in the northerly locations. In the Peace River District, these climate conditions, combined with the grey wooded soils, make the area suited for crops. Seventy per cent of British Columbia's wheat, oats, and barley are grown here. The district is one of Canada's prime producers of high-quality seed grain. The northern location and the great distance to the market at Vancouver have discouraged specialization in dairy cattle; many farmers raise swine as well.

Agriculture is not a major contributor to the economy of British Columbia, ranking below forestry, mining, and tourism. The rapidly increasing and expanding population is putting such a heavy demand on provincial agricultural production that the limited land available must be intensively farmed. Dairying, fruit and vegetable farming, as well as poultry and cattle ranching continue to dominate. But most of the agricultural production is for domestic consumption, and very little is exported. Increasing costs have all but wiped out the self-sufficient private farmer in favour of cooperatives and large corporate farms.

FISHING

If we consider the fishing done by the coastal Indians and the agents of the Hudson's Bay Company, we could say that the fish off the coast was

British Columbia's first natural resource. The fishing industry is now worth about $75 million annually, making it much less important than other primary industries. The establishment of a salmon cannery near New Westminster in 1870 made British Columbia salmon an important commercial product.

Salmon fishing is carried on between March and October. It is most successful when the salmon converge at the river mouths on their way to their spawning grounds. The Fraser, Skeena, the Nass rivers are the major sources of salmon fishing which is carried out either with gill nets stretched across the river mouth or with purse seines.

Once caught, the salmon must be processed immediately. Canneries are therefore located as close to the fishing grounds as possible. Salmon are not only high in nutritional value, but they also command a higher price per kilogram than beef. Halibut, second in importance to salmon, average 32 kg a piece when caught. They are packed in ice and taken to Vancouver or Prince Rupert for processing and marketing. Billing itself as "The Halibut Capital of the World," Prince Rupert boasts the world's largest fish cold storage plant that handles up to 85% of Canada's $40 million annual halibut catch. Rapid rail service distributes fresh halibut to eastern Canadian and American markets. Herring, cod, flounder, sole, and tuna are caught offshore in far smaller numbers, as are shellfish; shellfish contribute less than 2% to the annual value of the fishing industry.

Overfishing has recently been a problem because of highly efficient harvesting methods. Fishing for herring, for example, was halted from 1967 to 1971 because the supply was being slowly depleted. This has forced the Pacific Coast fishing industry to adopt strict conservation

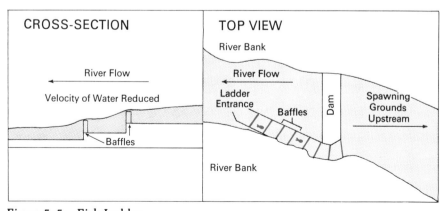

Figure 5–5: Fish Ladder

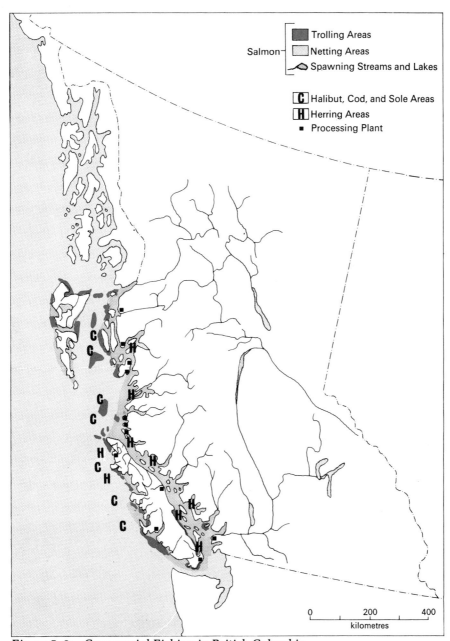

Figure 5–6:   Commercial Fishing in British Columbia

measures. The damming of the rivers for hydroelectric plants has proved disastrous for the salmon, which must travel up rivers to spawn. Logging, flow control, irrigation, and industrial waste have had a damaging effect on the waters of British Columbia and on the fish that must inhabit that environment. In addition, oil tankers plying the coast from Alaska present the constant danger of giant oil slicks, while competitive fishing by foreign countries has seriously reduced the stocks of several species of fish.

Fortunately, some steps are being taken to correct these problems. The offshore domestic fishing limit has been extended to reduce foreign competition. A licensing control has been instituted to reduce the number of fishing vessels and lessen competition. Fish ladders, such as the one at Hell's Gate on the Fraser River, have enabled the salmon to bypass obstacles like power dams to reach the upstream spawning grounds.

Chum salmon live three to five years and are only used for canning. Weighing up to 4.6 kg, they are silver with black specks and faint bars.

Figure 5-7: Types of Salmon
International Pacific Salmon Fisheries Commission

Pink salmon, also used solely for canning, have spotted backs and silver colour. They live for only two years and weigh up to 2.3 kg.

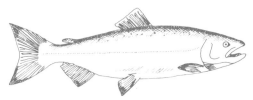

Sockeye, used solely for canning, live for four or five years and weigh as much as 3.5 kg. Slim and stream-lined, they have bluish-silver colour.

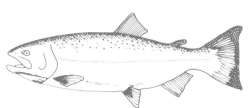

Bright silver and weighing up to 7 kg, coho salmon live three years and are sold commercially fresh, frozen, canned, and smoked.

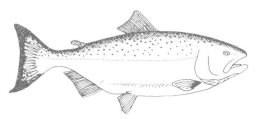

Chinook live five to seven years and grow to a whopping 55 kg. They are blue green and have lightly spotted backs. This salmon is mainly sold commercially fresh or frozen.

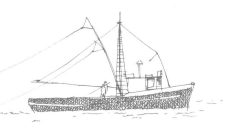

Trollers use as many as eight spools of trolling wire, made of stainless steel and led through long poles, two poles mounted amidship and two mounted in front of the wheelhouse. Each trolling wire has one or two sets of lures.

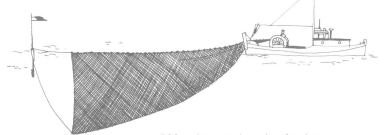

Gill nets are up to 500 m long and made of nylon twine. The mesh size depends on the type of fish to be caught. The net catches fish by the gills, thereby drowning them. A flag attached to a buoy marks the end of the net.

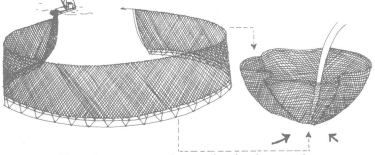

The salmon purse seine, made of nylon, requires speed. A skiff is attached to the end, then the seiner sends the net over the stern while the boat circles to meet the end of the net. The circle takes about an hour to complete; then the net is pursed at the bottom to trap the fish.

Figure 5–8: *Methods of Commercial Fishing*

Fisheries Association of British Columbia

Tins of British Columbia salmon being a common item in cupboards across Canada, it is hard to believe that the fish-products industry accounts for less than 5% of all the people employed in manufacturing in the province. Even with the addition of the fruit and vegetable processing in the Okanagan and Kootenay Valleys, the food industries hold down third position, far behind forest products and mining products.

But while the total shipments of food and beverage industries may be small by comparison, and of less monetary value than those of wood related industries, food processing in British Columbia has an enviable reputation for quality. This reputation seems capable of sustaining the industry, but food production nonetheless remains a risky business; many centres that rely on fish catches or crop harvests are trying to diversify their industries. The Okanagan Valley, for instance, is attempting to attract secondary industries in order to broaden its economic base and make the prosperity of the area less vulnerable to fluctuations in fruit production.

FORESTRY

British Columbia's forest is one of the major sources of the province's wealth: shipments are now valued at over $1 billion annually. The province has about 2% of Canada's forested area, yet supplies 25% of all the wood cut each year. The province has become a major world supplier of lumber and pulp and paper as well as supplying 100% of Canada's cedar roofing, 94% of its plywood, 75% of its softwood lumber, 22% of its pulp and paper, and 14% of its newsprint. Despite this heavy use of timber, both the government and forestry companies are well aware of their responsibilities in ensuring the supply of this raw material for the future.

The first sawmill was erected on the south end of Vancouver Island near Victoria; indications point to shipments of lumber to San Francisco as early as the mid-nineteenth century. At that time, the industry consisted of many logging camps located along the more accessible coastal margins of British Columbia, taking advantage of the natural harbours, the waterways protected by the mountains, and the adjacent supplies of Douglas fir.

Not until the completion of the railway, which provided inland transportation and a much broader market, did the forest industry take on any semblance of permanence. Today, the availability of power from inland hydroelectric plants and the vastly improved roads have served to move logging and milling operations to the interior of the province; these

Pacific Logging, Vancouver Island, B.C. A portable spar is used for loading logs onto trucks.

factors have also encouraged the participation of giant integrated corporations, such as MacMillan Bloedel at Prince George.

The climate, rough terrain, and size of the trees combine to make logging operations in British Columbia quite different from those in other parts of Canada. Loggers must cut roads through the rugged terrain, then solve the problem of cutting and collecting very large trees growing on steep mountain slopes. Therefore, special methods are used in the logging operations of British Columbia. The branches are removed and the top of the tree is cut off while the tree is still standing. Then large chain saws are used to fell the standing trunk. The fallen trees are then hauled up or down the slope by steel cables which are anchored to a strong, standing trunk that is used as a *spar*. Because the mountain streams are unsuitable for transporting such large trees, they must be loaded aboard logging trucks for delivery to the mills, or to some area of deep water where they can be collected into booms for towing to the mills. In some instances, self-dumping barges are used to move logs even more efficiently.

Because shipping facilities, a big market, and a large labour force are essential to the logging industry, the heavily populated Vancouver–Georgia Strait area has long been the hub of milling operations. Mills at Powell River, Elk Falls, Port Mellon, Nanaimo, and Woodfibre are never far from either the raw material or the manufacturing plant that buys the mill's product. Thus, the separate functions of logging, processing, manufacturing, and shipping are closely connected. Because British Columbia has abundant timber and because its wood products are in high demand, it is tempting to overexploit its forests. Stress on good management and reforestation practices ensures that new growth will always exceed cutting. Four trees are planted for each one cut; the practice of *leap frogging* or cutting only alternating strips of timber facilitates natural re-seeding.

Some new secondary industries are growing rapidly, based on processing those parts of the tree that a dozen years ago would have been

Cedar logs being unloaded in British Columbia.

discarded as useless. More efficent use of timber is also being emphasized, so that today well over 50% of the harvested timber is actually used. Twenty years ago the figure was only about 30%. Today, wood chips and sawdust (previously discarded as waste materials) are used in the manufacture of fibreboard, fireplace logs, perfume, fertilizers, charcoal, and insulating material. It is possible now to buy fertilizer made from tree bark (It may give a new aroma to the lawn and garden!), perfumes from the reprocessing of conifer needles, plastics created from wood resins, and particleboard made from compressed shavings and sawdust. These new products are made economically feasible by *manufacturing integration*. The largest integration complex operated by MacMillan Bloedel at Port Alberni on Vancouver Island consists of a series of interconnected wood-processing mills and plants. It is all part of an effort to reduce the wastage in the industry and to provide alternative products in the face of rising wood costs. In addition, the "integration" of large wood-processing complexes has increased efficiency and reduced waste.

Because the local market is limited, British Columbia exports over $2 billion worth of forest products each year. Over 50% of the exports go to the United States, while Japan and Western Europe (including the United Kingdom) each consume about 20% of the total. Because these markets are eager to guarantee constant supplies of timber and wood products, they have invested heavily in British Columbia's forest industry. This investment benefits the investors, but it also ensures a healthy trade pattern for Canada.

Considering the huge tracts of timber and the size of the lumbering industry, it is only natural that wood products should account for the great bulk of the manufacturing industry in the province. The products of British Columbia's sawmills and planing mills alone represent 70% of the lumber used by wood-related industries throughout the country. Pulp and paper and newsprint are the most valuable items, but construction, furniture manufacturing, boat building, and shingle production are a few of the other associated industries on which the province relies for financial security.

MINING

Although the discovery of coal on Vancouver Island in 1830 marked the beginning of the mining industry in British Columbia, the greatest incentive to develop and settle the province came with the Caribou Gold Rush in 1858. Any owner of a pick and sluice box could open a one-person

An abandoned gold mine in Hedley, British Columbia.

operation called a *placer mine*. Placer mining is a way of obtaining minerals from alluvial deposits; the minerals can usually be washed from these deposits. These placer mines soon exhausted the accessible surface deposits and were gradually replaced by the heavy equipment such as those used for *lode mines* which were operated by companies employing a large labour force. (A lode is a vein of mineral ore deposited between clearly defined non-metallic layers of rock.)

In the 1880s and 1890s, the discoveries of copper, lead, and zinc in the Nelson and Kootenay districts resulted in the establishment of mines that still provide much of the lead and zinc in Canada. The Sullivan mine at Kimberley is the largest lead-zinc-silver mine in the world and it, along with neighbouring mines, ships ore by rail to the world's largest smelting and refining works at Trail, B.C.

Mines that no longer yield deposits of gold, silver, copper, or other minerals have been abandoned. The towns built around them are today's *ghost towns*, the remnants of a temporary mining boom in the past.

Even the present mines at Kimberley are unable to supply enough lead and zinc to keep the Trail smelter operating, so that new supplies have to be sought further afield. As a result, Cominco Limited, one of the largest exploration and mining companies, now transports ore by water and rail from as far away as the Arctic. The large investments involved in the construction of the smelter at Trail and the improved transportation facilities have made the relocation of the refining process impractical, if not costly.

More efficient processing and increased international demand has renewed interest in some minerals. The Japanese need for coking coal (to supply their iron and steel industry) has stimulated mining in the old East Kootenay coal district. Molybdenum, mined along the coast, is processed and used in the aerospace industry. In fact, demand has been so great that the new superport of Roberts Bank to the south of Vancouver was constructed to handle the increased traffic.

In addition to primary mining activities, the secondary processes of refining and smelting are extremely important in British Columbia. Refineries and smelters, unlike wood-processing plants which can be relocated if necessary, require a huge capital investment for installation. Great care must be taken thus in choosing appropriate sites. While installations may at first be able to use raw materials from the immediate area, these supplies will in time become exhausted. The increased costs of bringing raw materials over great distances to keep a refinery or smelter operating may then not be justified. The giant complex at Trail, for example, was able to avoid such problems because it is serviced by a network of roads and railways.

The aluminum smelter at Kitimat has similar advantages. Located on Douglas Channel in the northwestern part of the province, the smelter stands in stark contrast to the surrounding forests and mountains. The channel itself is broad, deep, and surrounded by flat land, thus facilitating expansion of the harbour. The coastal location of the smelter permits Caribbean bauxite (a raw material used in aluminum production) to be transported via the Panama Canal, at fairly low cost. The creation of a tunnel through the coastal mountains has diverted the headwaters of the Nechako River to provide hydroelectric power at Kemano and, in turn, at Kitimat. Without this type of hydroelectric expansion, which began in 1950, the natural resource industries of British Columbia could scarcely have developed.

Despite the apparent optimism in British Columbia's mining industry, it has one critical problem: the ownership of natural resources. For some years now, both the federal and provincial governments have been proclaiming sovereignty. A practical difficulty arises when the federal government refuses to allow mining companies to claim provincial taxes as deductions on their federal tax returns. Many companies are obliged to pay double taxes. They are naturally reluctant to become involved either in new exploration or in expanding their existing operations.

Oil and natural gas did not even appear on the statistics charts in the mid-1950s, yet twenty years later they ranked second and fourth, respectively, in production value. Since the first discovery of these minerals in the Peace River District in the early 1950s, an extensive pipeline system has made oil and gas available to the populated south and southwest of the province; the value of this resource has therefore risen considerably. Increased exploration and the availability of new markets may influence the further growth of the petroleum and natural gas industries. Government-sponsored power dams and oil and gas pipelines from the Peace River District have promoted industrial development in the interior to a certain extent; as a result, they have attracted people away from the crowded coastal lowlands.

The economy of British Columbia, then, is essentially based upon the province's natural resources. An examination of British Columbia's economic development shows that the efforts of its population to use and process the natural resources of the environment have been successful. But the natural environment has in turn powerfully influenced the location of industries and people.

The rugged coastal Cascade Mountains surround numerous fiords, which serve as excellent sites for lumber and pulp mills, fish canneries, and port facilities. Many of these trench-like valleys of British Columbia form the natural mouths of important rivers and thus provide ideal sites for hydroelectric power stations.

Although most of the coastal trench is a flooded rift valley, a few areas are above sea level. The emerged sections include portions of the eastern shore of the Queen Charlotte Islands, the Gulf Islands, the east coast lowlands of Vancouver Island, and the Lower Fraser Delta. These areas are extremely important and have been intensively used. They contain the bulk of the region's manufacturing industries, the largest area of flat land in the province, and consequently over 50% of the total of British Columbia's farms and population.

Human contrasts are no less dramatic. British Columbia is home to about 2.2 million people, but almost 75% of the population is concentrated in the southwest corner of the province, around the Strait of Georgia. More than 50% of the total population lives in Vancouver, while portions of the interior are as uninhabited and isolated as when Captain Vancouver explored the coastline.

URBAN CENTRES

VICTORIA Beautiful gardens, tea at four, and riding the doubledecker bus to the Empress Hotel: many people think of Victoria in that way.

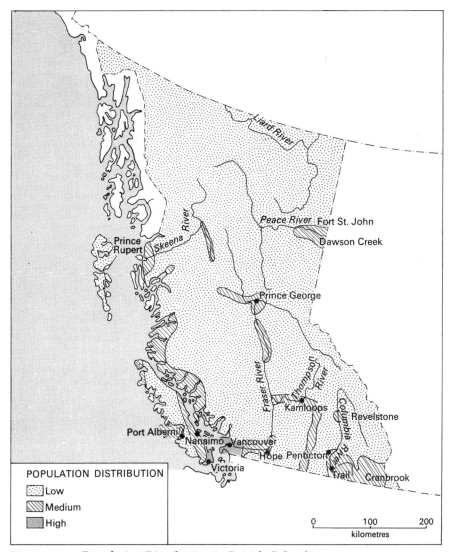

Figure 5-9: Population Distribution in British Columbia

Nevertheless, Victoria is also the capital of British Columbia and a strategic west-coast base for the Canadian Armed Forces, complete with one of the world's largest dry docks at neighbouring Esquimalt.

Victoria's deep, ice-free harbours attracted the Hudson's Bay Company in 1843; consequently, it became a small but vital gateway for coastal shipping. The discovery of gold in 1858 brought a large influx of people, so the city became a supply base for the mainland. Victoria was larger than Vancouver at the time of British Columbia's entry into Confederation in 1871 and so was proclaimed the provincial capital. No

British Columbia Government Photograph

The Causeway and Inner Harbour at Victoria, B.C.

British Columbia Government Photograph

City Hall, Victoria, B.C.

British Columbia Government Photograph

Government House, Victoria, B.C.

doubt many Vancouverites would have liked a second chance to be the seat of government after the completion of the Canadian Pacific Railway terminal on the mainland!

While Victoria remains an important port, employment in secondary industries is low. The three levels of government (federal, provincial, and municipal) altogether account for about 30% of all employment. Home for about 50% of the 400 000 inhabitants of Vancouver Island, Victoria features a blend of British and North American lifestyles, making it unique among the Canadian cities. The frantic pace of other Canadian metropolitan centres is not found here. Instead, this provincial capital offers solitude, beauty, and elegance. Its leisurely atmosphere combined with its warm sun almost year round make Victoria an attractive retirement city.

VANCOUVER Situated just north of the Fraser Delta and ringed by the coastal mountains, Vancouver is the third largest city in Canada and the largest metropolis in the West. But Vancouver did not always enjoy the distinction it does today. In the early nineteenth century, New Westminster was the recognized centre of settlement, while Vancouver was an insignificant sawmilling outpost. The community was originally called Granville but in the 1860s became known as "Gastown" after its hotel and saloon keeper, Capt. "Gassy Jack" Deighton. With the arrival of the railway in 1885, the town gained in size and prominence and was renamed "Vancouver." Through the decades, the original site of "Gastown" became a slum area near the docks. Recently, artists and business people have taken over the decaying buildings and have brought the historic area back to life with specialty shops, boutiques, restaurants, and nightclubs. The result is one of the major tourist attractions in Vancouver.

The rest of the city reflects its rapid growth in the twentieth century. Most of the business district is confined to the area between the lower end of the harbour and False Creek. Highrise apartments and office buildings now dominate the scene, particularly around English Bay. Expressways funnel traffic from the Fraser Valley to the downtown core and a massive bridge spans Burrard Inlet. Exclusive residential areas, like British Properties, climb the mountainsides in north and west Vancouver, while further urban sprawl extends to the eastern uplands of Burnaby and the flat delta areas of Surrey and Richmond to the south.

Variety in landscape and economic activities are not the only contrasts to be found in British Columbia. The people of Vancouver display a remarkable diversity as well. Part of Vancouver's appeal lies in its cosmopolitan nature. Just south of "Gastown" is "Chinatown," the

The campus of the University of British Columbia sits on the tip of Point Grey on the outskirts of the City of Vancouver, shown in the background.

George Allen Aerial Photos, Limited

second largest Chinese community in North America (after San Francisco) and a favourite with tourists. The original inhabitants of Chinatown came to Canada either to work the gold diggings or to help construct the transcontinential railway. Their descendants have remained important to Vancouver. Similarly, Europeans have left their mark on the city. Robsonstrasse, a two-block shopping mall, reflects the influence of Germans, English, and Scandinavians.

Vancouver's inner harbour is located on one of British Columbia's many fiords — Burrard Inlet. Deep, sheltered, and ice-free, the inlet provides the city with one of the largest natural harbours in the world, a decided advantage for Vancouver's important function. The city's use as a port was begun with the completion of the railway from Eastern Canada in 1885, but its potential was not realized until the completion of the Panama Canal. The canal provided a cheaper alternative to overland travel in transporting goods from the East to the West of the North American continent and vice versa; Vancouver therefore became a major port for goods bound from and to Central and Eastern Canada. In addition, grain from the Prairies destined for markets in Europe and Asia could be shipped more cheaply from Vancouver than from the St. Lawrence Seaway, so the harbour quickly became a break-of-bulk point for goods entering and leaving Canada.

Much of the industry in the harbour is based on the first-stage processing of raw materials. Oil refineries, fed by pipeline, are located at Port Moody; wood processing dominates the north arm of the inlet near New Westminster; canning centres around Richmond, while paper, lumber, and cement plants are found along the southern arm of the Fraser River. Drawn by the variety in manufacturing, culture, and lifestyle, many service companies have recently established major operations in Vancouver. Accounting, engineering, insurance, and consulting firms provide the expertise heavily relied on by the resource-based companies.

Vancouver and its environs boast two major educational institutions. The traditional stone and ivy of the University of British Columbia dominate most of Point Grey, while the futuristic glass and steel of Simon Fraser University shimmer on a Burnaby hilltop. A city with so much to offer is bound to draw people. Many tourists return as permanent residents, while entrepreneurs see Vancouver as the last frontier of private enterprise. The resulting expansion has created problems. Housing units are growing scarce and the costs are increasing rapidly. Job opportunities are few and unemployment, seasonally adjusted, is about 7%. Despite these problems, Vancouver remains one of Canada's most exciting and promising cities. How many patrons in "Gassy Jack" Deighton's saloon in 1867 could have guessed that they were sitting in the future commercial, industrial, and cultural centre of Western Canada?

TRADE RELATIONS

One of the most striking aspects of British Columbia's economic strength is its relative newness. Less than a century ago, the region was basically unexplored, isolated, and completely ignored in world trade. When William Van Horne selected Vancouver as the terminus of the transcontinental railway, he unwittingly unleased a giant. The opening of the Panama Canal in 1920 and the establishment of a steamship service to the Far East established the city a shipping centre. Since then, Vancouver has never looked back.

As Canada's largest Pacific port, Vancouver had become the centre for trade with countries that had previously found trade with Canada uninviting. When a Torontonian refers to the countries of the Orient, he is thinking of "The Far East." A Vancouverite sees the Orient as "The Near West." This distinction is all-important in understanding why British Columbia's trade relations seem isolated from the rest of Canada. Like most of the ports of China and Japan, British Columbia's major port is open all year. An additional factor in Vancouver's importance is the abundance of raw materials, available virtually at dockside. Leading industrial nations like Japan, whose own natural resources cannot be found in great quantity, find British Columbia's abundance of raw materials an irresistible blessing, at a price. Vancouver also offers the shortest crossing for vessels from the East. Road and rail facilities enable goods from the Far East to be distributed from Vancouver to the rest of the country with little difficulty. Since 1960, Japan has become one of Canada's major trading partners, competing with Europe and the U.S.A. for Canadian products, especially raw materials. Fully 70% of Canadian exports to Japan pass through the port of Vancouver; 50% of those exports originate right in British Columbia. Japan's need for coking coal for its steel industry, as well as concentrates (ore and metal) and forest products, has given the province a financial boost. British Columbia has become somewhat independent of the rest of Canada by more than geographical isolation. In addition to providing this valuable market, Japan has made significant investments in the domestic industries of British Columbia; Japan also exports considerable quantities of its manufactured products into the province such as motor vehicles, machinery, communications and scientific equipment, and textiles. So strong is this Oriental influence on the economy of British Columbia, that some people have been prompted to nickname the province "Japanese Columbia."

The approach to Vancouver Harbour was at first found to be too confining for large ships, but the coal producers of Western Canada had already signed a long-term export contract with the Japanese steel industry. The obvious solution was to build a "superport" especially for deep-draught supertankers at Roberts Bank, 24 km south of Vancouver. Bulk or "unit" trains were to provide the most effective means of handling goods at the terminus. A self-dumping bulk car can now empty itself in less than two minutes; thus, a long unit train can be completely unloaded in an incredible four hours.

Vancouver's deep-sea container terminal has operated for a number of years. Goods sealed in the containers can be transported by land, sea, or air, and never need to be unloaded from their container, a definite advantage in the handling of bulky cargo. But the experimenting goes on, even to the use of overland and undersea pipelines for the transporting of minerals, grain packed in capsules, or wood chips for future processing.

Economists are beginning to realize that Canada is a Pacific as well as an Atlantic country. As trade with Japan, the west coast of North America, Australia, and Southeast Asia increases, British Columbia could become a huge and prosperous funnel for this trade to and from the rest of Canada.

Skyline of Vancouver, B.C.

View of the spectacular glacier peaks of the Rocky Mountains in western Canada.

QUESTIONS

1. Study the cross-section of southern B.C., Figure 5-3. Identify the temperatures, precipitation, and vegetation at each of the four locations marked on the cross-section. What physical factors have influenced the climate and natural vegetation characteristics?

2. Why is the rainfall in the interior of British Columbia less than along the coast?

3. Assess the influence of British Columbia's relief on the transportation network and settlement patterns.

4. In what way is the Niagara Fruit Belt like the Fraser Delta? What problems are similar?

5. What are the problems associated with agriculture in the Okanagan Valley?

6. Why is it difficult for British Columbia to achieve self-sufficiency in agriculture?

7. Discuss some of the problems facing the fishing industry of British Columbia.

8. Describe briefly the historical location of sawmilling plants in the province. Why has there been a shift away from the original pattern of distribution?

9. What is an "integrated industry?" What advantages do they have?

10. What factors have revitalized British Columbia's mining industry?

11. What is meant by "double taxation" and how does it affect mining in British Columbia?

12. The development of modern port facilities and means of transportation are of prime importance to British Columbia's future. Discuss this statement with specific examples.

13. Can you suggest reasons why a company would decide to build a major aluminum plant on a remote section of the British Columbia coastline?

14. Why has a large smelter remained at Trail, when no major mineral deposits are left in the immediate area?

15. Describe the site and function of each of the following: Vancouver, Victoria, Penticton.

16. Summarize in the form of a chart the relationship between the historical events of British Columbia and the major steps taken toward the economic development of the province.

17. What has been the greatest influence on the economic development of British Columbia: the natural environment or the efforts of the population of British Columbia? Justify your answer.

RESEARCH

1. If you were an urban planner in British Columbia, how would you solve the problems of urban-rural land use competition and convince more people to live elsewhere in the province instead of in either Vancouver or Victoria?

2. Do research on the Haida, Kwakiutt, Nootka, and Tsimshian Indians, who used to inhabit the coast of British Columbia. Their past and present lifestyle has had a definite influence on the cultural atmosphere of the province. Discuss.

3. Each year, millions of dollars are invested in British Columbia's industries. If you were in a position to control some of the investment and capital, in which type of industry would you invest? Where would you locate the industry? Give your reasons.

6 THE PRAIRIES: AREAL DIFFERENTIATION

Traditional views of the Canadian Prairies as monotonously flat, wind-swept fields of wheat are changing. The Prairies of Canada, in fact, vary greatly in physical landscape and natural resources.

The Prairie provinces of Canada — Manitoba, Saskatchewan, and Alberta — contrast sharply to the Canadian Shield. As you drive west from the scattered lakes and bare-rock outcrops of northwestern Ontario, the landscape changes rapidly. The land becomes flatter and the forests disappear. You can see for hundreds of kilometres: you measure distances from the top of one dark red grain elevator to the top of another, a few kilometres down the road. Farmhouses, set back from the road, are hidden by trees which in turn are surrounded by a patchwork quilt of fields. This is the best-known image of the prairies and to a certain extent it is an accurate one. But the Prairies have great variety in their physical geography and economy.

RELIEF

The Prairies, for example, are not completely flat — they have areas of rugged hills and river valleys. Near the western edge of the Prairies, the foothills of the Rockies actually reach a height of 1500 m. Furthermore, while the Prairies are Canada's prime wheat-growing area, they are also rich in oil and natural gas; they also supply great quantities of potash used as fertilizer. Nor does everyone on the Prairies live on a farm. While many do, some of the most dynamic and rapidly growing cities in Canada are found on the Prairies.

The Prairies occupy the western interior of Canada. The area is bordered on the east by the Canadian Shield and on the west by the Rocky

Mountains. To the north is the Arctic; to the south, the U.S. border. It is to the south that the Prairies are least isolated. The southern edge is a political boundary only, for the Prairies are a natural extension of the Great Plains of the United States.

The Prairies actually rise from east to west in a gentle slope. In the east, the Manitoba Lowland section of the Prairies lies in the bed of an old glacial lake, so it is completely flat. To the west, the land rises gradually and is broken twice by two hilly ridges which stretch from north to south. These ridges are the Manitoba Escarpment and the Missouri Coteau. In several places, the somewhat monotonous prairie landscape is broken by a variety of landforms. For example, the Cypress Hills between southern Saskatchewan and Alberta stand well above the surrounding country. In addition, the Badlands, eroded by both wind and water along the Red Deer River, stand in striking contrast to our visual impressions of the Prairie landscape.

CLIMATE

The climate of the Prairies, while generally the same throughout the entire region, does have some variety. These variations have affected the way in which the land is used. The Prairies are dry for the most part and have extreme temperatures. Summers can be very hot, while mid-winter temperatures frequently plunge well below zero. The Prairies east of the Rocky Mountains, however, occasionally receive warm winds which descend the leeward side of the mountains. These winds are called *chinooks* and may raise temperatures by 9-14 °C within a matter of hours. Rainfall, however, does vary throughout the region. The northern and eastern Prairies receive from 350-550 mm of precipitation annually. The south-central Prairies, however, may receive as little as 280 mm of annual precipitation and experience near desert-like conditions.

SETTLEMENT

In comparison with other parts of Canada, the landscape of the Prairies has been influenced by human development for a very brief span of time. Although the Hudson's Bay and Northwest Companies carried on fur trading in the Prairies, it was not until 1812 that the first community or settlement was established along the Red River near present-day Winnipeg. However, problems such as flooding plagued the community's attempts at self-sufficiency and no large-scale influx of settlers followed immediately.

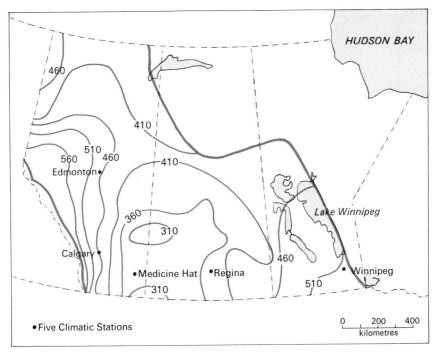

Figure 6–1: *Mean Annual Precipitation on the Prairies (mm)*

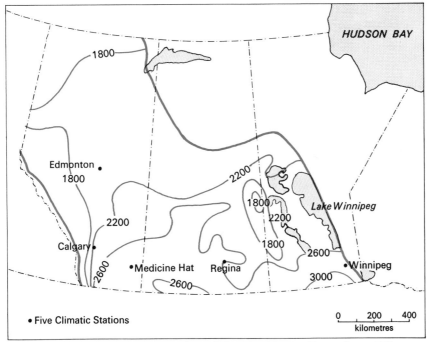

Figure 6–2: *Mean Annual Number of Growing-Degree Days above 7°C*

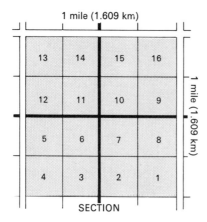

1 mile (1.609 km)

SECTION

Figure 6-3: Land-Survey Pattern on the Prairies

TOWNSHIP
contains 36 sections 260 hectares each
Every other section granted to the railway.
Two sections for school land.
One-and-three-quarters sections for
Hudson's Bay Company.

It soon became obvious that the rapid pace of settlement in the western United States might pose a problem for Canada. Movement north and south through the interior plains of Canada and the United States was so simple that Americans could have taken over the area. As a result, several explorers were sent by both the British and Canadian governments to assess the Prairies for settlement. The best known of these explorers, Captain John Palliser, was generally optimistic. However, he referred to the area in the southern Prairies which in fact receives minimal rainfall as "desert," generally useless for agricultural settlement. Despite the occasional pessimistic comments from surveyors the task of encouraging settlement throughout the Prairies was carried out. One phase of this settlement program was the actual surveying of the Prairies. Surveys ensured a fair distribution of the land; also, the government had more precise knowledge of the Prairies, allowing it to plan carefully for the region. Because of the relative flatness of the Prairie landscape, a square survey pattern was selected. Each square township was subdivided into 36 equal sections and each section contained 260 ha of land. Certain sections within each township were reserved for railway construction, schools, or the use of the Hudson's Bay Company. The remaining sections and sometimes parts of sections were then granted to settlers.

Certainly, choosing a particular section was simplified by the survey pattern used. However, it did little to encourage settlement in the first place. The real push — in fact, the single most important influence on the settlement of the Prairies — was the construction of the railway across the entire area. When the railway across the Prairies was being considered, it appeared likely that the construction of the line would occur in the more fertile belt to the north of Palliser's Triangle. However, an alert botanist, a member of the original survey team had noticed two important facts:

first, the rainfall, though sparse, came in the spring and early summer when it would be most needed by crops;

second, the growing season was actually longer than had been previously thought.

As a result and largely by chance, a southern route through the so-called "desert" was chosen. Thus, settlement was encouraged in an area which would otherwise likely have remained unpopulated. The southern route was relatively short and flat, thus reducing construction costs considerably. It eliminated in a very forceful way any concern about American settlers crossing the border to remain in Canada: troops and/or police could move much more quickly to the scene of an "invasion" by Americans.

By 1885, the first transcontinental railway had been completed across the Prairies. During the next ten years, additional branch lines were constructed. By 1915, two more transprairie lines, Canadian Northern and Grand Trunk Pacific, were built and the Prairies were settled at a rapid rate. While the Prairie railways were certainly important in encouraging initial settlement, their real significance lay in the movement of agriculture produce. In this, the railway network throughout the Prairies was unrivalled.

FARMING

During the late 1800s and early 1900s, settlers of many nationalities were attracted to the Prairies by the Canadian government's generous land grants. While each group tended to retain its cultural identity (and still does), all were united in a desire to establish a permanent and prosperous agricultural settlement. For the most part, the early settlers found plenty of flat land which was easy to clear, had good soils, and had an adequate growing season. Many settlers, however, were unprepared for the lack of trees and building materials as a consequence, severe droughts, and the shortage of surface water. In addition, European farming methods (which the immigrants were familiar with) were often not suitable for prairie agriculture. Neither their light wooden ploughs nor their seeds for crops seemed able to adapt to the environment. While the government was able to provide homesteads, a survey pattern, and a railway network for the settlers, it was unable to prepare them for the drought, insects, pests, and other hazards.

By the 1920s the Canadian Prairies had experienced an unprecedented boom in immigration; agriculture based on the cultivation of wheat had become the most significant aspect of its economy. But, as settlement throughout the Prairies became widespread, the problems associated with agriculture in the Prairie environment also became clearer. The lack of moisture as a serious handicap to farming quickly became apparent. As a result, farmers often left as much as 50% of their total cultivable land "fallow" or without a crop for one or more years in an effort to conserve moisture. This percentage is significant, in that a farmer who must leave 50% of the land "empty" each year must have a large amount of land in order to earn a living. Moreover, these larger farms also necessitated the use of machinery. Thus, the trend towards bigger or more extensive farms and increased mechanization became evident. (See cover photo.)

Various other methods were also used to conserve moisture and to reduce wind erosion which carried away precious topsoil. These methods included planting windbreaks, covering fields with straw, and strip farming (alternating planted and fallow fields).

Serious problems with wheat rust, a parasite which attacks grass plants and grains, occurred as well. Rust drastically reduces the size of the grain's kernels and thus reduces yields. Even with the development of more resistant strains of grain (for example, Red Fife, Thatcher, and Manitou), the spread of rust has not been far behind.

Despite such problems, however, wheat has continued to be a most important part of the economy of the Prairies. The lack of experience and capital tended to compound the ever-present problems of drought, wind erosion, and grain parasites. However, between the 1930s and the 1950s, dry-farming techniques became generally accepted and irrigation schemes were undertaken. In addition, the increasing use of fertilizers and pesticides helped to increase crop yields.

Today Canada's Prairie provinces are internationally recognized as producers of wheat. While the Prairies are not the largest single producer of wheat in the world, they certainly export more wheat than any place else. Although Canada's wheat yield is normally between 200-250 million tonnes annually, only 45 million tonnes are used domestically. Wheat sales to China and the U.S.S.R. have, for about the last twenty years, accounted for most of Canada's wheat surplus. At one point in the early 1970s, export demand dropped so drastically that Prairie farmers were paid by the Canadian government *not* to grow wheat. Ironically the following year the world suffered a wheat shortage.

Until recently, most of the wheat grown on the Prairies was of the *hard* variety. It has fine milling qualities and is used primarily to make flour for bread. However, the Chinese, who are among Canada's best customers, prefer the *soft* wheat variety, used for noodles and puddings. Soft-wheat yields are higher than those for hard wheat. Since Canada's wheat sales to China have increased so dramatically in recent years, Prairie farmers will probably grow more of the soft-wheat variety.

Because wheat is so important to the Prairies and therefore to Canada as a whole, it is necessary to maintain strong markets and fair prices.

A large part of the success in selling Canadian wheat abroad depends on the ability to move the wheat quickly and fairly cheaply from the producer to the consumer. A railway network plus storage facilities at Vancouver, Thunder Bay, and Churchill (the only Prairie ocean port) have greatly increased the efficiency of the grain-handling operation. Unfortunately, strikes and work stoppages can hamper or completely paralyze shipments at times. Even with the parts of the system functioning normally, the Prairie's total grain supply is not completely distributed for a full year after production.

IRRIGATION   Generally, precipitation on the Canadian Prairies is low: during dry spells, the lack of water can be critical. As a result, two alternatives are available to farmers who wish to cultivate these drier areas. One is to use the dry-farming techniques, such as strip farming and leaving

Figure 6–4: *Irrigated Areas on the Prairies*

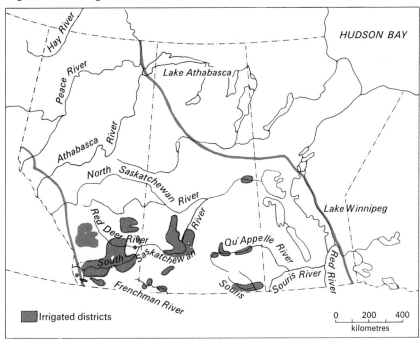

the fields fallow. The other method, more expensive but more reliable, is to irrigate the fields. About 30% of all Prairie wheat lands are irrigated. The development of irrigation projects has also encouraged a more widespread concern with water conservation, recreation, flood control, and, in the case of Saskatchewan, hydroelectricity.

The South Saskatchewan River project begun in the late 1950s was a particularly ambitious scheme to irrigate part of the so-called Palliser's Triangle. Two dams, which created a reservoir named Lake Diefenbaker, were built almost immediately. While the federal government assumed 75% of the total cost of the project, the province of Saskatchewan was responsible for the power station, irrigation system, and recreation facilities. Unfortunately, the costs have been staggering and farmers who practise dry-farming techniques seem reluctant to change their methods. The ultimate success of the project may lie in its ability to provide power for industrial development in south-central Saskatchewan.

Such projects certainly do not alter the landscape of the Prairies as a whole. However, they are important in that they can change local environments quite significantly and may even allow some farmers to experiment with new crops or even completely different types of agriculture, such as market gardening.

Farming (particularly wheat farming) on the Prairies has become "big business." Huge overseas sales have made investments in irrigation possible and as a result within the reach of more and more farmers. Research to find new, hardier, and more nutritious strains of wheat and other grains is being carried out. Wheat farms on the Canadian Prairies are much larger than ever before, so that the total number of farms has actually declined. Great emphasis is placed on large-scale use of machinery. As a result, many farm operations can be carried on with only a few people during harvesting.

RANCHING   Raising animals is another significant part of the Prairie economy. Herds of dairy cattle are raised close to urban centres, ready markets for milk and other dairy products. A similar situation exists for large turkey and chicken farms. The most important aspect of animal husbandry in the Prairies is the raising of beef cattle, called ranching. The importance of ranching increases from east to west in the Prairies, as rainfall declines and as the terrain becomes too rugged for crops (especially in Alberta). Ranching is also a highly specialized activity which requires extensive areas of grazing land. Prairie ranches often exceed 4000 ha: each head of cattle requires 20-24 ha for its own feeding. In most cases, only part of the ranchers' total land is actually owned by them, while the remainder is usually leased from the province.

OIL AND NATURAL GAS

Since the oil embargo by OPEC nations (Organization of Petroleum Exporting Countries) in the early 1970s and the concern over dwindling energy supplies, the Prairies have taken on a new importance. Not only are the Prairies Canada's single most important wheat-producing and ranching area, they also contain immense reserves of coal, oil, and natural gas. Unlike the metal-bearing igneous rocks of the Canadian Shield, the Prairies are underlain by layers of sedimentary rock. These horizontal rock layers are the remains of vast inland seas. The remnants of tiny invertebrates and acquatic plants settled layer after layer on the sea bed; over many millions of years, they turned into petroleum and natural gas. These formations of oil and gas, along with the potash deposits and coal seams trapped within the sedimentary layers, have completely altered the pattern of economic development in the Prairies (Table 6-2).

The Prairies hold vast reserves of coal. Alberta alone has about 70% of Canada's total coal reserves. Until recently, coal production had fallen drastically as other forms of energy, particularly oil and natural gas, became important. In the past few years, however, coal production in the Prairies has slowly but steadily increased. This growth can be explained partly by a genuine concern over future supplies of oil and natural gas, but most of the increased production comes from sales of coal to Japan. Japan, with limited natural resources, needs large quantities of coal for, among other things, its steel industry. In order to ensure long-term supplies of such basic raw materials, the Japanese are eager to invest great sums of

TABLE 6-1
Value of Fossil Fuel Mineral Production ($1000s)

	1972	1973	1974	1975	1976
Alberta					
Petroleum, Crude	1 247 064	1 894 724	3 004 334	3 254 971	3 531 100
Natural Gas	322 225	368 696	595 809	1 639 898	2 302 235
Coal	52 773	59 904	80 500	185 000	223 800
Saskatchewan					
Petroleum, Crude	219 212	246 057	443 840	389 746	435 675
Natural gas	8 663	9 044	9 014	5 878	8 250
Coal	6 356	8 500	7 300	8 900	12 900
Manitoba					
Petroleum, Crude	14 559	17 148	27 076	31 657	32 995

Source: *Quick Canadian Facts*, 31st Edition.

Gulf Oil Canada Limited

A drilling rig in Red Deer Valley, Alberta.

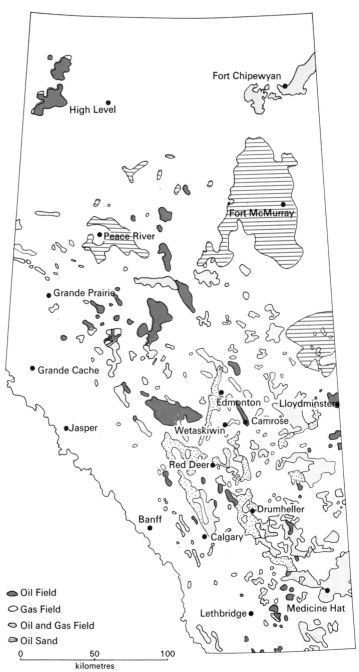

Oil Field
Gas Field
Oil and Gas Field
Oil Sand

0   50   100
kilometres

Figure 6–5: Locations of Oil, Gas, and Oil Sand in Alberta

money in mining projects abroad. As a result, Japanese capital has been partially responsible for encouraging exploration of new coal deposits and for stimulating production in existing coal mines. Interestingly enough, Ontario actually imports coal from the United States because transportation costs for Prairie coal are too high.

Among some other non-metallic minerals mined in the Canadian Prairies are salt, gypsum, and limestone. During the last decade, however, potash has taken on a new importance and continues to show dramatic growth.

The term potash, originally "pot ash," referred to the white residue left behind in iron pots after solutions of leached wood ashes were evaporated. Potash has long been recognized as a valuable fertilizer and much of the world's supplies, in fact, come from the Canadian Prairies.

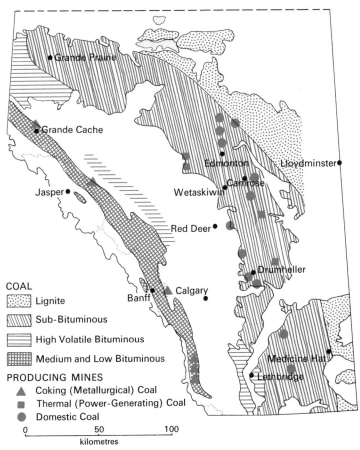

Figure 6–6: Coal Production in Alberta

In Saskatchewan, the main source of potash from the Prairies, potash ores were formed from salts deposited when ancient seas evaporated. Saskatchewan has the world's largest known deposits of high-grade potash. A large mine near Esterhazy, Saskatchewan, was the first potash mine in Canada. It opened in 1962 and produced 135 000 t in its first year. A number of mines are now in operation and it is hoped that, by 1980, production will reach 15 000 000 t.

Potash mining requires a large capital investment. For example, the cost of shaft construction alone for a typical potash mine costs about $50 million. Saskatchewan's potash mine operators estimate a total investment of over $1 billion. Thus, even a slight drop in market demand for potash can be critical. The entire potash industry is now concerned over what is called "double taxation": natural-resource industries are taxed by both the federal and provincial governments. This much taxation is a burden at the best of times, but, when business is in a slump, the effect is devastating. Furthermore, the industry was shocked in 1975 by the Saskatchewan government's announcement that it fully intended to take control of at least 50 % of the province's potash mines. Naturally, the large private firms which currently own the mines are worried by the announcement. They feel that the provincial government has permitted them to assume costly research and construction expenses, only to step in and operate the mines when they are assured of a profit. The Saskatchewan government, for its part, is worried over whether the owners of the mines will conduct business in the province's (and Canada's) best interests.

Nor is the wealth of the Prairies limited to the growing of wheat and the mining of coal and potash. The economy of the Prairies is remarkably versatile. Until recently, the vast oil and natural gas reserves of the Canadian Prairies have been largely taken for granted. Since the world oil crisis of 1973 and the subsequent rise in oil prices, Canada is looking at Prairie oil and natural gas with renewed interest. In the first half of the 1900s, even with oil discoveries at Turner Valley and Leduc, Alberta, demand remained low. However, the demand for oil has increased especially since the late 1960s; both need and concern for the future have necessitated continued exploration and development of additional oil and natural gas. Oil and natural gas, moreover, have become important in the manufacturing sector for such products as plastics and chemicals. As a result, the mineral-fuel industry is presently a significant source of income for the Prairies; this factor has justified the construction of oil and gas pipelines in Central and Western Canada.

Interest at the moment is focused on the Athabaska Tar Sands of northern Alberta. They probably hold the largest reserves of crude oil in

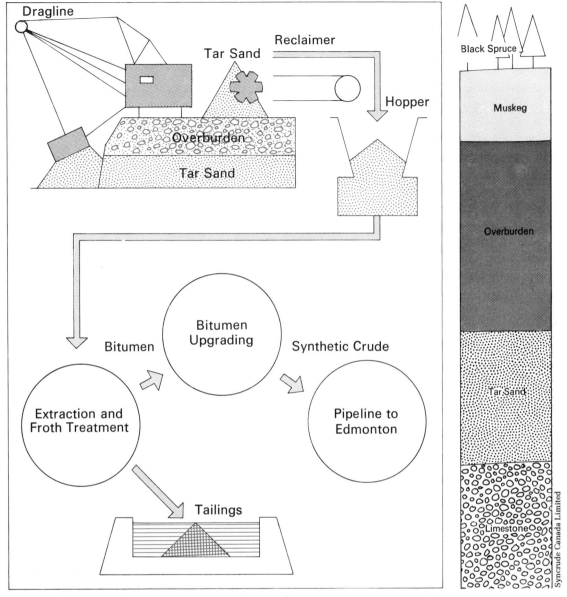

Figure 6–7:   *Flow Diagram (above left) or Tar-Sand Processing*

Figure 6–8:   *Cross-Section (above right) of Tar Sand*

the entire world. Little serious attention was paid to the oil sands until recently, first because procedures for extracting the oil from the tar sands were too difficult and costly to use; second, the need for oil from the Tar Sands became apparent only recently.

Many natural resources have remained unexploited simply because they have not been needed. This was the case with the tar sands in Alberta: they were not worked until 1967. The Great Canadian Oil Sands Company is currently extracting the oil by using gigantic rotating-bucket-wheel excavators which bite 75 t of sand every minute. Steam and hot water bathes the sand: 55 000 barrels of oil are "washed out" each day. In addition, Syncrude, a group of petroleum companies as well as the governments of Canada, Alberta, and Ontario, is operating 3 km north of the Great Canadian Oil Sands. It is hoped that Syncrude will be producing 125 000 barrels of oil a day by the late 1970s.

The tar sands are expected to meet Canada's energy needs for the immediate future at least. However, the costs are enormous — an investment of $1 billion is required for each project intended to produce 125 000 barrels a day. In order to reach a projected output of 1.5 million barrels per day by 1990, well over $12 billion will have to be expended. In addition, various environmental concerns, like air and water pollution from the exploitation of the tar sands, will require study as well.

URBAN PATTERNS IN THE PRAIRIES

The economy of the Prairies is now far more varied than just one hundred years ago when pioneers first began cultivating the soil. In much the

A view of the railroad in downtown Winnipeg (above left).

The business section of Calgary (above right).

An aerial view of Regina, looking east to west (left).

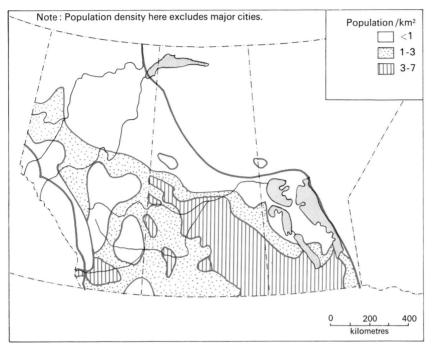

Figure 6–9: *Population Distribution on the Prairies*

same way, the settlements created by these same pioneers over a century ago would be almost impossible to recognize today. Initially, the centres which served the individual farms of the early settlers tended to locate along railway lines at intervals of about 12-24 km. This distance is roughly equal to that which could be covered by a wagon transporting grain from a farm to a central collection depot. Such centres existed partly to provide grain collection and storage facilities for the surrounding farms. They provided many other services as well. As time went on, such service centres typically provided functions such as a railway station, a hotel, general store, post office, curling rink, gas station, and a church — all clustered along or close to the main street. Housing was built for the people operating these services and often for retired farmers who had moved "into town." Although some of these towns have changed radically, hundreds of such settlements — each almost a carbon copy of the neighbouring town — are still scattered throughout the Prairies.

Although these small Prairie towns satisfied the everyday needs of the local farm community, they did not provide any specialized services. Frequently, then, one of these small settlements began to grow and

The Gulf Oil refinery in Edmonton.

Gulf Oil Canada Limited

provide more specialized services. These services might include a printer, a clothing store, a farmer's cooperative, a high school, a car and implement dealer, and possibly one or two restaurants. Such service centres grew in response to demands not only from the immediate area, but from a much larger surrounding area or hinterland. Obviously, a much larger population is needed to keep a clothing store or car dealer earning a profit than is needed to operate the only general store in town.

Inevitably, one or two of these more specialized centres grew into large urban centres or cities. These cities, in turn, influence large areas of the Prairies, perhaps entire provinces, like Winnipeg, Calgary, and Edmonton. In addition to being service centres for very large hinterlands, these cities have other specialty functions as well. Winnipeg, for example, has always been an important railway centre with large switching and stock yards. Winnipeg's growth has been somewhat hampered, however, by a limited market in eastern Manitoba and northwestern Ontario for its goods and services.

Calgary, Alberta, close to the Trans-Canada Highway and major railway lines, is an important manufacturing and distribution centre. In view of the renewed interest in Canada's oil and natural gas reserves, it has become a modern oil-boom city. The head offices of large oil companies, several new housing subdivisions, and a modern university campus all share the vigorous growth of the city.

On the other hand, Edmonton, surrounded by rich crop and pasture lands, is an important grain and livestock-marketing centre. In recent years, Edmonton has assumed many of the refining and manufacturing activities associated with the oil and natural gas fields as well as the mining areas to the north. Edmonton is also the capital of Alberta: the jobs necessary to administering the province have also helped to make Edmonton a thriving city.

While the large urban centres on the Prairies seem to be enjoying a period of unprecedented and dynamic growth, the situation is much gloomier for many of the small settlements. Costly "milk run" train routes, the Prairie town's lifeline, have been largely eliminated. More and more young people are leaving their farm homes in search of well-paid jobs in the cities. As a result, many small Prairie settlements are more isolated than ever before. Many are veritable "old folks homes" surviving on the demands of an elderly population and paid with monthly pension cheques. It is a tragic but apparently repetitious pattern across the Canadian Prairies.

THE FUTURE OF THE PRAIRIES

The changing settlement patterns of the Prairies are only one example of new vitality within this part of Canada. The growth of Prairie cities is matched by high expectations for wheat production and sales and by intense exploration for and increased production of oil and gas.

It has been suggested that the Prairies may in the near future play an active role in feeding the world's hungry. More than 75% of Canada's grain is shipped to 90 countries overseas; world stocks of grain are at their lowest levels since the end of World War II — enough to last only about one month! The poor developing nations of the world need grain desperately. In addition, more affluent nations, such as Japan, Europe, and the Soviet Union whose consumption of meat is steadily increasing, need more grain to feed their livestock.

It takes about 4 kg of food grain to produce 0.5 kg of beef and about 2 kg of grain to produce 0.5 kg of pork. Also, North Americans consume 90 kg of grain per capita each year — five times India's consumption. Prior to 1940, Western Europe was virtually the only grain producer that was not exporting a surplus. Now, the picture has completely changed. The United States and Canada are supplying the world with huge surpluses; that dependence can only continue to increase. It is possible for the Prairie provinces to increase their agricultural output greatly. This increase would require a large financial commitment to sophisticated irrigation techniques, widespread mechanization, as well as long-term research into grain growing techniques and the food needs of the world. It is possible for the Prairies to achieve the same status in the world of wheat as did the Middle East in the world of oil.

Neither can the significance of potash be underestimated. As an important component of fertilizer, potash is vitally important to the agricultural nations of the world who are attempting to increase their

TABLE 6-2
Net Value of Production by Top Four Industries in Alberta, Saskatchewan, and Manitoba

	1971		1972		1973		1974	
	$1000s	%	$1000s	%	$1000s	%	$1000s	%
Alberta								
Mining	1 479 769	38.7	1 787 838	40.2	2 423 170	41.8	4 200 684	49.4
Construction	895 412	23.4	998 632	22.5	1 098 782	19.0	1 484 164	17.5
Manufactures	755 246	19.7	849 473	18.1	1 016 776	17.6	1 318 276	15.5
Agriculture	564 022	14.7	655 782	14.8	1 073 220	18.5	1 284 031	15.1
Total for all industry	3 825 707	100.0	4 439 927	100.0	5 793 744	100.0	8 500 646	100.0
Saskatchewan								
Agriculture	801 762	47.8	798 852	45.9	1 336 622	54.0	1 988 358	56.1
Mining	348 321	20.8	355 820	20.4	426 131	17.2	670 307	18.9
Construction	231 115	13.8	252 642	14.5	324 165	13.1	402 733	11.3
Manufactures	209 965	12.5	244 221	14.0	291 979	11.8	373 242	10.5
Total for all industry	1 676 177	100.0	1 741 086	100.0	2 474 653	100.0	3 545 203	100.0
Manitoba								
Manufactures	534 472	39.2	599 790	39.1	720 739	35.7	906 434	38.4
Agriculture	303 504	22.3	330 270	21.5	538 297	26.0	584 838	24.8
Construction	282 674	20.7	316 096	20.6	408 216	20.2	439 370	18.6
Mining	147 921	10.9	179 124	11.7	230 361	11.4	274 982	11.7
Total for all industry	1 362 360	100.0	1 534 444	100.0	2 020 626	100.0	2 360 229	100.0

Source: *Quick Canadian Facts*, 31st Edition.

Ranching, the raising of beef cattle, is a highly specialized activity in the Prairies.

Agriculture Canada

Grain elevators in the Prairies.

View of a bucket-wheel excavator in operation at the Great Canadian Oil Sands, Limited, facilities near Fort McMurray, Alberta. The giant machine is 30 m high, 160 m long, and weighs about 1800 t. Electrically powered, it can mine approximately 100 000–120 000 t of oil sand per day.

agricultural output to keep up with the ever-increasing population figures.

Finally, Canada's oil and natural gas reserves in the Prairies will further ensure Canada's economic future. Production from the Athabaska Tar Sands will probably supply Canada's oil needs for many years to come. Thus, Canada's vulnerable position as an importer of mineral fuels would be considerably lessened. The traditional image of the Prairies as a vast, flat, windswept landscape dotted with farmhouses and fields of wheat is only partially true. Today the Prairies form a dynamic and exciting part of Canada's economy. To regard them as anything less is an outdated and grossly oversimplified view.

QUESTIONS

1. (a) On a blank piece of paper, draw a cross-section to illustrate the change in relief across the southern Prairies from Ontario to the foothills of British Columbia.
   (b) Label the following neatly on a cross-section:
   (i) the three prairie levels and escarpments
   (ii) Winnipeg, Regina, Medicine Hat and Calgary
   (iii) at each city, the total precipitation in millimetres, the mean annual temperature, the type of vegetation, and the soil type.
2. Why did the railways prove invaluable for settlement and farming in the Prairies?
3. Construct a fully labelled diagram to illustrate the original land-survey system introduced in 1869. List some of its disadvantages.
4. Development of Prairie agriculture since the 1900s coincides with the farmer's ability to adapt their farming methods to suit the Prairie environment. Discuss these adjustments under the following headings:
   (a) advantages and disadvantages to farm settlement
   (b) mistakes
   (c) coping with the environment.
5. Draw a vertical bargraph to illustrate the value of fossil-fuel production statistics (Table 6-1).
6. Draw three circle graphs to illustrate the value of fossil-fuel production statistics (Table 6-1).
   Prairie provinces (Table 6-2).
7. Briefly describe the sites and functions of the major cities in the Prairies.
8. Can the phrase *areal differentiation* be used to describe land use on the Prairies? In what way?

RESEARCH

1. Do research on the following topics:
   (a) Buffalo
   (b) Hutterite settlements
   (c) Ukrainian settlements
   (d) Native peoples
   (e) Pipeline construction
   (f) Tar sands
2. Debate the question, "Should the federal government or provincial governments control petroleum and natural gas resources in the West?"
3. A prime concern of the three Prairie provincial governments' economic policies has been to promote the diversification of industry by expanding secondary manufacturing and reducing their dependence on natural resource industries. Discuss.

4. How is the role of the Prairies changing in the overall economic development of Canada?

5. Research *either* the Hutterites or the Mennonites, two religious sects which have maintained their own identity throughout their settlement in the Prairies. Why did they come to the Prairies? What is unique about their lifestyles?

7 THE ONTARIO – ST. LAWRENCE LOWLANDS: CHOICE

The Ontario–St. Lawrence Lowlands Region has long been the focal point for economic development in Canada. This region faces serious problems both now and in the future; however, skillful decision making will be required to overcome them.

The lowlands of southern Ontario and Quebec, roughly between the Great Lakes and the Precambrian or Canadian Shield, is the economic centre of Canada. Here, in a line from Quebec City in the east to Windsor in the west, are the governmental, manufacturing, financial and commercial functions which affect the entire country. This lowland area is divided in two by an arm of the Shield called the *Frontenac Axis*. Each of the resulting subregions, the *Ontario Lowlands* and the *St. Lawrence Lowlands* and their major cities, Toronto and Montreal, are nuclei for the nation's largest concentration of population.

RELIEF

About 300 million years ago, this lowland area was covered by a shallow tropical sea. The silt on the bottom of this sea compressed into layers of sedimentary rock. Today, the outer edges of some of the more resistant layers of rock protrude above the surrounding countryside in long ridges, such as the Niagara Escarpment. However, the most significant single factor which has affected the physical landscape of the area was the action of glacial ice, which scoured and scraped the surface of the bedrock during *four* separate advances over the last one million years. Great hills of gravel were created when rocks were crushed and pushed ahead of the advancing ice. In the area of the present Great Lakes, deep depressions were created by the weight and scraping action of the ice. These depressions were later filled by melt water from the retreating glacier.

194

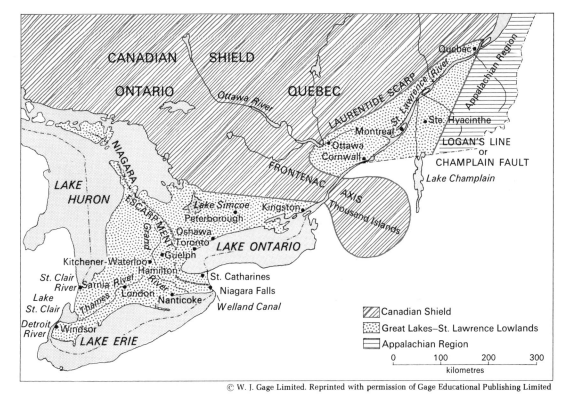

Figure 7–1:   Physiographic Regions of the Great Lakes–St. Lawrence Area

When the St. Lawrence Valley (which had been blocked by the retreating ice) eventually "opened," much of the water from the Great Lakes Depression drained away, leaving them as they are today. Large areas of sand and clay were subsequently exposed when the excess water drained away. Thus, the present landscape of the Ontario–St. Lawrence Lowlands is essentially made up of many of these glacial remnants — the Great Lakes themselves, morainic hills, ancient shorelines, and former lake beds.

CLIMATE

The climate of the Ontario–St. Lawrence Lowlands lacks the mildness and heavy precipitation of the west coast, but it is not as extreme as the Prairies or the Canadian Shield. The climate is somewhere in between. The extremes of climate in the inland locations are counteracted by the presence of the Great Lakes; in fact, the distinctive feature of the climate here is the high humidity. The region is the centre of interplay between

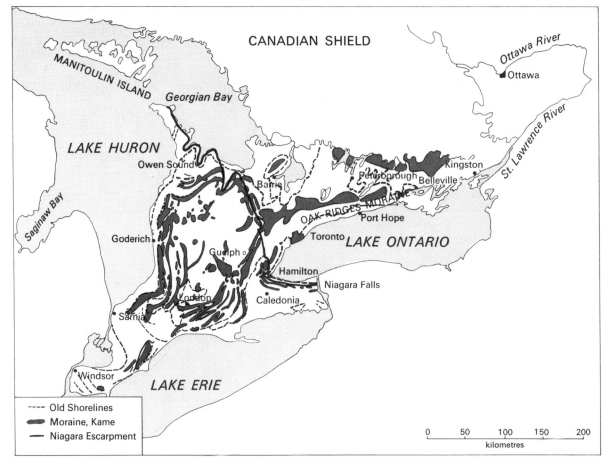

Figure 7–2: *Physical Features of Southern Ontario*

cold dry arctic air from the north and *warm* moist air from the Gulf of Mexico. The resulting storms usually move from west to east across the Great Lakes and along the St. Lawrence Valley. As a result, the typical weather pattern for this part of the country involves several days of dull, overcast skies often with rain or snow, followed invariably by as many clear, sunny days.

While the seasonal climate and daily weather patterns are generally consistent over the Ontario–St. Lawrence Lowlands, climate varies within the area itself. For example, Quebec City receives an average of over 250 cm of snow in a winter, while Windsor receives slightly over 100 cm. Similarly, the Windsor area is assured of a growing season of more than 220 days, probably 180 days being frost-free. On the other

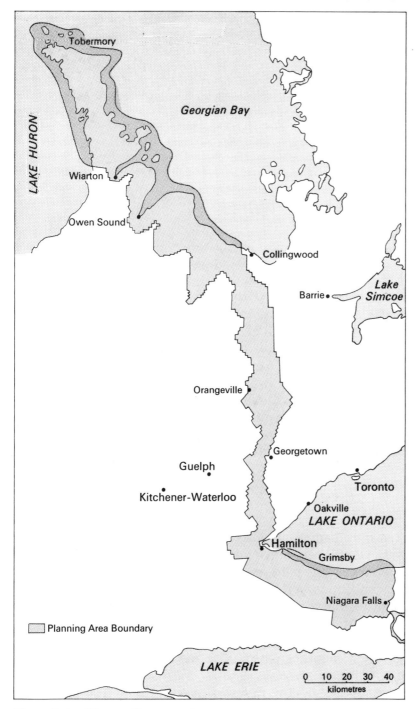

Figure 7–3: Niagara Escarpment

hand, the growing season in the Quebec City area is about 180 days, with only 120 days likely to be frost-free. These statistics partly explain the presence of specialty crops such as tobacco and soybeans in the southwestern part of Ontario. It is interesting to note that Montreal's snowfalls are usually about double those in Toronto; in 1974-75, Montreal spent over $20 million in snow removal.

AGRICULTURE

The way people use their land reflects their immediate needs as well as the tradition in which they have been raised. The pioneer farmers throughout the Ontario–St. Lawrence Lowlands depended on their land for all their needs. Although the use of the land was largely the same throughout the entire region, the allotment of land represented two completely different ways of life. In the Quebec portion of the lowlands along the St. Lawrence, land was divided so that each farmstead had water and/or road frontage. Therefore, farmsteads tended to cluster along the river. Long narrow farms called "long lots" or "rangs" resulted from this system of land division. This method of land distribution had the advantage of giving each farm easy access to a transportation route and also ensured that neighbours were close by. However, much of the farmer's time was then taken up in walking from one section of the "rang" to another. The quality of the soil often varied widely over the entire length of any one of these lots.

By contrast, the division of land in the Ontario section of the lowlands was based on a system of townships such as we have today. Because a great deal of experimentation occurred in the setting of township boundaries and because the townships were not always laid out in sequence, dimensions vary considerably even today. At present, while the original survey pattern imposed upon the Ontario–St. Lawrence Lowlands region is still very much intact, the agriculture is far from being at a subsistence level. The pattern of agricultural land use today reflects local climatic conditions, soil fertility, and market demand. Much of the area is devoted to livestock and dairying. However, specialized areas include:

(a) extreme southwestern Ontario, where light sandy soils and a long growing season encourage the cultivation of tobacco and some market garden crops;

(b) the Niagara Peninsula (and to lesser degree, the Collingwood area) where fruit is grown in the shelter of the Niagara Escarpment and close to the moderating influence of nearby water bodies;

(c) western Ontario, where corn production has increased tremendously to provide feed for livestock in the surrounding area.

What is not shown on the map of agricultural regions is that the total number of farms in the lowlands region has been declining in recent years. Farming is a business: larger, more highly mechanized farms are an almost inevitable trend. Many farms are becoming more specialized than ever before; that is, farmers concentrate on poultry, fruit, or dairying, for example, and are employing as much machinery as possible to maximize yields and increase efficiency. It is important to remember that barely more than a century ago virtually the entire population supported itself on an agricultural base; today less than 10% of the population of Ontario earns a living from farming.

Figure 7–4: *Agricultural Regions of Southern Ontario (Note the dense urban concentration in the Toronto-Hamilton stretch).*

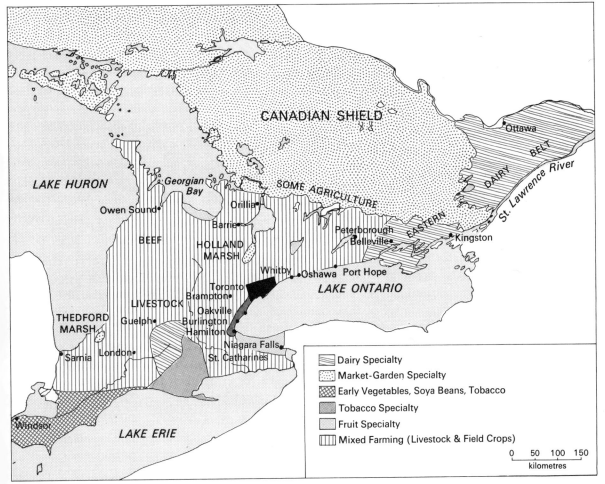

INDUSTRY

One cannot underestimate the significance of agriculture in the Ontario–St. Lawrence Lowlands area, but the dynamic growth of industry in this region is unparalleled. With this growth in the industrial sector of the lowland's economy has come a tremendous increase in population, focusing primarily on the two metropolitan giants, Montreal and Toronto.

This massive industrialization has occurred in the Ontario–St. Lawrence Lowlands for a number of reasons. The complex and versatile transportation network provides a stimulus to new industry and encourages established industries to remain. There is a great variety in the highway network, including the Macdonald-Cartier Freeway virtually from Montreal through to Windsor with excellent connection routes immediately south in the United States.

Air routes and airport facilities in the Ontario–St. Lawrence Lowlands are excellent. One of the busiest routes in the country connects Montreal and Toronto; the network of air routes in the busy northeastern United States is only an hour away via several different aircraft carriers. Two airports at Toronto and Dorval (just outside Montreal) provide the services of many of the world's major carriers. The recent opening of a third major airport at Mirabel, also near Montreal, provides international air services. Several regional carriers, such as Nordair, Pem-Air, and Otonabee Airways provide service between smaller centres such as Hamilton, Pembroke, Peterborough, and Kingston, as well as some points in the United States.

The railway lines of Canadian National and Canadian Pacific (Figure 11-5 in Chapter 11), which criss-cross the entire country, pass through this area. Montreal and Toronto have large switching yards. These railway lines are closely linked to a number of good harbours in the lowlands, particularly those at Montreal, Toronto, and Hamilton. Goods can be shipped by one mode of transportation and easily transferred to another at any one of these break-of-bulk points.

Perhaps the most significant factor in the transportation network of the lowlands was the construction of the St. Lawrence Seaway, completed in 1959. The existing waterway was deepened and new locks were built along the Seaway (Figure 11-3). As a result, traffic was increased between Quebec, Montreal, and the Great Lakes ports such as Toronto, Hamilton, and Welland. Ocean-going vessels, previously forced (because of the size of the locks) to terminate their journeys at Quebec or Montreal, are now able to enter the Great Lakes.

The nearness to large markets has been a factor in encouraging the

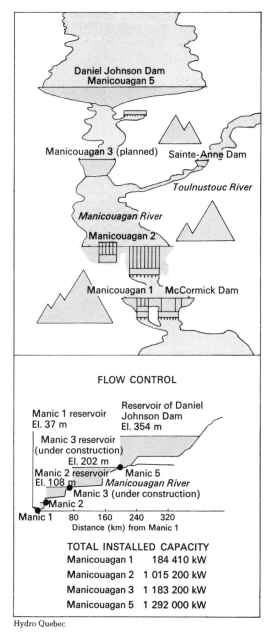

Figure 7–5: Manicouagan-Outardes Hydroelectric Complex

The Manicouagan 1 hydroelectric station was built as part of Hydro-Quebec's overall plan for development of the Manicouagan and Outardes Rivers. Construction of this giant hydroelectric complex began in 1959; when completed, it will comprise seven new powerhouses with a total installed capacity of 5 500 000 kW. Hydro-Quebec must always be in a postion to satisfy Quebec's demand for electricity, currently doubling every ten years. Three world records have been achieved on this project: Manicouagan 2, the world's largest hollow-joint, gravity dam; the transmission lines to Quebec and Montreal operate at 735 000 V, the world's highest transmission voltage in commercial operation; and, last but not least, the Daniel Johnson dam — the world's largest multiple-arch dam — will eventually impound a vast reservoir covering 1950 km².

The river flow at Manic 3 is regulated by Manic 5 reservoir, 120 km upstream. This reservoir, the largest artificial lake in North America, was created by the Daniel Johnson dam, 200 km from the mouth of the Manicouagan River. This river, which is 560 km long and drops 570 m altogether, flows from the Laurentian Plateau down through a deep valley in a rocky, uninhabited part of Quebec, then empties into the St. Lawrence with a flow averaging 100 m³/s. Manic 5 regulating reservoir has a surface area of 1950 km² and receives water from a region extending over 300 000 km², which is 64% of the river's catchment area. The reservoir's usable storage consists of the 20 m of water between elevations 334 m and 354 m.

growth of industry in the Ontario–St. Lawrence Lowlands. The largest concentrations of population in Canada are found in the lowlands, including two cities with almost three million inhabitants each. Furthermore, the densely populated northeastern United States provides another almost endless market; the movement of goods to these markets is facilitated by the transportation network. Even overseas markets, though distant, are accessible from the lowlands via the Great lakes and St. Lawrence Seaway.

Industry, even in these times of increasing automation, requires a large number of skilled and unskilled workers. The Ontario–St. Lawrence Lowlands has an abundance of people to fill these jobs. This region, because of its large population and complex urban growth, can offer additional training for workers to improve their skills and to enjoy the social, commercial, and recreational facilities provided by the large metropolitan areas such as Toronto and Montreal.

The Ontario–St. Lawrence Lowlands are ideally situated for obtaining raw materials. As an example, for the steel industry centred primarily in Hamilton, iron ore can be easily transported from the north shore of Lake Superior or the Duluth, Minnesota region. Coal can be moved quickly and cheaply from Kentucky, Ohio, Pennsylvania, and Virginia.

For the chemical industries clustered around the Cornwall-Brockville area and near Sarnia, the pipelines transporting petroleum

Figure 7–6: *Flow of Raw Materials into Hamilton's Iron and Steel Mills*

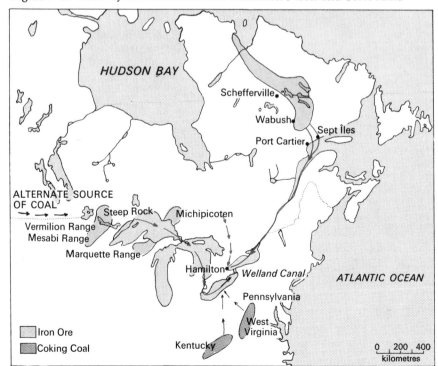

Phil Aggus and Son Ltd.

An aerial view of Hamilton's harbour.

from Western Canada terminate in the lowlands. Energy is still plentiful, despite ever-increasing demands placed on it by individuals and industry. The Great Lakes Basin itself provides hydroelectricity and water for cooling nuclear-powered generators.

Finally, industries are frequently attracted to a particular region because of the special service it can provide. In the Ontario–St. Lawrence Lowlands, the special functions provided by Montreal and Toronto, Canada's two largest metropolitan areas, cannot be discounted. They are the financial centres of Canada: Toronto's downtown core being dominated by the head offices of the Canadian Imperial Bank of Commerce, the Toronto-Dominion Bank, and the functional head office of the Bank of Nova Scotia. Downtown Montreal is dominated by the Royal Bank, the Bank of Montreal, and the Banque Canadienne Nationale. The head offices of many of Canada's leading accounting, legal, insurance, and advertising firms are also in the lowland region. Educational facilities (such as universities), stores, theatres, hotels, and so on, often required by large companies — and more often appreciated by their employees and families — are found in greatest number and variety in the two major urban complexes of this region.

The industrial development of the Ontario–St. Lawrence Lowlands corridor seems to follow a fairly consistent pattern. Textiles have traditionally been located in the Quebec portion of the corridor with chemical industries clustering around Cornwall and Brockville and in the western portion of the lowlands near Sarnia. Car and car-part manufacturers have established plants in the Toronto suburbs of Oshawa and Oakville as well as Windsor and St. Thomas. Steel making is, as mentioned, mainly confined to the Hamilton area. This pattern of industrial locations is not likely to change in the near future, simply because the factors which initially drew many industries to the lowlands are still in force — perhaps these factors are even more attractive than previously. Any negative factors which might affect an existing industry's location are likely to be counteracted by something called "industrial inertia." This phenomenon applies to industries so firmly established in a particular location that opportunities even more attractive elsewhere would not provide sufficient incentive to move.

URBANIZATION

In many ways, the Ontario–St. Lawrence Lowlands are an indispensable link in Canada's economic development. With the exception of British

Aerial views of Toronto, looking east on Bloor Street from Avenue Road. The photograph below was taken in 1956; the one on the opposite page, in 1976. Note the difference in the number of high-rise buildings in both photographs.

Northway Survey Corporation, Limited

Columbia — which is in a geographical sense almost closer to the western United States and Japan than to the rest of Canada — all parts of the country relate economically to one another and to the United States primarily through this lowland region.

The complex industrialization and urbanization of the Ontario–St. Lawrence Lowlands and its ability to attract a sizable population are all apparent indicators of success. However, the astonishing growth of this region has created many problems as well. Because of its varied employment opportunities, this region experiences population shifts from the farming areas to the cities. People also move into it from other parts of Canada; immigrants from other countries are attracted by the job opportunities here. Thus, tremendous pressure is put on this region to provide the necessary services and adequate housing.

Most people prefer to live in single-family detached housing. However, this kind of dwelling is becoming less and less feasible as the competition for land around cities such as Toronto and Montreal drives

Northway Survey Corporation, Limited

prices for houses and rents for apartments beyond the reach of most people. In Toronto, for example, about 40% of the existing housing is composed of single-family detached dwellings. Apartments and flats make up another 40%. Also, in Toronto, almost half of all families spend more than 40% of their income on renting when 25% has always been the accepted figure. Thus, the trend toward family-style apartments and condominiums may be in order. A continued emphasis on low-rent housing for lower-income groups would certainly be a social benefit for the entire region.

The highly urbanized areas of the lowlands also experience severe problems in providing transportation for their massive populations both within the cities and to points outside. Montreal and Toronto have expressways by which motorists can enter or bypass the downtown area. Commuter trains and buses link suburbs with the core. Both cities have subway systems. Nevertheless, the flow of traffic in this region continues to be a nightmare for drivers and traffic planners alike. Of course, other large Canadian cities also experience traffic problems, but the sheer size and population numbers in the Montreal and Toronto areas — indeed, the entire lowlands — make them extremely vulnerable. Consequently, transportation experts are looking at a great variety of alternative plans which will reduce traffic flow at peak periods. Some of these alternatives are:

(a) limiting growth in the downtown areas and encouraging the decentralization of some existing and all new businesses;
(b) car pools;
(c) staggered working hours;
(d) expansion of existing mass transit along routes not now being used to capacity.

Another serious problem closely related to the population pressure in the Ontario–St. Lawrence Lowlands region is the competition between various types of land use. This situation has become especially critical in the area of the Niagara Peninsula below the escarpment. Here, soils and climate combine to create ideal growing conditions for delicate fruits such as cherries, grapes, and peaches. Unfortunately, this area is equally attractive for housing subdivisions and for manufacturing industries, since it is close to Hamilton and Niagara Falls. It is also served by the same road and railway services which connect Toronto with the whole Niagara Region. The entire issue is complicated because prices for sprays and fertilizers, machinery, fuel, and labour have risen tremendously over the last decade. These price increases have not been matched by the prices farmers are being paid for their fruit. For example, sweet cherries brought 48¢/kg in 1974 but only 33¢/kg in 1975. Also, the number of peach- and pear-processing plants in Canada has declined from 19 to 4 in the nine years between 1965 and 1973.

Decisions which involve changes in existing land use must be carefully weighed and must be made only after all relevant factors and alternatives have been studied. Every sector of society must reassess its priorities and decide whether agriculture land is more valuable (in the broadest sense) than industrial land, whether housing projects can encroach on recreational land, or whether various land uses can perhaps compromise in a satisfactory way.

Finally, as the Ontario–St. Lawrence region continues to urbanize and grow, attention will have to turn to the problem of governing such a complex area. The original structure of government was designed to serve an agriculturally based society. Now it is obvious that too many small local jurisdictions and no central planning agency exist to coordinate their activities and encourage cooperation. In the most densely populated region of the lowlands around Toronto, the Ontario government restructured the local jurisdictions to create the new regional governments of Hamilton-Wentworth, Halton, Peel, York, Durham, Niagara Falls, as well as several others in northern and southern Ontario.

By law, these regional governments must develop a regional plan for their own area and they are responsible for providing "hard" services such as water, sewage and garbage disposal, and police protection. The local councils within the regions have the responsibility for passing by-laws controlling the zoning of land according to the regional plan. That is, the regional plan sets out the desired land use, such as "residential," and the local council determines whether single-family dwellings or multiple housing will be built and exactly what densities of population will be permitted.

TCR* Goals and Principles

The TCR document listed 12 goals for the region against which to consider the "vital social implications" of growth. It also listed five development principles designed to help achieve the goals.

I Goals

1. To facilitate the achievement of the Region's economic potential,

consistent with the overall provincial interest and development.
2. To preserve the unique attributes of the regional landscape.
3. To minimize the urban use of productive agricultural land.
4. To minimize the pollution of water and the atmosphere.
5. To facilitate and maintain a pattern of identifiable communities.

* Toronto-Centred Region.

6. To provide best possible accessibility for the movement of people and goods.
7. To provide essential transportation, water and sewer facilities at minimum cost consistent with overall benefit.
8. To maximize opportunities for using specialized services and facilities.
9. To develop in a manner consistent with the needs arising from long-term population trends, particularly the scale of growth and anticipated changes in household size and composition, and in age distribution.
10. To develop a manner consistent with emerging and probably future technological innovations, i.e. to facilitate, adjust to, and receive the benefits of such possibilities.
11. To develop in a manner consistent with the needs arising from social changes resulting from future economic and technological developments, e.g. changing patterns of leisure.
12. To develop the Region in a manner that provides flexibility.

Figure 7–7: The Toronto-Centred Region, Zone 1

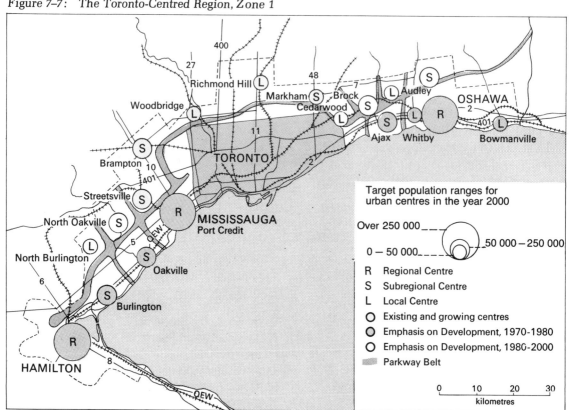

Design for Development — The Toronto Centred Region — 1970, Queen's Printer for Ontario

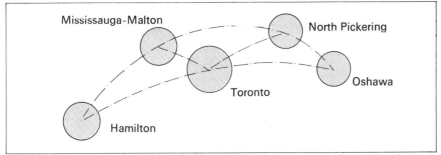

Design for Development — The Toronto Centred Region — 1970, Queen's Printer for Ontario

Figure 7–8:   The Five-Pole Structure

Figure 7–9:   The Toronto-Centred Region

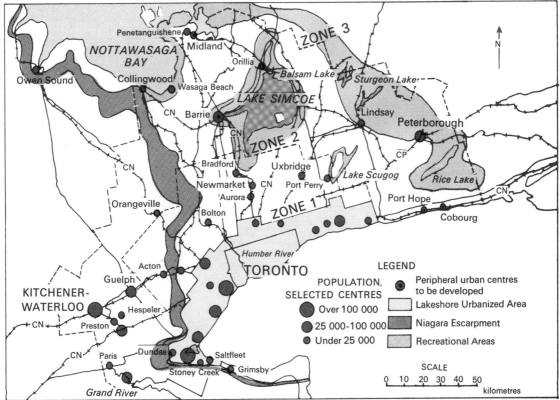

Design for Development — The Toronto Centred Region — 1970, Queen's Printer for Ontario

TABLE 7-1
Projected Population and Employment in the year 2000

Urban Centre	Functional Class	Urban Population	Service Employees	Manufacturing and Construction Employees	Total Employed
Hamilton	2	700	317	133	450
Burlington	4	150	38	27	65
N. Burlington	5	75	11	5	16
Milton	6	20	2	1	3
HAMILTON SUBREGION		945	368	166	534
Mississauga	2	440	188	66	254
Oakville	3	200	79	22	101
N. Oakville	4	150	29	7	36
Erin Mills-Meadowvale	4	270	66	19	85
Brampton-Bramalea	4	280	62	27	89
Malton	6	35	24	40	64
Georgetown	6	40	6	4	10
MISSISSAUGA SUBREGION		1415	454	185	639
Oshawa-Whitby	2	450	193	52	245
S. Pickering	4	120	25	11	36
N. Pickering	3	200	129	26	155
Ajax	4	120	22	14	36
Bowmanville	6	35	4	3	7
Audley	5	70	14	10	24
Columbus	4	150	36	11	47
OSHAWA SUBREGION		1145	423	127	550
Aurora-Newmarket	3	75	58	20	78
Woodbridge	6	20	2	11	13
Richmond Hill	5	95	15	8	23
Markham-Unionville	6	35	3	6	9
NORTH SUBREGION		225	78	45	123
Toronto[1]	1	932	461	149	610
West Metro[2]	3	540	113	121	234
North Metro[3]	2	768	212	121	333
East Metro[4]	3	660	184	89	273
TORONTO SUBREGION		2900	970	480	1450
TOTAL URBAN PLACES		6630	2293	1003	3296
REST OF COLUC		524	—	—	217
TOTAL COLUC		7154	—	—	3513

Note: Population figures are given in thousands.
[1] Central Toronto includes City of Toronto and East York.
[2] West Metro includes York and Etobicoke.
[3] North Metro includes North York and the north Metro fringe.
[4] East Metro includes Scarborough and Milliken.
Source: Design for Development — The Toronto-Centred Region — 1970 Queen's Printer for Ontario.

II Principles
1. The principle of linearity, which seeks as far as possible to align urban places along a series of more or less straight paths to take maximum advantage of parallel routes for transporation and services.
2. The principle of functional efficiency, which seeks a best set of political, economic, and social relationships for all urban and rural places.
3. The principle of decentralization, which emphasizes (i) the importance of metropolitan centre influence, and (ii) a logical distribution of urban places within a metropolitan region.
4. The principle of space conservation, which stresses, on a per capita basis, adequate open space and recreational requirements.
5. The principle of natural resource conservation, which stresses the need for careful use of land, water and air.

Source: Design for Development — The Toronto-Centred Region — 1970, Queen's Printer for Ontario.

This urban complex will be a Toronto-centred region; plans include the division of the area into three zones:

Zone 1: the heavily urbanized corridor for the region. This corridor is planned to house 71% of the total population by the year 2000.

Zone 2: the "commutershed" where urban growth is discouraged and agriculture encouraged. This area is to have 4% of the total population by the year 2000.

Zone 3: the peripheral zone dominated by conservation and recreation areas, with Barrie and Midland as the growth centres. This area is to house 25% of the total population in 2000.

Toronto Centred Region Zone 1 plans for the development of two tiers of urban communities parallel to the lakeshore and separated by a Parkway Belt. The 23 urban places would differ in size and function, but they would be dominated by five major cities.

It should be noted that in order to effectively house the expected population and to complete the second tier, a number of new communities will have to be established. In the interim, these sites — North Burlington, North Oakville, Audley, and Columbus — are to remain as active agricultural areas.

Between the two tiers of cities lies the Parkway Belt, an area of 233 km² that is to serve as the transportation and utility corridor linking the urban zone together. In addition, the Parkway Belt serves to preserve

An aerial view of Montreal with the Bonaventure Expressway in the foreground and Mount Royal in the background.

open space, create recreational areas, and break the urban populations into distinct units.

Further plans include the preservation of ecologically sensitive areas such as river valleys, waterfront sites, and in particular, the Niagara Escarpment. The Escarpment, a unique combination of hills, cliffs, waterfalls, and unusual rock formations, will be protected by stringent land-use regulations to preserve the history and ecology of the area, but permit other compatible land uses as well.

No one can dispute the significance of the Ontario–St. Lawrence Lowlands in the economic development of Canada. Other parts of Canada

Convention and Tourist Bureau of Metropolitan Toronto

A view of Toronto's CN Tower with the city landscape in the background (left).

An aerial view (below) of Hilton Works, Basic Steel Plant of the Steel Company of Canada, Limited. Note that much of this property has been created by dumping fill. In order to increase its steel production, the company has had to develop a second site at Nanticoke, on the north shore of Lake Erie.

Stelco

predominate from time to time: such is the case with oil and gas exploration in the Far North or with recent reports of the rapid growth of western cities such as Edmonton and Calgary. However, the Ontario–St. Lawrence Lowlands have, since the early days of Upper and Lower Canada, consistently been the focal point in the economic development of the country. Unfortunately, this region must also at this moment and in the future face serious problems which may hamper its continued prosperity. An ever-increasing urban population, a shortage of reasonably priced housing, overworked transportation systems, and pollution of the air and water are among a few of its problems. But the situation is far from hopeless: thoughtful decision making in the decades to come will ensure the continued growth and prosperity of the entire lowlands region.

QUESTIONS

1. Prepare a map of the Ontario–St. Lawrence region.
   Mark on and label the following:
   (a) all major rivers and lakes
   (b) the boundaries of the region
   (c) the major cities from Quebec City to Windsor
   (d) the Queen Elizabeth Highway (QEW)
   (e) The Macdonald-Cartier Freeway (Highway 401).

2. Describe the effects of glaciation on the lowlands region.

3. What are the advantages and disadvantages of the "long lot" system of surveying?

4. Briefly describe the factors favouring industrialization in the Lowland region.

5. What is "industrial inertia"? How is it significant?

6. What are the current problems facing the Ontario–St. Lawrence Lowlands?

7. What factors have contributed to the overwhelming importance of the Ontario–St. Lawrence Lowlands in the economy of Canada at the present time?

RESEARCH

1. Make a scrapbook of newspaper articles about the industries of this region.

2. Draw a large map of the region and mark on the locations of the important industries with appropriate symbols.

3. Prepare to debate either for or against the government plan to control the development of the Toronto Centred Region.

4. Respond to the question posed by a government advertisement to the people of Ontario, "Is there any place you'd rather be?"

8 THE CANADIAN SHIELD: RESOURCE MANAGEMENT

The Canadian Shield is extremely rich in natural resources. The successful development of these resources will depend on the delicate balance of the three primary elements of the Shield — the people, the resources, and the environment.

The Canadian Shield: a vast frontier of rock, lakes, forests and scattered, isolated towns abruptly carved out of the landscape. The Shield is a stranger to most Canadians. It is "way up north" to the great majority of Canadians who live along Canada's southern border; it is difficult to imagine either the vitality or the potential of the area.

RELIEF AND DRAINAGE

As a physiographic region, the Canadian Shield is a huge crescent-shaped area of Precambrian igneous and metamorphic rock, with Hudson Bay at its centre. With an average elevation of about 650 m, it is wedged between the Prairies to the west and the Great Lakes and the St. Lawrence River to the south and east. In much of the Shield, the rock is actually exposed, or overlain by only a few centimetres of soil. The Shield is a direct result of four periods of glaciation, during which the ice exerted a tremendous downward force on the land surface. It is estimated that ice which is 3.2 km thick exerts a downward pressure of about 3.5 billion tonnes per square kilometre. The ice, in its advances and retreats, scraped off and carried away most of the topsoil in the Shield. Many glacial features, such as drumlins and eskers, however, remain on the landscape of the Canadian Shield. Only very small areas of soil suitable for agriculture are found in the Shield. One of these, the *Clay Belt* in northeastern Ontario and northwestern Quebec, represents the remains of a glacial lake.

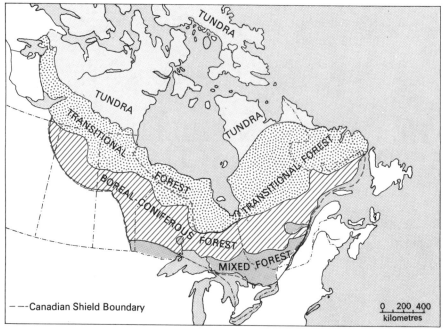

Figure 8–1:   Vegetation of the Canadian Shield

More than 30% of the Canadian Shield is covered with water. Several major river systems drain the Shield and the landscape is dotted with countless small lakes. Broadly, three main watersheds are distinguished:

(i) the rivers draining towards Hudson and James Bays, Ungava Bay, and the Arctic Ocean;

(ii) the rivers flowing to the Great Lakes, St. Lawrence River, the Atlantic Ocean, and the MacKenzie River;

Figure 8–2:   Cross-Section of the Canadian Shield

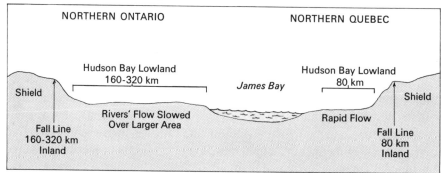

(iii) the Churchill-Nelson system which flows across the Shield in the Nelson Trough.

All of the rivers within these three systems vary greatly in their lengths and potential for use. In Quebec's Eastern Shield area, the point of farthest navigability (fall line) of its rivers is within 80 km of sea-level. Thus, powerful fast-flowing rivers, suitable for hydroelectricity, are created within that relatively short gradient. A similar situation exists along the MacKenzie River. On the other hand, in Ontario the fall line lies between 160 and 320 km inland. Rivers consequently tend to move more slowly with the more gentle gradient. Finally, those rivers draining toward the Arctic Ocean, through extensive lowland areas which receive little precipitation, have minimal potential for hydroelectric power development.

While the rivers of the Shield have never been used for the transportation of bulky commodities (for example, iron ore), since the 1700s they have been valuable as fur-trading routes and as a means of access to and from logging areas. Even before 1900, G. M. Dawson, director of the Geological Survey of Canada, had recognized the real importance of the Shield's drainage systems as:

> . . . a gathering ground for many large and almost innumerable and small rivers and streams which in the source of power they offer in their descents to the lower adjacent levels, are likely to prove in the near future of greater and more permanent value to the industry of the country.

Certainly, the slow-moving rivers of the southern Shield were adequate sources of power for the development of industry in southern Ontario and Quebec. However, as industry expanded in the south, forestry and mining became important farther north. It thus became economically necessary to harness the northern rivers to serve the forestry and mining industries requiring large amounts of energy.

CLIMATE

In much the same way as the physical landscape of the Shield has affected its use by people, the climate of the region is significant as well. The climate of the Shield displays sharp contrasts between brief, clear, and often very hot summers and long, cold winters. Because Hudson Bay is frozen for much of the year, its moderating effect on the climate of the Shield is reduced. Even though winter temperatures on the Shield can reach levels well below 0°C, little of the dampness can make temperatures even farther south seem bone chilling.

Precipitation in the form of rain and snowfall decreases in the Shield from east to west and from south to north. While the southern rim of Quebec receives over 1000 mm annually, the tundra of northern Manitoba gets only about 380 mm. Unfortunately, although precipitation is adequate, a frost-free period of about 80 days does not permit large-scale agriculture, except in a few isolated areas such as North Bay and Chicoutimi. Here the frost-free period may extend to 120 days. Nevertheless, agriculture in the Canadian Shield is a chancy business at best; obviously, it is not a major part of the economy of the Shield.

RESOURCES OF THE CANADIAN SHIELD

HYDROELECTRIC POWER   One of the most significant contributions of the Canadian Shield to the country's economy has been to provide hydroelectric power. Hydroelectricity has served industrial developments both here and in parts of the United States as well. When hydroelectric power was first introduced in the late 1800s, it could be transmitted over a distance of only 2-3 km. Although Sherbrooke in Quebec was the first urban centre to use hydroelectric power in 1888, long-range power transmission had been hampered by the lack of large transformers. One of the first of these transformers was the 11 000 V transformer on the Batiscan River in Quebec: it was able to transmit power to Trois Rivières, 30 km away.

While early hydroelectric projects had been privately developed, the early 1900s saw the creation of the Ontario Hydro Electric Power Commission and the Quebec Streams Commission (later the Quebec Hydro Electric Commission). The development of hydroelectric power became very much a provincial responsibility.

In 1900, Shawinigan Falls on Quebec's Maurice River was the first of the major hydroelectric-power complexes. Power was transmitted over a remarkable 144 km distance; electricity became available to the urban population of Montreal and to various industrial complexes as well. Although the significance of the Maurice River installations has dwindled to a great extent, it nevertheless represents an important first step in the history of hydroelectric power on the Shield. It is now overshadowed by installations such as the Saguenay Valley complex, which has increased in size as the power demands of the Aluminum Company of Canada have grown. By 1960, the Saguenay Basin was producing as much power as Niagara Falls and was transmitting its surplus to Quebec City.

Many major hydroelectric complexes have since been established

Figure 8–3: *Hydroelectric-Generating Stations in the Canadian Shield*

on various rivers throughout the Shield. The Bersimis Project, 560 km east of Montreal, was completed in 1960. This project involved the construction of two dams, a road, a tunnel, and the town site of Labrieville. It is significant as the first hydroelectric project entirely engineered and financed by the province of Quebec.

Hydro Quebec's massive Manicouagan-Outardes River Project includes seven generating stations on the two rivers. This project will increase power to 75.8 MW and exceed the St. Maurice power capacity by four times. The most significant aspect of this project is the Daniel Johnson dam, which is about 230 m high and 1230 m long. It also includes a reservoir five times larger than Lake Mead at the Hoover dam in the United States. Aluminum cables are used to transmit the electricity to distant industrial markets and to the Baie Commeau area for use in aluminum smelting and the pulp-and-paper industry. (See Fig. 7-5).

Other hydroelectric projects on the Shield include installations on the Ottawa and Madawaska Rivers, the Abitibi Canyon and the Wanapitei River, the Seine River and Lake of the Woods in northwestern Ontario. New high-voltage transmission lines make it possible to transport power fairly efficiently from remote areas of the Shield to various industrial centres. However, in the case of Ontario, all potential power sites have

Figure 8–4:   James Bay Hydroelectric Project

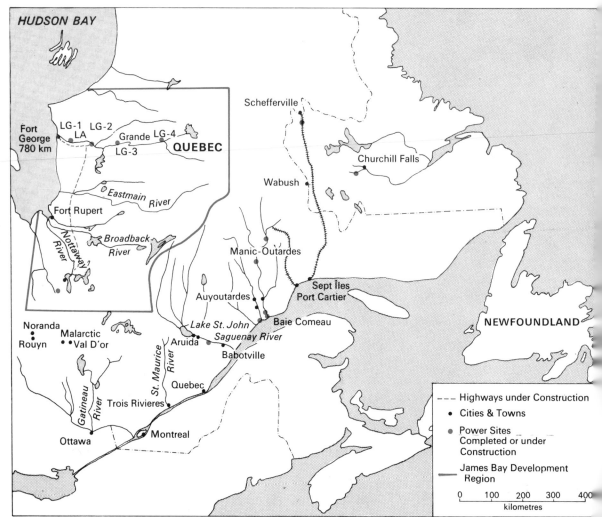

been used and alternative sources must be sought to satisfy the ever-increasing demands for power.

Undoubtedly, Canada is a world leader in terms of hydroelectric power, both in its modern equipment and in its efficient installations. Two of the most massive hydroelectric projects ever conceived are located in the eastern Shield. They are the Churchill Falls complex in Labrador and the James Bay Project in northern Quebec.

Churchill Falls, with a spectacular drop of approximately 80 m, is one-and-one-half times as high as Niagara Falls. The main reservoir will cover an area almost four times the size of Lake Ontario. Eleven turbines at the site will, by the late 1970s, have a generating capacity of 5.2 MW. The sheer size of the complex, privately funded by Canadian and American capital, makes it one of the most remarkable hydroelectric installations in the world. The availability of power may make the area more

Figure 8–5: Churchill Falls Hydroelectric Project

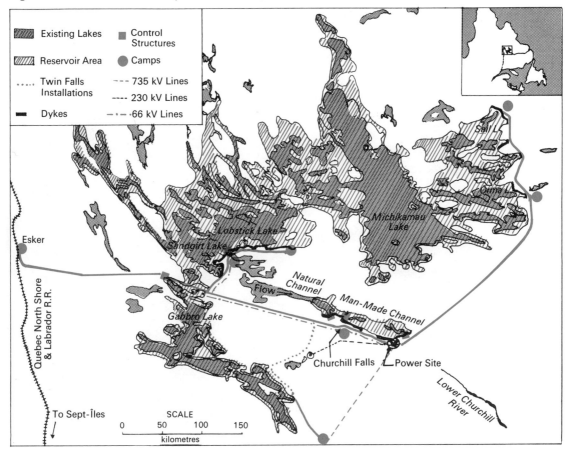

attractive to new industries. Hydro Quebec will also purchase this power for possible export to the northeastern United States and perhaps Ontario.

Quebec's James Bay Project, announced by the provincial government in 1971, is the largest and most expensive hydroelectric project ever

The Abitibi Canyon Generating Station is on the Abitibi River in the James Bay watershed, 104 km north of Cochrane. This plant has the highest dam used for hydro-electric power in Ontario — 95 m from deck to bedrock — which concentrates a natural fall of about 10 km upstream. It has a capacity of 210 000 kW from five units.

Ontario Hydro

undertaken in Canada. It involves the diversion of five rivers — the La Grande, Great Whale, Eastmain, Broadback, and Nottaway. It is hoped that the project will be completed in the mid-1980s; it will have a capacity of 10.3 MW. This capacity may be increased to 16 MW if additional rivers to the south of the La Grande can be harnessed in the future. This project alone would represent about 33% of Canada's existing hydroelectric capacity.

The goals for the James Bay Development Corporation are even more ambitious. They involve the creation of an entire economic infrastructure (system of communications, public services, etc.) based on the hydroelectric project. Included will be the construction of a complex communications and transportation network, the exploitation of mineral and forestry resources, and the development of tourism.

Several features of these projects make them particularly significant for the whole of Canada at this time:

(i) The financing of these projects involves enormous sums of money. In the case of Churchill Falls, the cost is about $950 million. For the James Bay project, the cost will likely exceed $12 billion. Of this amount, about $400 million will be for transportation and communications alone, including the building of the road from Matagami north to Fort St. George as well as airports at Matagami, Fort St. George, and other sites.

(ii) Great concern has been expressed, particularly in the James Bay project, about changes in the environment. The inhabitants of the area, mainly the Cree and the Inuit, were especially concerned about the destruction of their traditional hunting and fishing grounds. In protest, they launched a series of law suits which reached the Supreme Court of Canada. As compensation, the Quebec government has settled with the native peoples by offering to pay $225 million in order to transfer some territory directly to the Cree and Inuit and to make other major changes in the project itself.

(iii) Careful consideration will have to be given to future energy policies both for Quebec and the country as a whole. The availability of energy has become a matter of grave national concern. Thus, it is likely that the federal government will be eager to play a major role in the distribution of hydroelectricity from these massive new projects. This role is particularly true in the case of hydroelectricity being transported from Canada into the United States.

MINERAL WEALTH   The Canadian Shield is rich not only in hydroelectric potential but in its abundance of minerals as well. Because the

Canadian Shield is composed mostly of igneous rocks, it contains large quantities of metallic minerals. Some of these metallic minerals (or metal) are lead, zinc, copper, gold, silver, and nickel.

Many dreamers hoping to "strike it rich" in the Shield have been disappointed. But, many others with knowledge, perseverance, and good luck have seen their "finds" develop into large-scale mining operations. Exploration for minerals in the Shield now is certainly much more sophisticated than it once was. Complicated instruments, mapping techniques, and air photographs (some taken by satellite) make exploration for minerals a much more scientific process. However, the days of the old prospector with pick and mule have not disappeared completely. Now the "prospector" is quite likely to be either a geologist or an employee in the exploration department of a large mining company. The mule has been replaced by the automobile, and by aircraft where locations are isolated.

Gaspé Copper Mines, owned by Noranda Mines Limited, is a good example of the old and new. The mine actually began operations in the mid-1950s after an exploration program which lasted 20 years and involved extensive mapping and drilling work. However, the five Miller Brothers of Sunny Bank, Gaspé, first stimulated interest in the area. On several occasions, the brothers had found pieces of copper ore in the York River and, in 1921, they organized a prospecting party to find the source of the ore. In attempting to stalk a partridge for their lunch on one of these expeditions, they literally fell over the broken rock of Copper Mountain.

Figure 8–6: Minerals in the Canadian Shield

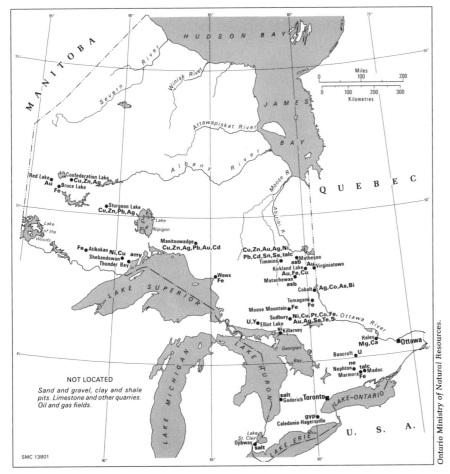

Figure 8–7: Minerals in Northern Ontario

Au (Gold); Fe (Iron); Cu (Copper); Zn (Zinc); Ag (Silver); Pb (Lead); Cd (Cadmium); Ni (Nickel); Sn (Tin); Se (Selenium); Pt (Platinum); Co (Cobalt); Te (Tellurium); U (Uranium); Y (Yttrium); Ne (Neon); S (Sulfur); Bi (Bismuth); Mg (Magnesium).

About 35 years later this became the site of Gaspé Copper Mines.

The best known and probably the most productive mining area of the Shield is the Sudbury Basin in northern Ontario. Nickel and copper are mined here by International Nickel and Falconbridge Mines Limited. Only slightly farther north and east are the copper and gold mining areas of the Rouyn-Noranda. Other highly productive mining areas in the Shield include the gold mines at Kirkland Lake, Timmins, and Red Lake and nickel at Thompson, Manitoba. Most of Canada's uranium is found at Elliott Lake on the north shore of Lake Huron. Vast reserves of iron ore lie along the Quebec-Labrador border and on the north shore of Lake Superior near Atikokan.

When metallic ores are brought to the surface after they have been mined, they are normally smelted at the site or at a nearby installation in order to avoid the high cost of transporting bulky quantities of ore. Smelting is a process whereby the metallic ore is subjected to various physical and chemical processes (such as extreme heat) to remove impurities and to concentrate the metallic content. This "concentrate" is then shipped for further refining into nickel pellets, powder, or copper cakes, for example, usually at some distance from the particular mine site. The International Nickel Company of Canada sends its nickel concentrate to Port Colborne for refining. Falconbridge Mines Limited, on the other hand, has found it most advantageous to ship its concentrates to its refinery in Norway.

The mining of iron ore has become increasingly sophisticated as well. While estimates of iron ore reserves in the Canadian Shield are in the billions of tonnes, the ore is largely of low-grade quality. This factor plus the distance involved makes its shipment costly and uneconomical. A process called "pelletizing" smelts and concentrates the iron ore to produce iron ore pellets. These pellets are of a high quality and have the advantage of being easy to load and transport. Another advantage of these pellets, particularly in the operations in Quebec and Labrador, is that they do not freeze in low temperatures.

An aerial view of Inco's Port Colborne, Ontario, Nickel Refinery.

George Hunter

International Nickel Company

The Sudbury Basin contains twenty producing mines operated by the International Nickel Company of Canada, Limited, and the Falconbridge Nickel Mines, Limited. From this source comes more than half of the world's nickel output, a large part of the world's supply of platinum group metals, and one-third of the entire Canadian copper production.

Almost without exception, a town grows around a mine site, particularly if the mine is a large one or if more than one producer is in the same vicinity. Many of these towns begin as planned communities created by the company operating the mine. Two examples of recently planned mining communities are Thompson, Manitoba, where nickel is mined by the International Nickel Company of Canada, and Manitouwadge in northwestern Ontario where copper is mined at the Geco mine by Noranda Mines Limited.

Housing is provided for the employees; schools, hospital facilities, parks, recreation centres, and shopping are also available. These *company towns* usually depend solely on the life of the mine for their existence. The disadvantages of this dependence can be seen in the town of Elliott Lake: it thrives while the demand for uranium is high, but is almost a ghost town when demand declines. On the other hand, centres such as Rouyn-Noranda (which serves several mine sites and has a population of almost 30 000) can survive because they provide services other than those directly related to one particular mine. In fact, since 1972, work at the Great Horne Mine, Noranda Mines Limited's richest ore body, has been phased out. Anticipating exhaustion of the ore body, Noranda Mines Limited has enlarged the capacity of the Horne Smelter and is now involved in custom smelting work for customers from all over North and South America. Even without the Great Horne Mine, the

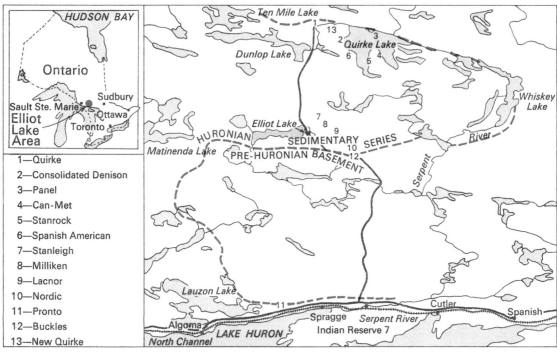

1—Quirke
2—Consolidated Denison
3—Panel
4—Can-Met
5—Stanrock
6—Spanish American
7—Stanleigh
8—Milliken
9—Lacnor
10—Nordic
11—Pronto
12—Buckles
13—New Quirke

Figure 8–8   Uranium mining in the Elliot Lake Area

An aerial view of Inco's Thompson Mine and plant-site area, Thompson, Manitoba. Part of the city of Thompson is shown in the background.

Below right: Driving a crosscut at one of Inco's mines in the Sudbury District. Driving one of the sublevel crosscuts, which extend the full width of the ore body, this three-boom drill jumbo is driven by an air-cooled diesel engine with an oxy-catalytic exhaust scrubber.

International Nickel Company

Gulf Oil Canada Limited

employment pattern remains largely unchanged and exploration in the surrounding area has been greatly stimulated.

Mining is without doubt the most significant factor in the economy of the Canadian Shield. Canada has achieved international status for its volume of mineral production and the techniques used in mining and processing ores. But it would be a mistake to assume that no rich ore deposits have been left undiscovered. Many are known but are not being developed because the demand for and prices of the metals involved are too low. As a result, some potential mines have simply been overlooked. Texasgulf Canada Limited's Kidd Creek mine near Timmins is a good example of an overlooked deposit. The area, already dotted with mine sites, had been thoroughly mapped and studied for years, but it was not until the 1970s that the discovery (of zinc, lead, copper, and silver) was actually made and a new mine brought into production.

FORESTRY

The Canadian Shield is a vast area of lakes and rivers, great expanses of igneous rock, and extensive forests. The waterways, as we have seen, have been harnessed for hydroelectric power. The barren rocks supply the world with a wealth of minerals. And the forests of the Shield have been a focus of economic activity as well. Lumbering became important on the Shield in the early 1800s. By the middle of the nineteenth century, sawmills powered by hydroelectricity from the Shield were operating in the St. Maurice and Ottawa River valleys as well as along the shores of Lake Huron and Georgian Bay.

In the late 1800s, Canada began making paper from wood. For many years after that, the pulp-and-paper industry expanded rapidly, especially as American demands for newsprint continued to increase. It was about the time that lumbering on the Shield began to decline that growth in the pulp-and-paper industry began to accelerate. However, British Columbia has now taken over in supplying world markets with high-quality lumber.

In addition to the presence of vast stretches of forests, the Shield has other advantages favourable to both the lumbering and pulp-and-paper industries. Waterways are important for transportation although roads are becoming more significant for transporting pulpwood. The abundance of hydroelectricity on the Shield is available to power both sawmills and pulp-and-paper installations.

Although improved road and rail transportation and more efficient transmission of electricity have allowed lumbering industries to locate with more freedom than in the past, large quantities of water are still needed to remove waste materials. Thus, lumbering and pulp-and-paper communities are heavily concentrated along rivers in northeastern Ontario and along the north shore of Lake Superior. These communities — for example, Marathon and Kapuskasing — are much like the mining towns of the Shield. While they have the same facilities, they are also vulnerable when market demand and prices fall.

While production in the lumbering industry of the Shield has obviously declined, its importance should not be underestimated. Ontario's lumber industry ranks third among all the productive Crown lands, still stands as the leading producer of pulp, and is second only to British Columbia in sawmill production.

TOURISM

Tourism also makes use of the natural resources of the Shield. The tourist industry will probably become more significant in the near future: leisure time is increasing and the costs of using that time are increasing as well. Moreover, a great interest has developed in recent years in conservation and the proper use of the natural environment. A network of scenic parks has been established throughout the Shield in response to the increasing popularity of both camping and canoeing. It is probable too, that as the Muskoka and Haliburton cottage areas of the southern Shield become more and more crowded and as building-code requirements become stricter, people from urban areas south of the Shield will look north for vacation properties.

CONCLUSION

The Canadian Shield remains very much Canada's Frontier — a land still largely untouched, but nonetheless having a remarkable impact on the economy of the country as a whole. It is a seemingly barren land except for the trees, yet it is becoming modern: with technology and improved communications, the Shield is beginning to yield to the pressure of growth from outside. Through developments in mining, hydroelectricity, and tourism, the natural resources of the Canadian Shield are being used to foster economic growth throughout the rest of the country. Until now, development in the Shield has been mostly a blend of people, resources, and the natural environment. In the face of intensified economic activity and growth, the balance between these three elements must be maintained, even improved.

QUESTIONS

1. On a map of Canada, mark the boundary of the Canadian Shield. Label the major rivers in the Shield and mark in the major hydroelectric-power sites. Shade in the area involved in the James Bay Project.

2. List several physical characteristics that distinguish the Shield from other physical regions of Canada.

4. Compare the climate of the Shield with those of other parts of Canada.

5. The development of primary industries on the Shield closely paralleled the development of power resources. Write a brief essay describing the relationship of industry and power in the Shield.

6. List the factors that contributed to the growth of forest industries in the Shield.

7. In chart form, summarize the major mining centres in Manitoba, Ontario, and Quebec. Additional references may be used to complete the chart. Make use of the chart headings given below as a guide.

Chart Headings
Mining Centre
Major Mineral(s) and Use
Town Site

8. Explain why the Shield is no place for farming.

9. Why have so few people ventured north to live on the Canadian Shield?

10. What advantages do you think are associated with life in the Shield? What are the disadvantages?

11. Suggest potential obstacles to development in the north of the Shield.

12. Discuss the contribution of the Canadian Shield to the economy of Canada.

RESEARCH

1. Write a research paper on one of the following:

   (a) James Bay Power Project
   (b) Nelson River Power Project
   (c) Quebec-Labrador iron-ore discovery
   (d) The Sudbury Basin: A geological wonder!

2. Debate: Is industry responsible and concerned enough about the physical health of their workers and the environment?

3. Debate: Should native peoples receive more compensation for their lands and better employment opportunities when large-scale resource development affects their livelihoods?

4. Many urban areas of the Shield perform unilateral functions related to the Shield's resources. Choose *four* major urban areas and describe the development of each as a resource centre. Include a description of their sites.

9 THE ATLANTIC REGION: SUPPORT OF LIFE

The Atlantic Region of Canada is perhaps the most fragmented and in many ways the most isolated region of Canada. The Atlantic provinces will have to pool their resources in order to achieve long-term economic growth and stability.

The Atlantic Region is full of striking contrasts in landscape, economic development, and lifestyles. The landscape is stunningly scenic, from the bleak, rugged outcrops of Newfoundland to the flat, green fields of Prince Edward Island. Economic development ranges from the small fishing boats anchored in the harbours of Newfoundland to a highly sophisticated car-assembly plant in Nova Scotia. Home for a Maritimer can be a quiet picturesque fishing village or a busy port city.

THE PHYSICAL ENVIRONMENT

The Atlantic provinces comprise the coast of Eastern Canada south and east of the Precambrian Shield. Newfoundland is separated from the three other Atlantic provinces (Prince Edward Island, New Brunswick, and Nova Scotia) by the Gulf of St. Lawrence. Prince Edward Island, Nova Scotia, and New Brunswick are more popularly referred to as the *Maritimes*. The Atlantic provinces are virtually surrounded by water and are isolated not only from the rest of Canada but from each other as well. The region is actually quite small, having less than 3% of Canada's total land area. According to the 1971 population census, the total population of the entire Atlantic region was about two million, approximately 10% of Canada's total population.

The landscape is rugged and varied with great expanses of forest. Where Precambrian rock underlies the region, minerals such as copper, gold, lead, and iron ore are mined, particularly the iron ore in Newfound-land. In central New Brunswick and Nova Scotia, sedimentary rocks are responsible for the formation of large coal deposits as well as substantial quantities of salt and gypsum. Because of the ruggedness of the land-scape, agriculture as an economic base is severely limited; road and rail routes tend to follow the river valleys or hug the coastline. This factor has also influenced the distribution of population in the Atlantic Region. Population is not only small but also highly dispersed.

The climate of the Atlantic region is as varied as the landforms. The nearness of the Atlantic Ocean has a moderating effect on the climate. In particular, mid-summer and mid-winter temperatures are not as extreme as those in the Prairies. Basically, the climate of this region results from the interplay of *cold* continental air masses from the northwest and *warm*

Figure 9–1:   *Mean Annual Frost-Free Period (days) in the Atlantic Region*

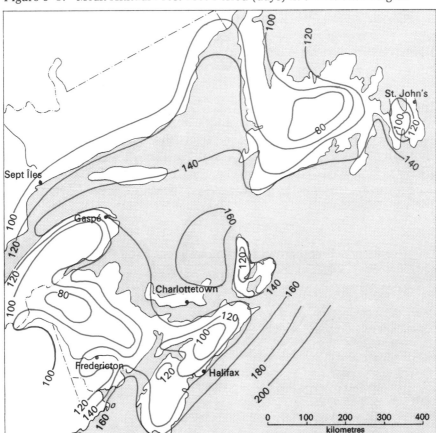

maritime air masses from the south. Thus, heavy precipitation (sometimes 1520 mm annually), strong winds and unpredictable temperature changes often occur. Temperatures during the summer range from 10°C to 18°C in the interior of New Brunswick and Nova Scotia. During winter, drift ice and icebergs driven south by the cold Labrador Current present a very real hazard to all forms of shipping, particularly when the icebergs are accompanied by dense fog for which the area is well known.

The heavy rainfall in the Atlantic provinces has created soils which are badly leached: that is, the valuable soil nutrients are washed deep into the soil so that they are beyond the reach of the roots of crops. These infertile soils cover much of the Atlantic region. The most fertile soils are found along the flood plains of rivers, as well as along the north shore of the Bay of Fundy in New Brunswick.

THE ECONOMY OF THE ATLANTIC REGION

The Atlantic provinces were settled early during the mid-nineteenth century because of their unique position for sailing vessels from Great Britain and Europe. Initial economic growth was based on the products of fishing and forestry which were mainly destined for the overseas market. This period may well have been the most prosperous for the Atlantic Region.

As settlement spread across Canada and the United States, the Atlantic provinces found themselves far from the mainstream of economic activity in Canada. Restrictions were placed in their dealings with their logical trading partner, the northeastern United States, by a Canadian policy to protect domestic markets. As a result, Canada's Atlantic prov-

TABLE 9-1

Producer's Shipments of Various Minerals, by Province, 1973

	Nfld.	N.S.	N.B.	P.E.I.	Canada
1. Copper (tonnes)	8 647	3	10 310	—	908 241
2. Iron ore (1000s of tonnes)	24 398	—	—	—	52 358
3. Lead (tonnes)	8 444	291	44 011	—	376 939
4. Zinc (tonnes)	8 695	—	192 563	—	1 352 074
5. Gold (troy ounces)	14 345	—	5 202	—	1 954 340
6. Silver (troy ounces)	572 918	22 838	3 568 678	—	44 487 589
7. Gypsum (1000s of tonnes)	809	6 178	92	—	8 389
8. Salt (1000s of tonnes)	—	752	—	—	5 565
9. Sand and Gravel (1000s of tonnes)	6 466	11 348	9 553	1632	233 461

Source: *Canada Year Book 1975.*

Nova Scotia Communication and Information Centre

An aerial view of a container pier in Halifax.

TABLE 9-2

Value of Metallics, Non-Metallics, Fuels, and Structural Materials Produced 1973 ($1000s)

	Metallics	Non-Metallics	Fuels	Structural Materials	Total
Newfoundland	335 831	25 325	—	13 350	374 506
Prince Edward Island	—	—	—	1 680	1 680
Nova Scotia	156	24 060	15 568	21 935	61 719
New Brunswick	132 798	4 162	3 434	21 961	162 355

Source: *Canada Year Book 1975.*

TABLE 9-3

Value of Mineral Production, 1963-72 ($1000s)

	Nfld.	P.E.I.	N.S.	N.B.
1963	137 797	798	66 539	28 343
1964	182 153	831	66 228	48 678
1965	207 558	599	71 007	82 164
1966	244 020	1 063	85 596	90 208
1967	266 365	1 775	52 544	90 440
1968	309 712	977	56 940	88 452
1969	256 936	452	58 562	94 593
1970	353 261	640	58 159	104 791
1971	343 431	978	60 138	107 134
1972	290 610	1 097	57 520	119 930
1973	374 506	1 680	61 719	162 355

Source: *Canada Year Book 1975.*

TABLE 9-4
Atlantic Region Agriculture, 1971-72

Province	Farm Income Total ($1000s)	Farm Income Net ($1000s)	Commercial Farms	Subsistence Farms	Total Farms
Newfoundland	—	—	282	1 427	1 709
Prince Edward Island	44 017	11 810	2 780	3 577	6 357
Nova Scotia	70 147	19 819	2 568	7 053	9 621
New Brunswick	64 151	18 886	2 603	6 103	8 706
Atlantic Region	178 315	50 515	8 233	18 160	26 393
Ontario	1 573 869	478 179	63 667	46 220	109 887

Source: Statistics Canada.

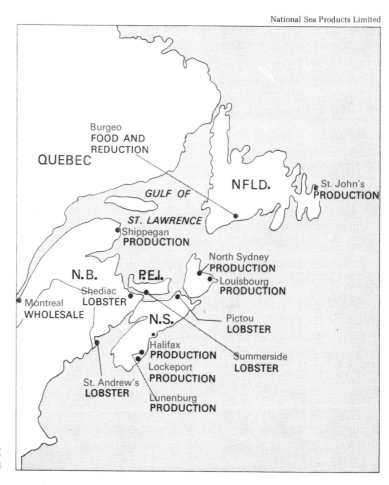

National Sea Products Limited

Figure 9-2: Fish Processing
Plants in the Atlantic Region

inces now find themselves among the country's chronically poor and caught in a vicious cycle of poverty and underdevelopment that is difficult to break. Even in Nova Scotia, southern New Brunswick, and the Avalon Peninsula of Newfoundland, where capital investment and construction exceed levels elsewhere in Canada, unemployment is higher and wages lower than in the country as a whole. Throughout the remainder of the Atlantic provinces, unemployment is double and average incomes are well below the figures for the rest of the country.

PRINCE EDWARD ISLAND

To the casual observer, probably the most prosperous of the Atlantic provinces appears to be Prince Edward Island. It is about 5160 km² in size; its population is approximately 112 000, according to the 1971 census. Although it does not possess the natural prerequisites for industrial development, it has prospered by emphasizing fishing, agriculture, and, more recently, tourism. During the past few years, Prince Edward Island has indeed made very rapid strides in economic development.

Fishing in Prince Edward Island earned a record $12.5 million in 1975; most of this amount resulted from excellent lobster catches. Because Prince Edward Island is not involved in offshore fishing to any great extent, it has been largely unaffected by declining catches throughout the North Atlantic. Unfortunately, however, fishing in the Maritimes is still very much a seasonal occupation, thereby causing a great amount of unemployment in the fishing industry for much of each year.

Agriculture in Prince Edward Island is largely based on mixed livestock farming and the cultivation of mainly potatoes and hay. Prince Edward Island in fact produces about 50% of Canada's best-grade potatoes for local consumption as well as for exporting. Although incomes from livestock have risen dramatically, farmers have had to face increased costs in labour and equipment in recent years; as a result, agricultural development has slowed down. Of late, a more serious problem for agriculture in Prince Edward Island has been a decrease in the number of farmers willing to continue farming as their primary occupation. In the last six years, the number of farmers in Prince Edward Island has actually declined by 50%. Presently only 12% of the total work force on the island is engaged in agriculture. Assistance in the form of grants from the provincial government is an attempt to reverse the trend.

Until recently, Prince Edward Island has been largely without industry. The provincial government has been encouraging industry to locate here, particularly light industry. Two industrial parks are being established on the island, one in Charlottetown and a smaller one in Summerside. Existing industries include a french-fried potato processor, several fish-processing plants, and a handful of metal works.

Prince Edward Island's prosperity is also enhanced by a willingness on the part of the federal government to pour large sums of money into various projects. The minute area and small population of Prince Edward Island provide an ideal location for microstudies. Islanders often find themselves unwittingly testing various federal schemes. While generous housing grants have been warmly welcomed in the island, attempts to consolidate fragmented farm holdings and to develop road-construction projects have antagonized islanders, who feel that their traditional lifestyle is being threatened.

NEW BRUNSWICK

New Brunswick occupies the mainland part of the Atlantic provinces closest to the industrial heartland of Canada and the United States. It is south of the St. Lawrence River and Gaspé, and is bordered on the west by the state of Maine. To the south is the Bay of Fundy and on the east is the Northumberland Strait, which separates New Brunswick from Prince Edward Island. Physically it is a complex area. The interior of New Brunswick consists of uplands, with elevations of over 600 m in some areas. This upland area, as is the case in the interior of Newfoundland, is largely uninhabited and is heavily forested. About 50% of New Brunswick's land area consists of lowlands, often very flat and marshy. The valley of the St. John River, which flows along New Brunswick's western border, meets the Bay of Fundy at Saint John, the province's most urbanized area. The Saint John River Valley is New Brunswick's prime agricultural zone, where both soil and climatic conditions permit the growth of specialty crops, including corn and potatoes. The climate can be severe throughout the rest of the province. Annual precipitation varies from 800 to 1200 mm; yearly snowfalls exceeding 250 cm are not unusual.

In recent years, New Brunswick's economic growth has far outstripped that of the remaining Atlantic provinces. Since the early 1970s, New Brunswick's growth has been more impressive than that of the entire country, indicating that, in one province at least, the effects of Canada's general economic slowdown were hardly felt at all.

New Brunswick has tended to be aggressive in its policies of economic growth. In particular, increased construction in New Bruns-

Saint John Valley, New Brunswick.

wick aided by increases in spending have contributed to higher incomes and decreased unemployment. Construction projects include:

(i) major public works schemes to improve highways in and between Saint John and Moncton, New Brunswick's most prosperous and highly developed corridor

(ii) a $200 million expansion at the Irving Oil Refinery, which will double its output by 1977 to 250 000 barrels (40 000 m³) a day. It will then become the largest refinery in Canada and one of the largest in the Western Hemisphere

(iii) the construction of a 24 km pipeline across St. John. This pipeline will join the Irving Oil Refinery to a gigantic thermal electric plant at Lorneville, near the city.

Other projects in New Brunswick include a port complex at Lorneville, a nuclear-power station in the same area, and huge office-shopping complexes in Saint John and Moncton. In addition, capital expenditures have stimulated expansion of the pulp-and-paper facilities and mining operations in the interior.

Mineral resources are extremely important to New Brunswick. Production of minerals in New Brunswick reached a value of $250 million during 1976 and shows great potential for the future. Mining is particularly significant here because the 4000 jobs it provides are for the most part in the northern, chronically underemployed, part of the province. It is interesting to realize that in New Brunswick mining is the only natural-resource industry which appears to grow steadily and continually. Agriculture, forestry, and fishing are all faltering as income-earners. Fishing is relatively insignificant to the overall economy of New Brunswick, bringing in only about $20 million annually: those who wish to fish for a living are suffering financially because of depleted fish stocks, thereby adding to the number of unemployed workers.

Agriculture is based largely on mixed farming and livestock, with potatoes as a significant specialty crop. A drastic decline in potato prices during the early 1970s, however, played havoc with farm incomes and substantial government assistance was required to help relieve the situation. Finally, the importance of forestry to New Brunswick cannot be underestimated, earning about $400 million for the province in 1975. Forestry added the most money to the provincial economy for that year. Strikes, declining demands, depleting forests, and environmental damage have, however, made its future growth seem less promising. Mining, as the province's second-largest income earner, holds more potential.

By comparison with the other Maritime provinces, New Brunswick has been astonishingly successful in generating economic growth from within the province. Much of the province's present success can be at-

Fredericton, New Brunswick.

New Brunswick Department of Tourism

Moncton, New Brunswick.

New Brunswick Department of Tourism

tributed to the province's willingness to participate actively in promoting and sustaining province-based projects.

NOVA SCOTIA

The peninsular province of Nova Scotia has more potential for economic development — and it has been relatively successful in attracting foreign investment — than either Prince Edward Island or Newfoundland. Joined to New Brunswick in the north by a narrow isthmus, Nova Scotia includes not only the peninsula itself but also Cape Breton Island. The two are joined by the Canso Causeway, which was completed in 1955.

The northern half of the Nova Scotia Peninsula generally consists of scattered lowland areas, the best known of which is the Annapolis Valley which grows specialty crops, as in the Niagara region of southern Ontario. Much of the remainder of Nova Scotia consists of uplands. Precipitation is heavy, although it is lighter in the interior than along the coast. Annual precipitation figures range from 1000 mm to 1600 mm, most of it falling as snow and freezing rain. The best combination of moisture and warmth is found in the Annapolis Valley, where fruit (particularly apples), corn, and even tobacco are grown. Other lowland areas, climatically unsuited for such specialty crops, emphasize mixed farming, dairying, and poultry.

As might be expected, the population of Nova Scotia tends to be clustered in the lowland areas, with concentrations around Sydney in Cape Breton and Halifax-Dartmouth on the east coast of the mainland. The entire east and southeast coasts of Nova Scotia are a series of deep fiord-like harbours (much as in Newfoundland) with Halifax at the centre. Today, this cluster of shipping with all its associated functions is the largest urban centre in the Maritimes. This Halifax-Dartmouth cluster has enjoyed an unprecedented spurt in economic growth in recent years — growth unequalled by the remainder of the province. The Halifax-Dartmouth area is the scene of a major building boom involving apartment blocks, commercial complexes, and transportation terminals. New port facilities and a terminal for the handling of bulk-container shipments provide the fastest service between North America and Europe. Unfortunately, the province as a whole has suffered in the general economic slowdown in North America and a more restrictive government-spending policy in Canada.

Manufacturing is of primary importance in Nova Scotia. This province is probably the most industrialized of all the Atlantic provinces. Nova Scotia has been particularly successful in attracting foreign capital to finance industrial developments within the province. Nova Scotian

Nova Scotia Communication and Information Centre

An aerial view of two bridges in Halifax.   *Annapolis Valley, Nova Scotia.*

industry has attracted investment, first, by using the province's own natural resources as raw materials for foreign-based industries: an example is Stora Kopparberg of Sweden, which owns Nova Scotia Forest Products Ltd. Second, Nova Scotian industry has received investment by attracting firms which have no bearing whatsoever on the local natural-resource base, but which pour money into the economy of Nova Scotia by using the province's utilities and labour pool. Good examples here are the plants of Volvo (Swedish) and Michelin (French).

Volvo and Michelin are remarkable success stories. They are both companies which could very likely operate at a profit in virtually any location. That they have chosen Nova Scotia is a combination of excellent selling and good fortune for the province. Volvo has been in Nova Scotia since the early 1960s and markets its finished automobiles in Canada and the United States. Despite the high cost of transportation and of importing materials, it continues to operate successfully. Michelin too has enjoyed profitable growth in Nova Scotia; with expansions planned at both its plants, it will employ about 3000 people.

Over twenty years ago, Nova Scotia led the Atlantic Region in providing money for the continued establishment of manufacturing industries: it has lent money to well over 100 firms during that time. It is a trend that has proven successful for Nova Scotia; other Atlantic provinces have followed suit.

Interestingly enough, very few local companies use the region's natural resources. One exception is National Sea Products Limited, which processes fish under the brand name of "Highliner." Fishing is not a major profit-making enterprise in Nova Scotia, as reflected in the situation at National Sea Products Limited. Although sales from 16 plants throughout the Maritimes and the United States totalled almost $100 million, the company lost over $1 million in 1975. While declining markets and increasing costs were contributing factors, the real problem was the depletion of fish stocks that has plagued Newfoundland.

The single most significant item in the economy of Nova Scotia is coal mining. Mining operations are carried on primarily in Sydney on Cape Breton Island. These mines were originally developed in coal seams running out under the ocean. As time went on, the distances between the pithead and the coal face increased to the point that mining became both inefficient and unprofitable. Cape Breton coal was therefore not able to compete with sources elsewhere, particularly in the United States. In 1965, when over 10 000 people were employed in coal mining and in the related steel industry, Dominion Steel and Coal Corporation (DOSCO) decided to close the mines. The coal mines were subsequently taken over by DEVCO (The Cape Breton Development Corporation) and administered by the federal government. The steel mills came under the control of the province as SYSCO, or Sydney Steel Corporation. By the mid-1970s, despite massive capital expenditures, SYSCO found itself at a virtual standstill, losing $40 million in 1976 alone. Despite the bleak outlook for steel, coal mining in Nova Scotia has become profitable at last. Although fewer workers are employed than 10 years ago and considerable amounts of capital have been expended, the coal industry should continue to enjoy steady growth in the years to come.

NEWFOUNDLAND

Newfoundland, in both landscape and economy, provides the most striking contrast to Prince Edward Island. It was the most recent province to become part of Confederation, having joined only in 1949. Newfoundland (especially Labrador) is generally a bleak, barren landscape underlain by Precambrian rock. Parts of central Newfoundland are virtually uninhabited, while most of the population live along the deeply indented fiord-like coastline, particularly around the Avalon Peninsula. In the northern part of Newfoundland, near-tundra conditions make agriculture impossible. Mean summer temperatures in the south reach only 16°C; the number of frost-free days each year is only 70. Even the rugged uplands of New Brunswick have about 100 frost-free days a year. Precipitation is high, particularly along the coast, with snowfall often exceeding 250 cm annually.

As might be expected, Newfoundland's economic base is virtually without agriculture. For many years, fishing was the leading source of income for Newfoundland. During the 1950s and 1960s, when foreign deep-sea fishing fleets began fishing on an extensive scale, the fish stocks depleted drastically. Some species were depleted by 50% in the space of only a year or two. One solution adopted by the federal government was to place limits on the quantities of fish caught. As a result, people reaching their quotas quickly — and it often happened — were without work for the remainder of the fishing season. In 1977 both the Canadian and U.S. governments established the "200 mile" (320 km) fishing limit to ensure that foreign fishing vessels would not encroach on their coastal waters and to enable fish stocks to replenish themselves. But there is no guarantee that the 320 km limit would be respected by foreign fishing fleets (See Page 106).

The largest share of Newfoundland's income comes from forestry and mining. In the island of Newfoundland, it is estimated that, out of the total area of 112 260 km², over 36 200 km² are classified as productive forest. The principal commercial species of trees are the black spruce and balsam fir. In fact, forestry is important to the whole of the Atlantic Region: it provides substantial employment in related activities as well. Forestry alone accounts for 50% of the exports from the region. Large-scale pulp-and-paper operations are found in Corner Brook, Grand Falls, and Stephenville. Currently a $50 million forestry management program is underway, aimed at increasing productivity and improving reforestation techniques.

Unfortunately, several problems plague Newfoundland's forestry industry. First of all, a number of lengthy strikes have made for lower earnings for labour and companies in the last few years, and all major companies have been seriously affected by these strikes; second, although new stands of timber are being developed on the island, some timber is now being cut in Labrador and shipped to mills in Newfoundland. The transportation costs involved here are extremely high, making the operation less profitable. In fact, the mill at Stephenville lost $25 million in 1976 alone.

In view of these problems, the Newfoundland forestry industry must work doubly hard in order to compete for world markets. To achieve a more competitive position necessitates a highly mechanized operation and, as a result, a small labour force: it must become a *capital-intensive* industry. Thus, although the forestry industry employs large numbers of workers indirectly, the actual employment in the mills is small. Those phases of the forestry industry that do require more workers (the

Hundreds of picturesque fishing villages, called outports, are scattered along the coastline of Newfoundland.

labour-intensive industries, such as cutting timber) seem to be the least attractive kinds of work.

However, Newfoundland earns from natural resources its greatest profits, which in 1975 totalled $35 million. Most of this amount comes from the mining of iron ore. Several years ago, the Wabana Mines on Bell Island were forced to close because the lower-grade ore was unacceptable for smelting. However, new sources of high-grade ore in Labrador have considerably revived the industry. A huge complex at Wabush now provides a steady flow of high-grade ore.

Investors are also interested in potential offshore natural gas and oil reserves: exploratory work is being carried out jointly by French and American interests. If oil or gas is actually found, the interesting issue here will be over the jurisdiction of the resources themselves. Newfoundland, of course, hopes to control any discoveries itself, but the federal government will likely insist on its constitutional right of ownership of offshore natural resources.

The brightest aspect of Newfoundland's future probably lies in its potential as a supplier of hydroelectricity. Churchill Falls is a superb example of such potential. Development in Newfoundland could also be based on nuclear power.

CONCLUSION

The future of the Atlantic Region is difficult to predict. Certainly, many of the ingredients for sustained economic development are present. Prince Edward Island has a strong agricultural base and has become an important tourist attraction in recent years. Newfoundland has hydroelectric potential and vast reserves of iron ore. Nova Scotia has been successful as a coal producer and has made impressive strides in attracting foreign investment to the province; and New Brunswick has a fairly strong industrial base and a healthy mining sector as well. One feature common to much of the Maritimes is the abundance of excellent harbour facilities, particularly in Nova Scotia and New Brunswick.

However, potentially serious problems are highly visible in the Atlantic Region. The population of the Atlantic Region as a whole is small and widely scattered throughout the four provinces. Even urban centres in the Atlantic Region are small by comparison with cities in the rest of Canada; thus, the markets for goods produced there are limited. The culture and economics of the Atlantic Region are diverse: each province has its own geography, its own history, its own set of economic strengths and weaknesses. No one characteristic seems common to all — except the isolated villages dotting the coasts of the four provinces. The two inland cities of significance are Moncton (a transportation and distribution centre) and Fredericton (a government and university complex).

While certain specific areas such as Halifax and St. John are highly industrialized, industrial development in the region as a whole is minimal. Maritimers cannot live and grow on agriculture, fishing, and forestry alone. The industrial base must be broadened for the Maritimes to achieve long-term economic growth and stability.

The federal government has been generous in its financial aid to the Atlantic Region. It has been said that the federal government contributes about 50% of the provincial revenue to each province, a figure twice as high as the national average. Funding by government agencies such as DREE (the Department of Regional Economic Expansion) has also considerably widened the economic base. At the 1976 annual conference of provincial mine ministers, energy experts suggested that with an initial investment of $100 million, the old Wabana iron ore mines could be transformed into gigantic oil-storage tanks as a safeguard against future oil restrictions. Presumably, the economy of Newfoundland would be transformed as well in the process.

In recent years, the developing nations of the world have begun to realize that their real strength lies in unity. It is not beyond the realm of possibility that the Atlantic Region, which has long considered itself the most underdeveloped region in all of Canada, may unify its many parts and pool its resources; in fact, provincial premiers in the Region have met from time to time to discuss unification of the Atlantic provinces. Such an Atlantic Community would be a formidable force indeed — each province could strengthen the weakness of others and together they could broaden the entire regional economic base to a point where no one province would be as vulnerable as at present.

QUESTIONS

1. What are the effects of the rugged Maritimes landscape on
   (a) agriculture?
   (b) transportation routes?
   (c) distribution of population?
   Give examples.
2. What are "leached" soils? What other parts of Canada might have the same problem of leaching? In what parts of Canada does leaching probably not occur?
3. What natural conditions make the waters surrounding the Atlantic provinces ideal for fishing?
4. Why is Prince Edward Island's farming population dwindling? What could be done to counteract it?
5. What problems face the forestry industry in the Maritimes, especially Newfoundland?
6. How has Nova Scotia encouraged manufacturing there?
7. Why have New Brunswick's natural resource industries failed to keep pace with the dramatic growth experienced in other areas?
8. In what ways are the Maritime provinces isolated
   (a) from one another?
   (b) from the rest of Canada?
9. Compare the number of subsistance farms with the number of commercial farms in Table 9-4. Compare the average farm income of the Maritimes with the average farm income of Ontario. Summarize briefly the physical and human factors that explain the pattern revealed by your comparisons.

RESEARCH

1. Prepare notes for a debate in which you must defend the advantages of a union in the Maritime provinces.
2. Design a brochure that advertises the tourist attractions of the Atlantic Region.
3. Do research on the following topics:
   (a) The Acadians
   (b) Supertankers and the Atlantic oil refineries
   (c) Pulp-and-paper companies of Newfoundland
   (d) The future of tidal power of the Bay of Fundy.

10 | THE CANADIAN ARCTIC: THE LAST FRONTIER

Largely uninhabited and, until recently, largely undeveloped, the Canadian Arctic is a vast storehouse of natural resources, despite its harsh environment. The exploitation of these natural resources must be approached with caution, skill, and respect for both the natural environment and the native peoples of the North.

For centuries, Canada's Arctic has attracted a steadily increasing stream of people willing to challenge its barren landscape. Their motives have varied. For the early explorers, it was the search for a Northwest Passage through the Arctic Islands that would connect the Atlantic and Pacific Oceans to provide a shorter route to the Far East. For those who came later, the attractions centred on whaling and fur trading. By the end of the nineteenth century, the focus was on Canada's Northwest, where gold had been discovered along the Yukon River. Now, with worldwide concern over diminishing natural resources, the discovery of oil and minerals in Canada's North has renewed interest in the region.

However, the Canadian Arctic has not always been challenged by "outsiders" alone. A fairly large native population of Indians, Métis, and Inuit live permanently in the Arctic; they are becoming increasingly vocal about the manner in which outsiders use the North. The Canadian Arctic is one of the last frontiers for Canada and for the world as well. Science and industry now have the means not only to develop the resources of the Canadian Arctic but to minimize the effects of the harsh environment as well. Here, as in the Canadian Shield, it will be the mutually beneficial relationship between the three basic elements — *resources, people,* and *environment* — which will ensure the harmonious development of the Canadian Arctic.

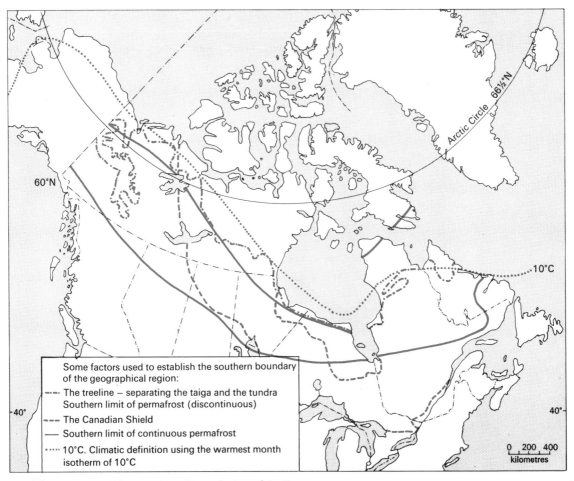

Figure 10–1: *The Arctic — Boundaries of Its Features*

DEFINING THE CANADIAN ARCTIC

The physical geography of the Canadian Arctic is bleak (yet varied), hostile, and even challenging. However, before discussing the actual landscape of the Canadian Arctic, it is necessary to establish its boundaries as precisely as possible. This is a very difficult problem simply because many parts of Canada which are not considered part of the Arctic have many of the characteristics of the Far North. For example, students might suggest that the Arctic is extremely cold, but the fact is that the Prairies can experience similar low temperatures. Low precipitation in

Canada's Far North can be matched by rainfall figures on the Prairies. Finally, the Arctic is usually thought to be a region in which no trees will grow. However, many mountainous areas of Canada are without trees, yet they would not be considered as part of the Arctic.

On its simplest level, the Canadian Arctic is usually thought to be that part of the country north of 60° latitude. In an attempt to be more accurate and to enable comparisons between locations, Louis Edmond Hamelin, a Canadian geographer, has established what he calls a *Circumpolar Index*. It is not limited to one characteristic such as coldness, which applies to other areas as well. The Circumpolar Index uses a variety of characteristics generally associated with the Far North and gives each of these characteristics a value. For example:

    (i)   a location with a latitude of 90°N scores 100 out of 100
   (ii)   permanent pack ice scores 100
  (iii)   pack ice for 4 months scores 20
  (iv)   an airfield at least 1600 km away scores 100
   (v)   more than one flight per day scores 0.

Thus, out of a possible score of 1000, Melville Island receives 865, Churchill (Manitoba) receives 450, and Chibougamau (Quebec) receives only 183. By comparison, Reykjavik in Iceland has a score of 127, and Narvik in northern Norway receives 112. In Canada, Hamelin considers the boundary between the Arctic and the so-called South to be a line joining those locations with circumpolar index values of 200. Allowing for local variations, certain specific features appear over and over again. Some of these features are a water temperature at or near 0°C, the presence of perpetually frozen ground, low temperatures for long periods of time (although not necessarily colder than more southerly latitudes), and the absence of trees. While Canadians tend to think of the Arctic as anything north of the Arctic Circle (which is not incorrect), it is important to realize that local conditions can substantially change what are generally known as Arctic features.

THE ARCTIC LANDSCAPE

Although climatic features throughout the Arctic are somewhat similar, the landforms are varied. Generally speaking, the Arctic landscape consists of glacier-covered mountains in the east and flat lowland areas in the west. The entire area has been scoured by glacial erosion; glacial features are therefore found throughout the Arctic. Gravel beaches are many kilometres long and may sometimes reach heights of over 100 m. Sand and gravel ridges, called *eskers*, have been found inland. Arctic land-

A stream issuing from under the ice on the northern margin of the icecap.

Arctic cotton.

forms, without vegetation, are much more noticeable than they would be in southern Canada where they are covered by trees and underbrush.

There is nothing unusual about most of the landforms in the Arctic. Mountains and lowlands are found in the Arctic, as in other parts of Canada and the world. However, a few features are unique to the Arctic landscape: they result directly from the severity of the climate. These features are *permafrost, pingoes*, and *patterned-ground* phenomena.

Permafrost refers to soil or rock whose temperature remains consistently below 0°C. Areas of permafrost in the Arctic reach depths of 300 m, while scattered areas to the south may only extend a few metres. The presence of permafrost is a significant feature because of its potential instability. These frozen soils can damage structures built on them when the top layer of soil thaws and shifts. In addition, drainage is hampered by the frozen ground (See Page 11).

Another landscape feature unique to the Arctic landscape is the conical hill with a central core of ice. These conical hills are called *pingoes*; they may reach heights of 50 m. They exist in great numbers around the Mackenzie River Delta. Finally, the constant freezing and thawing over much of the permafrost zone creates geometric patterns of circles, ovals, polygons, and stripes which tend to resemble a turtle shell especially when viewed from an aircraft. Such a feature is described as *patterned ground*.

THE ARCTIC CLIMATE

While certain features of the landscape are unique, the climate of the Canadian Arctic is not. Because the low temperatures of the Canadian Arctic can be more than matched in other parts of the country, the climate

Pingo in the flood plain of Mala River, Borden Penninsula, northern Baffin Island.

Geological Survey of Canada, Ottawa

Polygonal ground, Old Crow Plain, Yukon Territory. Note the isolated spruce trees along the margin.

Geological Survey of Canada, Ott

of the Arctic can be distinguished mainly by *the duration of the low temperatures*. Snow can fall virtually any time during the year. Throughout the Arctic, annual averages of only about 76 cm of precipitation are received. Since this amount is the equivalent of only 76 mm of water, the Canadian Arctic is actually a desert. Heavy snowfalls are more imagined than real — snow accumulates and remains on the ground because of the persistently low temperatures. Deep drifts often occur in the absence of a protective vegetation cover.

SETTLEMENT IN THE ARCTIC

The Canadian Arctic has not been settled like the rest of the country. The native Inuit and Indian populations of various origins have shifted back and forth across the Arctic: only recently have they settled in particular areas. The Inuit seem to have passed through *four* fairly distinct stages since their apparent origins about 3000 years ago. In the earliest period, nomadic hunters drifted across the Canadian Arctic from Alaska. This particular group, sometimes called *Pre-Dorset*, was significant because it made small and remarkably delicate stone tools such as scrapers and spears. They were followed by the *Dorset* group, which covered a wide area of the Arctic from Melville Island to Greenland and the northwestern part of Newfoundland. Their economy, like that of the Pre-Dorsets, was based on hunting and fishing. They surpassed the previous group technologically, however, with their use of polished slate and with their ability to create minute yet detailed carvings. A third migration, the *Thule*, shifted from Alaska to Greenland about eight or nine hundred years ago and apparently had some contact with Viking settlers. This group was particularly well adapted to the Arctic environment. They used dogs, constructed winter villages from slabs of stone, bones, and sod, and also hunted whales.

The most recent group, the *Central Eskimo* (now *Inuit*), can be traced back to the eighteenth century. They too led a nomadic life; they hunted walrus and seal, mainly because the Europeans were killing the whales. The Central Eskimos have been influenced by Europeans in another way: the sewing needle, introduced to the Inuit in the mid-nineteenth century, changed Inuit clothes-making.

However, it must be remembered that the Arctic's capacity to support any kind of life is exceedingly low. Probably at no time have more than 20 000 people simultaneously occupied the entire area. The limiting factor in the Inuit and Indian occupancy of the Arctic has been starvation, a condition that has encouraged the exploitation of all edible resources within the area.

The residential section of Inuvik. Note that the houses are raised on stilts above the ground.

Great numbers of scientists still tend to divide the native population, particularly the Inuit, into coastal and inland groupings. However, increasing evidence indicates that the Inuit population has in fact adapted to the whole of the Arctic, not to any specific area within the Arctic. The Inuits have adapted to the environment by using all available resources: they concentrate on gathering food available in great quantities or at certain times of the year. Resources, such as caribou, beaver, seal, walrus, polar bear, and various fish, have all been significant sources of food, of clothing and shelter (skins), and of tools and decoration (bones and sinew).

Until the arrival of the Europeans, the Arctic environment and its native population existed in a reasonably harmonious state. As the non-native population increased, particularly in recent decades, their influence on the native people became more and more pronounced. It was through these so-called outsiders, working for the government in mining projects and other similar activities, that many of the Indians and Inuit gradually gave up their nomadic lifestyle in order to achieve a more settled life. Many became apprentices, artisans, interpreters, labourers, and so on. With these new roles came the assurance of an outside source of income and the choice of an alternate way of life. Now, it is becoming increasingly clear that the native people of Canada's Arctic are concerned not only about the loss of their traditional ways, but also about the real value of the lifestyle which seems to be replacing them.

ECONOMIC DEVELOPMENT IN THE ARCTIC

Interest in the Canadian Arctic is probably greater now than ever before. This interest has been largely stimulated by concern over dwindling mineral resources and the increasing cost of energy supplies. The Arctic has shown great potential in both areas. Unfortunately, despite reserves of minerals and fossil fuels, certain problems make the exploitation of these resources difficult in an Arctic setting.

(i) **Climate**. The prolonged intense cold of the Canadian Arctic presents difficulties in working and living conditions. It is often too cold to work outside; as a result, life in the Arctic tends to be indoors and in a fairly confined space. Climatic conditions play havoc with

Figure 10–2: Settlement in the Arctic

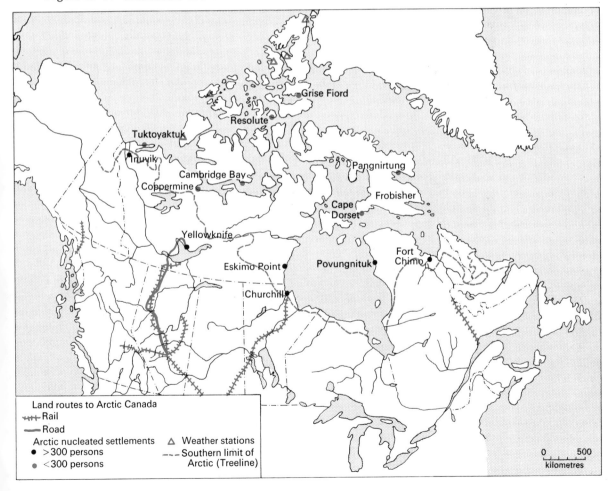

Land routes to Arctic Canada
+++ Rail
— Road
Arctic nucleated settlements   △ Weather stations
● >300 persons   --- Southern limit of
● <300 persons   Arctic (Treeline)

0   500
kilometres

construction projects as well. When frozen soil or permafrost thaws, the ground becomes unstable; therefore, buildings can be considerably weakened because the ground shifts. In addition, water and sewage transmission becomes a horrendous task in permafrost zones. Often, buildings are established on piles with water and sewage moving through above-ground insulated boxes called "utilidors."

(ii) **Distance.** Distances from mine sites or oil and gas fields in the Far North are not just a few hundred kilometres but more likely a few thousand. These distances are over large areas of barren uninhabited landscape. It is often difficult to justify the construction of transportation routes in such circumstances unless the resource involved is likely to bring great financial gain.

(iii) **Transportation (Land and Water).** The moving of goods in the Canadian Arctic involves both the long distances mentioned above and tremendous costs. Bulky goods such as iron ore and petroleum are most economically moved by water, but shipping by water is not always possible in the Arctic. Delays because of poor weather, unused capacity on the return voyage, high insurance rates, and the lack of docking facilities for ships and tankers are all factors contributing to the high costs of transporting goods in the Far North. Also, until submarine freighters become a common mode of Arctic transportation, the shipping season is limited. Railways will likely prove to be the best means of transporting cargo such as metal concentrates. Railways, however, necessitate a level of construction (more complicated than a road, for example, which can be anything from a trail to a superhighway) and a commitment to provide track, railway cars, and other facilities at all times.

As far as land transportation in the North is concerned, railways seem to be superior to but also dependent on roads. Railways provide the means of moving goods, but roads are essential during rail construction and for the subsequent "opening up" of the surrounding area.

Air Transportation. The helicopter and the Canadian-made Beaver and Otter aircraft are being suggested for the transportation of light yet valuable goods such as uranium concentrates. These aircraft have proven themselves invaluable in the exploration of the North: it would be reasonable to consider extending their usefulness.

Pipelines. Finally, pipelines as a means of transportation in the Arctic have received a great deal of publicity lately. Their usefulness would be limited to moving liquids such as oil and

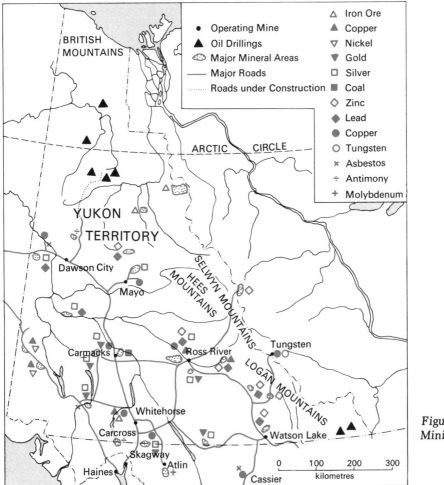

Figure 10–3:
Mining in the Yukon

natural gas. Maintenance is an obvious problem, because distances
are so great and climatic conditions so severe in the Canadian
Arctic. In addition, permafrost would necessitate building a
pipeline above the ground or an insulated one under the ground;
either type, the native population insists, will do great harm to the
delicately balanced northern environment.

MINING IN THE CANADIAN ARCTIC   Almost no comparison can be
made between mineral exploration and mining as it was during the
Yukon gold rush of 1890s and as it is today. Not only is it a much more
sophisticated industry — using computers, laser beams, and satellite
photography — but it also employs 250 000 Canadians directly in mining operations and adds significantly to Canada's Gross National Pro-

duct. Mining has contributed substantially to the present high level of activity in the Canadian Arctic.

Prospectors on their way to the Klondike and Yukon Rivers were actually the ones to discover the Yellowknife gold camp at Great Slave Lake and silver-radium deposits on Great Bear Lake in the 1930s. During this period as well, bush flying, which made previously remote areas much more accessible, had a great effect on exploration in the North. Since that time, numerous mines have come into existence in Canada's Arctic, particularly in the Yukon and the Great Slave and Great Bear Lake areas of the Northwest Territories. Among the largest producers are United Keno Hill (silver, lead, zinc, and cadmium), Pine Point Mines (lead and zinc), and Giant Yellowknife Mines (gold).

Several mining ventures are planned for the Arctic Islands. Nanisivik Mines on northern Baffin Island will be financed by private sources, including Canadians, Germans, Dutch, and the Canadian government. Production of 1500 t/d of lead and zinc will likely begin during the late 1970s. The federal government will build the town site, dock area, airport, and roads. Another potential mine site is the Polaris deposit on Little Cornwallis Island. A final decision on bringing the mine into operation is pending; at the time of writing, it is likely that production could begin soon.

One of the most spectacular mineral deposits anywhere in the world is Mary River Iron Mountain, a mountain of iron almost 600 m high on Baffin Island. It is owned by Baffinland Iron Mines (backed by Hudson Bay Mining and Smelting, among others). This mountain has hundreds of millions of tonnes of reserves. Development is hampered by the short shipping season, but it is hoped that huge ice-breaking vessels will solve the problem. This reserve is matched by Crest Iron Deposits on the border between the Yukon and Northwest Territories. Discovered in the early 1960s by Standard Oil of California, this deposit is not as rich as Mary River, but it is believed to have over 32 billion tonnes of ore. While the main problem facing Mary River is the shipping season, the lack of economical energy is holding back development of Crest Iron. Mineral exploration and mining in the Canadian Arctic provides numerous examples of potential resources being identified and studied but remaining undeveloped until their profitability can be assured.

In the area of oil and natural gas exploration, however, Canada's Arctic has been more consistently in the news during the 1970s. Major drilling sites are found in the shallow area of the Beaufort Sea, near the delta of the Mackenzie River, although many other Arctic Islands are involved as well. Companies such as Imperial Oil, Dome Petroleum, and

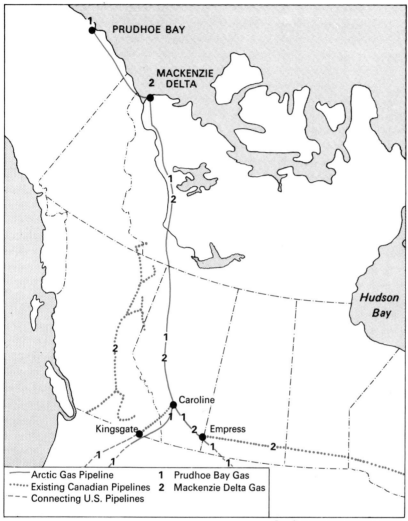

PRUDHOE BAY

MACKENZIE
2 DELTA

Hudson
Bay

Caroline

Kingsgate

Empress

—— Arctic Gas Pipeline	**1** Prudhoe Bay Gas
······ Existing Canadian Pipelines	**2** Mackenzie Delta Gas
– – – Connecting U.S. Pipelines	

Figure 10–4: Pipeline from the Arctic

Canadian Arctic Gas Study Limited

Panarctic Oil are among those financing the staggering costs of the various projects.

Each drilling hole may cost as much as $3 million when special drilling islands or vessels are required. Needless to say, success cannot be guaranteed. But high costs are not the only concern. Equipment must be transported over thousands of kilometres from either Calgary or Montreal; climatic conditions are extreme; total darkness prevails from November to January; and the shipping season is limited to only a few weeks.

It is impossible to discuss oil and natural-gas exploration in the Arctic without reference to the Mackenzie Valley Pipeline, the means by which natural gas could be moved from the Mackenzie Delta and Prudhoe Bay to Central Canada.

Both the drilling program and the proposed pipeline have come under scrutiny from environmentalists who fear irreversible changes in the natural landscape and adverse effects on the natural life. One major concern has been the "blow out" or explosion which would contaminate Arctic waters and be exceedingly difficult to clean up. This particular concern has led to the building and installation of "blow-out preventers" (at a cost of $1.1 million each) to be installed on the ocean floor near the Delta to control high pressures.

Arctic Gas, the company responsible for the pipeline proposal, is also aware of the public's concern and has made a number of studies of alternative methods of transporting the gas and of minimizing the damage to the environment. Alternate means of transportation include transporting liquefied natural gas by rail, ocean tanker, and even aircraft. Transportation by pipeline is by far the most feasible method. Gas in the underground pipeline can be chilled to avoid thawing the permafrost; the ground above the pipeline can be revegetated to minimize surface erosion. No decision has yet been made on the actual construction of the pipeline. An inquiry, headed by Mr. Justice Thomas Berger of the Supreme Court of British Columbia, has, since 1975, studied the impact of the pipeline. His recommendations, published in May 1977, include a ten-year waiting period before constructing a pipeline through the area in order to allow time to settle the land claims of the native peoples.

Perhaps the most difficult problem facing mineral and oil exploration (and particularly the pipeline proposal) in the Canadian Arctic is the hostility of the Indian and Inuit populations. The native population feels that contacts with outsiders encouraged them to abandon their traditional ways and to become aliens in their own land. Non-native business executives (largely from Canada and the United States) are the "power brokers" in the economic development of the Far North, but they fail to revere the Arctic lands the way the native peoples do. The feeling is simply that outsiders can always return to southern Canada or the United

The Mackenzie Valley Pipeline Research Project near Inuvik, Northwest Territories.

Gulf Oil Canada Limited

States when the oil and mining "booms" are over. The native population will have no such options and will at some future date be left with an environment virtually destroyed by outsiders.

COMMUNITY ORGANIZATION

The organization of settlements in the Canadian Arctic provides an interesting additional study of a region which has always been based on a hunting and gathering type of economy. Settlements in the Far North tend for the most part to be communities planned by outsiders and lack any sense of change or of adaptation to the natural environment.

The smallest and most insular of these settlements are probably the technical stations, such as those created by the Distant Early Warning (DEW Line) project. These stations involve a small working force of single men who spend no more than six months to one year at the station. The duties of the people involved are clearly defined; the food, recreation, and shelter is fairly standard and no relationship usually exists with the native population.

Somewhat larger are the service settlements, such as Sugluk and Povungrituk, which are usually organized and operated by government agencies. Here, several hundred Inuit as well as a handful of whites share the social services and amenities.

Communities such as Churchill, Manitoba, are complex settlements which may provide a variety of functions in the Far North. These functions may include transportation, grain shipping, and military services, among others. These settlements often include large numbers of transient males and substantial native neighbourhoods, often composed of Inuit brought from other areas.

Finally, the typical mining town (found across the Canadian Shield as well) is completely planned to service the population of the mine site. Yellowknife is a good example of these "instant" company towns. However, it has since developed to become the territorial capital.

Towns of the North show an interesting aspect of life in the Canadian Arctic, primarily because they have not evolved and they really represent the image of southern Canada simply transplanted into a northern (and foreign) environment. These towns have no suburbs to speak of — people are effectively contained within the town itself and town sites themselves tend to be similar. Because many of these towns are simply replicas from southern Canada, often little thought is given to the environment in which these towns must grow and develop. Suggestions have been made which would encourage clustered dwellings, indoor shopping, school facilities, and so on, but the actual implementation of these suggestions remains to be seen.

CONCLUSION

The Canadian Arctic, as well as the Canadian Shield, remain as Canada's primary sources of economic wealth for the future. And, like the Shield, successful development will occur only with a harmonious relationship between the land, the people, and the resources themselves. Unfortunately in the Arctic, the future of the environment is delicately balanced. Vast areas are required to support life. Because the plant life grows much more slowly in extremely cold climates, damage to the environment can be widespread and difficult to remedy. Also, public concern is growing for native rights and ownership of land in the Far North. These concerns will undoubtedly affect developments in the Arctic for years to come.

QUESTIONS

1. Why is it difficult to establish boundaries for the Arctic region?

2. What is the Circumpolar Index? In what ways is it a useful device?

3. Describe the effects of (a) glaciation and (b) low temperature on the landscape of the Arctic.

4. What factors hamper the exploitation of Arctic resources? Give examples.

5. What are the concerns of the Arctic's native population regarding economic development? Why has their concern become much more vocal in recent years?

RESEARCH

1. Suggest ways in which Arctic settlements could be more satisfactorily adapted to the northern environment.

2. Read the recently published report of the Berger Commission that studied the feasibility of an Arctic gas pipeline. Discuss some of the arguments for and against the construction of the pipeline.

3. Assume that you have been hired as a member of a team of scientists to do research along the Arctic coastline. Make a list of the equipment you feel you would need to survive at your destination. What hardships would you expect to face?

4. Transportation in the Arctic remains a problem. What are the advantages and disadvantages of the following transportation links to the North: aircraft, road, rail, pipeline.

5. Make a list of all the reasons why people go to the Arctic to live. Make a list of all the reasons why people do not want to go to the North. Some experts have predicted that the Mackenzie Valley will have a population of three million in the next century. Do you think that this is likely to happen? Why?

6. Prepare to debate for or against the resolution that, "The Inuit are being assimilated too quickly into the white culture."

PART THREE:
FROM SEA
TO SEA—
AND BEYOND

11 | THE TIES THAT BIND THE REGIONS INTO A NATION

As the other chapters have shown, Canada is a hard piece of land to unify and to make work together. Our regions vary greatly in their natural resources, history, and culture. Average income and lifestyles differ from region to region. All of these differences lead to the two great problems that the people of Canada face all the time. We must work together to have Canada function as an independent nation. And we should see to it that every Canadian has the chance to have a decent standard of living. Over the long run, pulling our diverse regions into a single nation has been, and still is, our most serious concern.

DIVISIVE FACTORS

VASTNESS   One problem to overcome is size. The country is so big: about 6000 km from east to west and almost 5000 km from south to north. In the North where travel is difficult in any case, the land is broken up by countless streams, ice caps, mountains, lakes, and bogs.

The size of the country is made even more noticeable by the small number of people. It is odd that the second-largest country in the world should have only 23 million people, which is just 10% of the population of the United States. Not only do we have very few people, but also these people have become grouped in and around a few large cities; as a result, even in the settled south, wide gaps separate the clusters of population. (See Figure 3-1 in Chapter 3.)

PHYSICAL BARRIERS   Many of the gaps between the groups of people are caused by landforms and bodies of water. In Newfoundland, most of the people live on the east coast; the interior is relatively uninhabited and broad water bodies separate the island from the mainland. The Gaspé highlands and the state of Maine come between the Maritimes and the

264

St. Lawrence Lowlands. In fact, just one valley, the Madawaska, carries almost all the land traffic *within Canada*, between the Atlantic provinces and the rest of Canada. The term "within Canada" has been stressed because the shortest route from Montreal to the ocean ports is through the United States. The Canadian Pacific Railway takes the direct shortcut, right through Maine, from Montreal to Saint John, New Brunswick. The huge Montreal refineries obtain their oil by a pipeline from the closest Atlantic port, Portland, Maine.

The greatest physical barrier in southern Canada has been the 1600 km extent of the Canadian Shield. Those hard rocks alternating with lakes and muskeg cost the builders of the Canadian Pacific Railway more problems and money than did the Rockies. Worst of all, the Shield is located right in the middle of Canada, between the industries and markets of the East, and the farms and oil of the West. Fortunately, the Great Lakes have supplied a waterway to bypass the worst part of the Shield, but all other forms of transportation have had to contend with the long stretch of hard rock. People are continually tempted to avoid the area entirely by moving through the United States instead.

The Prairies are only lightly populated; between Regina and Calgary the population density drops to as low as one person per square kilometre, a density as sparse as that of the Sahara Desert in Africa. Calgary and Edmonton are separated from the Pacific coastal cities by almost 1000 km of mountains. It should surprise no one that regional loyalties are so strong in Canada

CULTURAL DIVERSITY The peoples of Canada are diverse. To an outsider Canada might well look like an accidental collection of many peoples, each with its own culture, outlook, and sense of history. Even among the Francophones, the Acadians of New Brunswick and the *habitants* of Quebec are culturally distinct from one another; cultural variations exist inside Quebec as well. In southern Ontario the Anglophones of the Ottawa Valley have their own accent; Toronto, the Niagara and Bruce Peninsulas, Essex-Kent, and the Holland Marsh are all unique in their own ways (and they have their own accents too). Nationally, lifestyles among the residents of Newfoundland, Saskatchewan, and British Columbia differ markedly, to give only the most obvious examples. Probably the cultural differences among these provinces are greater than those between some European countries as, for example, Austria and Switzerland, or southern France and northeastern Spain.

PROXIMITY TO THE UNITED STATES To make the divisive factors worse, the well-known pull to the south seems to attract each region of

Canadian Pacific Public Relations and Advertising Photographic Services

The Canadian Pacific on Field Hill crossing the Kicking Horse River.

The Canadian Pacific at Stoney Creek Bridge, B.C.

Canadian Pacific Public Relations and Advertising Photographic Services

Canada to its neighbouring part of the U.S.A. Physical geography does not *force* anyone to move or interact north-south, but it certainly makes it easier, whether along the Columbia River or Lake Champlain. Sometimes the easiest route between parts of Canada runs through the U.S., as in the case of goods from southern Ontario seeking an eastern port. On the other hand, the shortest route between Buffalo and Detroit passes through Ontario; the only land route to Alaska also runs through Canada. Many of the largest American cities are near Canada. The closest big city to Halifax is Boston, to southwestern Ontario are Buffalo and Detroit, to the eastern Prairies is Minneapolis, and to British Columbia is Seattle. Toronto is closer to Detroit, and almost as close to New York City (the world's greatest financial centre) as it is to Montreal. Many Canadians have relatives in the United States; it is common for Canadians to retire to Florida or California. (Even climate increases the American pull!) The United States is the world's wealthiest single market. It looks as if it were willing to absorb all that Canada has to offer, whether it be oil, nickel, lumber, or hockey players. The huge financial resources of the United States make it seem as if the Americans could buy out Canada, simply by offering Canadians more for their land or resources than Canadians would wish to refuse. The United States has ten times the population of Canada and that population is highly productive. It is probable that Canada will always be at a disadvantage in numbers and therefore money (See Fig. 3-2).

UNIFYING FACTORS

In their attempts to help develop a sense of Canadian identity, politicians, teachers, and artists have used the connection of the British Commonwealth. Thus, our political system and traditions differ from those of the Americans. Most Canadians are united in not wanting to be American, or even in being mistaken for Americans. (In Europe, the only group of travellers who flaunt their flag all over their jackets, lapels, and backpacks is the Canadian.)

Anti-Americanism is popular with some, but most people recognize that, if Canada is to remain united, it must develop a strong, positive patriotism instead of depending on a negative feeling. More and more, Canadian history and literature are being emphasized in the schools. The federal government, especially through the Canada Council, has been trying to help support Canadian art, Canadian music, and Canadian films.

Ever since Confederation, the federal government has been trying to tie us all together. Indeed, it could be said to have been the main function of the federal government all along. From the first years, Ottawa has been concerned with the two basic matters of establishing sovereignty over all the land and of promoting the means of knitting us all together.

SOVEREIGNTY   Sovereignty means the international acceptance of Canada's legal right to control the land. The great West and North that Canada inherited from Britain after 1870 were almost empty of European peoples: in some cases, lands had not even been "discovered" yet, much less explored. As the United States filled up, Americans badly wanted to spill across the border into the open land. The Royal Canadian Mounted Police (originally the North West Mounted Police) established Canadian sovereignty on the Prairies. Later, the Mounties kept the peace in the British Columbia and Yukon gold fields. The claims to the Arctic islands were made secure only after 1900, notably by Captain J. E. Bernier. However, the Canadian control of the islands was not made real until after 1945 when a number of airfields, posts, and weather stations were built, with American help, as far north as Alert, 83°N.

Although sovereignty has been fairly well established by now, many people fear that the better portions of the land are being lost to Canadians through foreign ownership and takeovers. This fear has become acute along the Nova Scotian coastline, in Prince Edward Island, along the Great Lakes, and in the Prairies. Efforts are being made in several provinces to limit ownership of prize lands to permanent residents of those provinces. This has clearly raised the issue of *nationalism versus money.* If we have to think first of profit and of money entering the economy, then obviously the free sale of land to the highest bidder should be allowed. If, however, the land is to remain under the control of Canadian citizens, then perhaps sales to outsiders should be restricted. Unfortunately, money is far more plentiful outside than inside Canada. Considering, too, the few people that live in Canada, the odds are that foreigners, rather than Canadians, will wish to buy the best land. In this sense, being patriotic costs money. One further point to notice is that much of the legislation proposed would limit ownership to the people *of that province.* Here, then, is another sign of provincialism existing within Canada.

RESOURCE DEVELOPMENT   The same issue of nationalism versus money appears in the debates over the development and sale of natural resources. Especially now in the case of oil and natural gas, one side urges that they be sold at the highest price possible to bring more money into the economy and allow for further exploration; the other side urges a slowdown on sales because of the belief that the fuel resources should be saved for Canadians in the future. It is clear, too, that the development of Arctic oil and gas depends on amounts of money beyond the Canadian ability to supply. Developmentalists, the people in favour of developing resources now, are seeking foreign financing and markets to build the necessary pipelines, but the nationalists fear that foreign money may increase foreign control of the fuel industry and sell off a non-renewable resource too quickly.

The fundamental problems of keeping complete sovereignty are that 23 million Canadians cannot afford to develop their own resources because of the difficult topography, vast size, and severe climate, and that Canadians form only a small and widely scattered market. Two hundred and thirty million Americans, 250 million West Europeans of the Common Market, and over 100 million Japanese have the money, the business organization, and the markets. Canada wants the money to further the development of all aspects of its economy, but it also wants to control the development and plan for the future. It's not easy to achieve a balance!

TRANSPORTATION **Waterways.** In a country as big as Canada, a good transportation network has always been considered essential to unity. Historically, some authors have said that Canada is a result of

An aerial view of the Welland flight locks

St. Lawrence Seaway Authority

pre-existing transport systems. The fur traders from Montreal followed the Great Lakes and the Saskatchewan River System. Later, the Hudson's Bay Company organized all of Central Canada from the shores of Hudson Bay as well as British Columbia from the Pacific Coast. Canada can thus be thought of as the combined result of three waterway systems: The St. Lawrence–Great Lakes, the Hudson Bay–Arctic, and the Fraser–Pacific Coast.

In Canada, 338 430 people (out of a total of 8 626 925 employed)

Figure 11–1: Major Fur-Trade Routes

were listed in 1971 as employed in "Transport Operating Occupations." That is, one out of every twenty-five working Canadians was driving a truck or working on a train, ship, or airplane. Of course, as many people again were needed to keep all the lines, railway yards, docks, and airfields open and in operation. The proportion was lowest in Ontario and in Saskatchewan, where it was only one out of thirty. It was highest at the ends of the country, in the Yukon and Newfoundland where one out of every sixteen was working on some ship, truck, train, or plane. Transportation is particularly important in the North because most of the necessities of life, and other supplies as well, must be brought in from the South. Also, hospitals and schools are few and far apart; the non-native residents make frequent trips "out" to the South.

Certain cities show up as being very closely tied to transportation. Tops on such a list would be Thunder Bay, Ontario, the lake port and railway centre. Also high in their "transport" employment are the east coast ports of St. John's, Newfoundland, and St. John, New Brunswick.

Of the total freight moved within Canada in 1974 — some 712 million tonnes — about one-seventh, 118.5 million tonnes, was moved by coastal shipping. Ships moved between Canadian ports carrying logs along the British Columbia coast, ores and grain through the Great Lakes, and fuels and ores along the St. Lawrence. In addition, the St. Lawrence Seaway carried 26.5 million tonnes between Canada and the United States. Most of this cargo was iron ore being sent to American steel centres and coal being shipped to Hamilton and Toronto.

If the route is direct and free of obstacles, water transportation is the cheapest and most efficient way to transport goods. It can even outcompete pipelines because natural waterways need not be constructed; also, the costs of maintenance are lower. A typical ship can carry the freight of many long freight trains and of thousands of airplanes. Therefore, water is the favoured way to ship goods which move in great quantities, such as wheat, oil, ores, and coal, or which have low value per mass, like sand and gravel.

Canada is blessed with the longest coastline in the world and, on the eastern side, by a long entrance into the continent. The eastern provinces of Canada are even given "water" names, Maritime or Atlantic, showing their close ties with the ocean. A long waterway extends almost 4000 km into the North American land mass; located along this route are numerous ports with a variety of functions. St. John's, Newfoundland, being the farthest point east, acts as the closest service centre for the hundreds of ships on the fishing grounds. To the west and south is Halifax, on the open ocean, and behind it is St. John, on the Bay of Fundy. These cities act as major ports on mainland North America. Continuing westward, the broad St. Lawrence estuary gradually narrows down to Quebec City.

Along the now somewhat winding St. Lawrence River, ocean ships can reach Montreal, almost 2000 km by water from St. John's. At that point, the St. Lawrence Seaway begins and allows the ocean-going ships to reach the two great ports at the western end of Lake Ontario, Hamilton and Toronto. The Welland Canal provides an entry into Lakes Erie, Huron, and Michigan; the Soo Locks, into Lake Superior. Finally, at Thunder Bay, "the Lakehead," a ship is much of the way across the continent.

The Seaway system allows for the shipment of bulk materials cheaply, especially iron ore from Labrador to Hamilton, Buffalo, and Cleveland, wheat from Thunder Bay to the ocean ports, pulpwood from the Shield, and coal from the Applachians. This traffic is so great that, of the seven leading Canadian ports in tonnage, all but one are along this route. (The only exception is Vancouver, which monopolizes the Pacific

Figure 11–2: St. Lawrence Seaway and Great Lakes

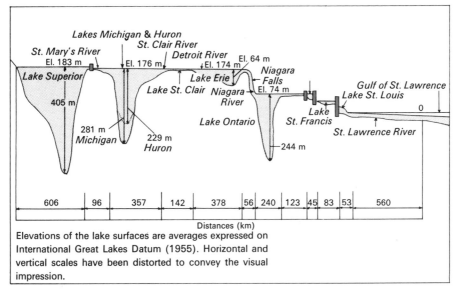

Figure 11–3: Cross-Section of Great Lakes and St. Lawrence Seaway.

trade.) Highest in tonnage is Sept Îles, with 22 million tonnes in 1972. If we add its close neighbour, Port Cartier, the figure of the Labrador-Quebec iron-ore harbours reached 37 million tonnes in 1972.

The Seaway's value goes beyond these statistics because it allows Canadian goods to avoid the worst of the Shield, the part "north of Superior." It is as if Canada, "cursed" with that hardrock barrier, was given a way around it. The dams of the Seaway are also capable of producing more than two million kilowatts of hydroelectricity.

The Seaway does have its problems, however. As ocean-going ships become larger, the locks have become too small to accommodate many of them. It also takes a great deal of time for ships to move inland and pass through all the locks. Containers, the new method of handling goods in big "boxes," are so efficient that it is becoming ever more economical for ships to unload containers at the east-coast ports for the railways or trucks to carry them further inland. It is now possible for the container ships to make many more trips across the oceans: the ocean ports do not have the problems of ice.

The east-coast Canadian port system has had an interesting sequence of ups and downs in importance. The first European contacts were with the Atlantic provinces, such as with places in Newfoundland and Port Royale, Nova Scotia. Later, as the great rivers were explored, the *voyageurs* made Montreal their base for water-borne traffic all the way to the

The city of Montreal and the harbour facilities.   Canadian Pacific

Rockies. Then in the nineteenth century as the clipper ships and the new steam ships were developed, the Maritime provinces took back the lead in oceanic shipping and the Halifax-born Cunard Line dominated the North Atlantic trade. In this century the enlargement of the St. Lawrence River route and the Seaway led to the decline of the Maritimes and the growth of Montreal and the interior ports. Now with containers and huge tankers, the advantage seems to be returning once again to the Nova Scotia and New Brunswick shores. The basic question remains: Is it worthwhile for the shipping companies to spend the extra time needed to reach Toronto, Sarnia, or Thunder Bay? In shipping, time is indeed money, because time controls the number of loads the ships can carry.

Hudson Bay acts as another extension of Atlantic shipping routes into the interior of Canada. Unfortunately, the ice-free season is only four months long and the Shield surrounds the Bay. Only two railways (no roads) reach the shore of the Bay. Hudson Bay may be located in the middle of Canada, but it is almost completely cut off from Canadian economic life. The only modern port on the bay, Churchill, exports the wheat of the Prairies. The total shipping, 580 171 t in 1975, ranks only 47th among Canadian ports (just behind Midland, Ontario). Despite its low totals and its small population of 1604, Churchill does serve a valuable function in Canada; when the shipments of wheat begin each year, they seem like an avalanche of freight and must be transported as quickly as possible.

In the channels of the North, ships pay their annual calls to the posts scattered among the capes and islands. The tonnage total is very small, but shipping is nevertheless essential to the existence of the settlements and to the well-being of their inhabitants. It would require hundreds of expensive airplane flights to carry the freight transported by just one of these ships.

The fiords of the British Columbia coast contain many deep harbours. A number of specialty ports, dealing in lumber or bauxite have been built. However, just one city, Vancouver, controls most of Canada's Pacific trade. Because of this, and because of the growing importance of Japan as a trading partner, Vancouver has replaced Montreal as Canada's leading ocean port. This high tonnage has come to be based on the export of wheat (to China for example), coal (mostly to Japan), and lumber products (to the U.S.). The port of Vancouver has kept up with modern developments. The old harbour now includes a large container port; more impressive yet, the Roberts Bank Superport, just off the Fraser Delta, has been built. Here the water is deep enough for the largest ships and the coal transports can load and reach the open ocean quickly.

Table 11-1 lists the main Canadian ports in terms of the tonnage

TABLE 11-1
The Principal Ports of Canada, 1972

	Total Tonnage	% Outbound	% International
1. Vancouver, B.C.	34 898 000	80	78
(with New Westminster)	37 918 000		
2. Montreal, Que.	25 514 000	39	40
3. Thunder Bay, Ont.	23 094 000	96	20
4. Sept Îles-Pte Noire, Que.	22 324 000	95	81
5. Port Cartier, Que.	15 088 000	77	81
6. Quebec, Que.	14 835 000	39	68
7. Hamilton, Ont.	12 681 000	5	63
8. Halifax, N.S.	11 716 000	48	78
9. Saint John, N.B.	10 318 000	41	81
10. Sarnia, Ont.	8 086 000	36	64

Source: Statistics Canada, *Shipping Report 1974* (Part 4: Origin and Destination for Selected Ports).

handled. As you can see, ports function in different ways. Because so much of Canadian freight is bulky, many of the ports are one way. Notice that at Thunder Bay and Sept Îles practically all the freight moves outward. This is no surprise since Thunder Bay ships out wheat, barley, and iron ore; at Sept Îles, except for some inbound fuel oil, all the freight is iron ore. The same is true in reverse of Hamilton, Ontario, where almost all the freight (95%) is coming in. This one-way traffice is not ideal, because it means that the ships are empty on the run *to* Thunder Bay and Sept Îles and *from* Hamilton; half their round-trip is "wasted."

Vancouver also functions mostly as a one-way port. The outbound figure of 80% would be even higher if we took out of the "In" column the two million tonnes of logs, lumber, and newsprint that are towed or barged into Vancouver from the lumber towns along the British Columbia coast. Ships make the long runs to Vancouver empty to load up on coal, wheat and barley, timber, sulphur, potash, and rapeseed. As a general rule, it takes more workers to handle goods coming in than goods going out, so that a port like Vancouver will have fewer people employed by the port than would one like Montreal.

Of course, total shipping is a somewhat unsatisfactory measure of a port's relative importance. Oil, coal, ores, and grain all weigh a lot but need very little labour in loading or unloading. Manufactured goods, on the other hand, require more careful handling and storage; thus, they add more to the economy of a port. The containers carry most of the manufactured items in water-borne traffic. Further, container traffic is far more balanced between In and Out than is bulk traffic. For example, of their container freight, Montreal has 57% going out and 43% coming in; Halifax, 51% out and 49% in.

Table 11-2 shows the ranking of Canadian container ports. On this list Vancouver drops to fourth place and the Seaway ports disappear. The

TABLE 11-2
Canadian Container Ports, 1972

	Tonnes of Container Freight
1. Montreal	1 226 000
2. Halifax	1 070 000
3. Quebec	696 000
4. Vancouver	567 000
5. Saint John	364 000

Source: *Canada Year Book 1974.*

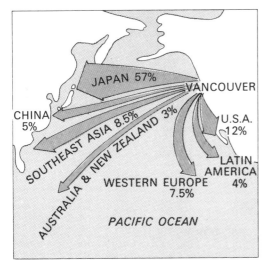

Figure 11–4: The Export Trade
of Vancouver.

high position of Montreal and Halifax suggest the continued importance
of Europe in our oceanic trade.

Railways. The principal means of freight movement in Canada is
still the railway. After a long period of dominance, the railways have seen
their share of the tonnage drop to about 32% of the total (262 million
tonnes in 1976). The principal competition lately has come from the
pipelines, which are in many ways unlike the other forms of transportation. If we exclude the pipelines, with their heavy flow of oil and natural
gas, then the railways carry about 44% of all the freight moved.

Even that number does not give an accurate picture because railways
carry their freight further, on the average, than do trucks or pipelines.
(The few long pipelines are more than balanced by the dozens of short
lines.)

Table 11-3 shows the main categories of freight carried by the Canadian railways in 1972, while Table 11-4 lists the major goods.

You will notice how important the mines, the grain fields, and the
forests are. Numbers 5, 10, and 11 all come from trees and total over 36
million tonnes. The very high figure for iron ore is impressive because
most of it is shipped on just one railway, the Quebec North Shore and
Labrador, which carries the ore from the Labrador-Ungava iron mines to
the docks at Sept Îles. Note too that the railways ship mostly bulk
materials. All the machinery, new automobiles, farm equipment, and
other metal products total only nine million tonnes, less than 4% of the
freight carried.

Of all the forms of transportation, the railways have had the greatest

TABLE 11-3
Main Categories of Freight Shipped by Rail

	Tonnes (1972)	%
1. Raw materials	111 575 000	47
2. Manufactured goods	76 247 000	32
3. Agricultural products	40 723 000	17
4. All others	9 365 000	4
	237 910 000	100

Source: *Canada Year Book 1974.*

TABLE 11-4
Principal Commodities Shipped by Rail

	Tonnes (1972)	%
1. Iron Ore	37 850 000	15.9
2. Non-Metallic Minerals	25 624 000	10.8
3. Wheat	20 229 000	8.5
4. Coal	14 011 000	5.9
5. Pulp & Paper	13 955 000	5.9
6. Other Metallic Ores	13 862 000	5.8
7. Petroleum Products	13 036 000	5.5
8. Other Grain & Cereals	11 865 000	5.0
9. Potash & Other Fertilizers	11 670 000	4.9
10. Lumber	11 336 000	4.8
11. Pulpwood	10 944 000	4.6
	158 758 000	67.0

Source: *Canada Year Book 1974.*

role in uniting the settled parts of Canada. In fact, in the western half of the country, the railway brought in people and fostered settlement. The entry of British Columbia into Confederation was contingent on the construction of a railway. However, the Canadian Pacific Railway (now CP Rail) from Montreal to Vancouver, did much more than assure Canada of a Pacific coastline. It created the first surface east-west route entirely within Canada; as a result, it strengthened Canada's claim to sovereignty over the Prairies. The government was able, by means of the railway, to extend law and order to the vast plains. The railway led to the opening up of the wheat fields; it gave birth to new cities like Calgary and Regina; and, beginning with Sudbury, it unlocked the immense mineral wealth of the Shield. The CPR proved that, despite all the barriers, Canada could be united and its regions could work together.

Both nationalistic and economic motives seem to have been at work in the routing of the Canadian Pacific Railway. The decision to blast a route across the Shield instead of hooking up with the already built U.S. midwestern railroads came from the desire to have the entire route in Canada. In the Rockies, the Kicking Horse and Rogers Passes were used instead of the much easier Yellowhead Pass in order to run the line closer to the boundary. This route stopped the traffic of the southern Prairies from being lost to the Great Northern Railroad in Montana. In southeastern British Columbia, the Kootenay, Columbia, and Okanagan valleys all led southward into Washington State. To tie those areas to the rest of Canada, another CPR line was built west from Lethbridge, Alberta, through the Crows Nest Pass, then up and down all the ridges between the valleys. Just as the Shield route led to the accidental discovery of the Sudbury ores, so this difficult and expensive line led to the development of the lead and zinc ores around Trail, the Okanagan orchards, and the coal beds which are now supplying Japan. Sometimes nationalism pays!

The Saskatoon area, Saskatchewan. Canadian National

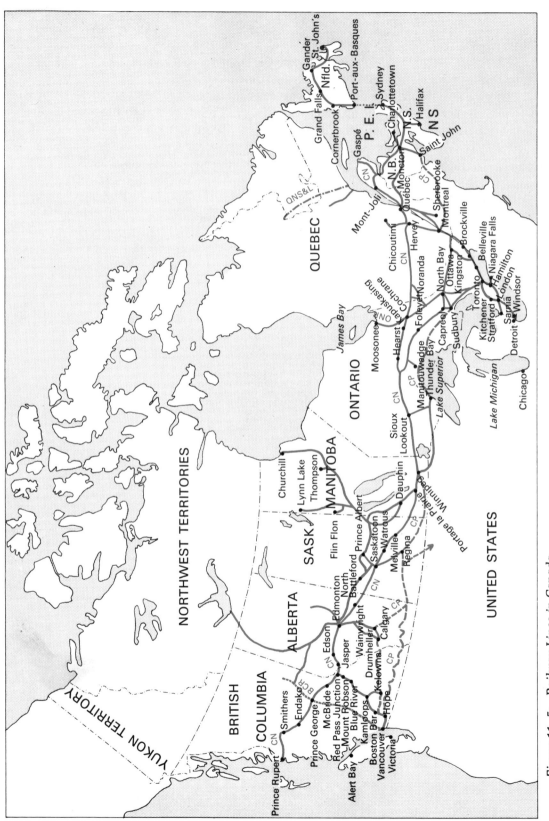

Figure 11–5: Railway Lines in Canada

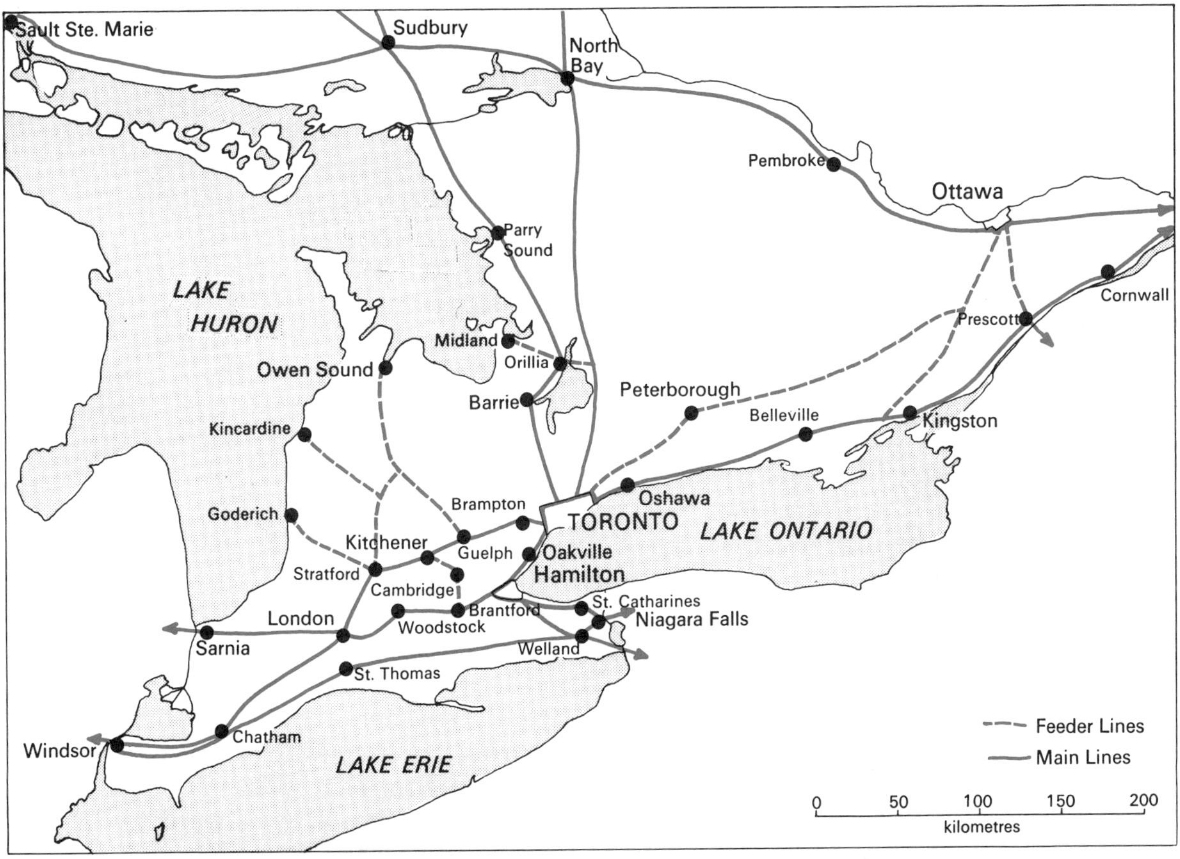

Figure 11–6: *Railway Lines in Southern Ontario*

The Canadian railway network is made up of two great systems with a few smaller lines supplementing them. The three main nodes on the transcontinental network are Vancouver, Winnipeg, and Montreal. With the exception of a CN branch to Prince Rupert, all the lines to the Pacific coast terminate at Vancouver. From that great port eastward the lines follow three paths heading for the Yellowhead, Kicking Horse, and Crows Nest passes and the cities just beyond them: Edmonton, Calgary and Lethbridge. Moving eastward the lines gradually converge, passing through the mid-Prairie cities of Saskatoon (CN) and Regina (CP), until they all come together at the mid-Canada node, Winnipeg.

Eastward from Winnipeg the lines again fan out along three routes: to Thunder Bay for trans-shipment to lake steamers, across the Shield (CP), and through the Clay Belt, north of the Shield (CN). Eventually, these lines and the ones from southern Ontario converge again at Montreal. Beyond Montreal the lines diverge again, into a southerly route across Maine (CP), and an all-Canadian route through Madawaska (CN). The lines come together again at the smaller node, Moncton, from where the Canadian National runs through Nova Scotia; via ferry, bus (passenger) and a narrow-gauge line (freight) across Newfoundland to St. John's.

One of the oddities of the Canadian rail network is that the busiest traffic of all does not occur along this basic trunk system but rather off to the side, in southern Ontario. Here Toronto serves as the great node. It is joined to the east-west corridor by the CP to Sudbury, the CN to North Bay and Montreal. Southwestward from Toronto, a radial system of lines serves to connect the rest of the country with Canada's greatest concentration of manufacturing and with the United States via Detroit and Buffalo.

The rail corridor runs east-west, parallel to the boundary with the United States. Even at its northernmost point, Edmonton, it is only about 500 km from the border. Over the years a series of lines have been built northward, at right angles to the basic network to reach certain sites of importance, such as the iron mines of Labrador. Thus, the Ontario Northland has been built from North Bay to the southern tip of Hudson Bay at Moosonee, and a long CN branch line from Saskatchewan to Churchill on Hudson Bay. In Alberta, tracks have been built from Edmonton northward to Great Slave Lake and Lake Athabasca, northwestward to the Peace River country. In British Columbia, the British Columbia Railway has been extended along the upper Fraser River into the northern interior of the province.

Canada is one of the few developed countries which continues to build railways. The railway is still seen, therefore, as a means of welding the country together, to bring the "empty" lands of the North into closer contact with the settled parts of Canada.

The railways have been so important that the question of freight rates has had its impact on the unity of the country. Before the development of trucking and pipelines, the railways had almost a monopoly on transportation in the parts of Canada away from navigable water. The federal government became deeply involved in the questions of freight rates. Although the aim of the government was to prevent the railways from setting unfair rates, the western provinces long complained that the rates set favoured the East over the West. The West claimed that the rates helped Montreal rather than Vancouver, and kept manufacturing concentrated in Ontario and Quebec. With the rise of other forms of

transportation, the railways complained of being overregulated. Therefore, in 1967, Parliament passed the National Transportation Act which
set up the Canadian Transport Commission. The railways can now set
their own rates, subject to supervision by the Commission.

Highways. Because their importance had been mostly local until about
1950, highways have had only a small impact on Canadian unity. It was
not until the 1950s that the federal government became actively concerned with the need for a good transcontinental highway system. As in
the case of the CP 70 years before, the Shield proved to be the major
physical barrier. The first east-west highway avoided the worst of the
hard rock area by running due north from North Bay to the Clay Belt and
following it westward through Kapuskasing to Nipigon, Thunder Bay,
and Winnipeg. This route, however, was much too roundabout for any
truckers or tourists driving from southern Ontario to the West. Hence,
most of these people took the short cut through the United States.

   To provide a more direct route and to open up the rough but scenic
areas "North of Superior," the Trans-Canada Highway was blasted

A main interchange on the Macdonald-Cartier Freeway in Toronto.

Ministry of Transportation and Communications

Courtesy of Department of Highways, Province of Manitoba, Canada

The Trans-Canada Highway at the Manitoba-Ontario Boundary.

through the rock to connect Sault Ste Marie with Thunder Bay. The highway was made truly Trans-Canada in the 1960s with a direct route from St. John's to Victoria. Except for the people in southwesternmost Ontario, the most direct route east-west was now entirely within Canada. It had been built at great expense; Canadian nationalism had paid the price. But "the price was right," because it allowed thousands of Canadian travellers the opportunity to see and sense the extent and grandeur of their country.

This new east-west highway opened new ground in only a few places. West of Montreal, the Trans-Canada Highway closely follows the route of the CP; east of Montreal it follows the CN. The principal cities of the railway axis are thus the main cities of the highway axis as well: Vancouver, Calgary, Regina, Winnipeg, Thunder Bay, Sudbury, North Bay, Ottawa, Montreal, Quebec, Moncton, the Sydney ferry, and St. John's.

As was the case with the railways, a number of roads have been built northward from the main axis to penetrate into the Near North. To date, no highway has reached Hudson Bay, although roads to its southernmost part, James Bay, are underway in both Ontario and Quebec. The most important roads northward have been built out of Edmonton. During

World War II, the Alaska Highway was built some 3000 km through the Yukon to Fairbanks, Alaska. Within the past few years, a major road has been constructed to Yellowknife, at the northern end of Great Slave Lake. This latter road follows the Mackenzie River for a few hundred kilometres and may in the future be extended along the Mackenzie to Inuvik at its mouth.

Trucking handles about 25% of all freight carried in Canada (172 million tonnes in 1974.) This figure is very high when one considers that the heavy bulky materials, like iron ore, coal, petroleum, wheat, barley, and lumber, are all carried by water, rail, or pipeline. Truck runs tend to be short, but more expensive than rail or ship. However, trucking is flexible, convenient, fast, and of critical importance in supplying the daily needs of cities. Over nine times as many employed persons are listed by the Canadian census as "truck drivers" than work on railway trains.

Pipelines.   Pipelines have become significant in achieving national unity because they are the means of transporting oil and natural gas. They accounted for 196 million tonnes, or over 25% of all the freight moved in Canada in 1974. The Shield has again been a problem because it lies between the wells in Alberta and Saskatchewan and the markets in southern Ontario. Even more than the highways, the pipelines have had to face the difficulties of the hardrock, because the pipes have to be buried; therefore, trenches had to be blasted for hundreds of kilometres into crystalline rock. At the same time, no transport method is more vulnerable and yet more necessary to a nation's security than a fuel-carrying pipeline. (See Figure 4-15.)

When the first major natural gas pipeline was built, it was kept within Canada, despite the cost. The route chosen was close to that of the CN east from Winnipeg, north of Lake Nipigon, then slightly north to take advantage of the Clay Belt. Thus, it avoided some of the worst areas of the Shield.

The oil pipelines have also taken the easier route south of the lakes: this route allowed for quicker and cheaper construction as well as direct access to the huge United States market. The pipes run around both ends of Lake Michigan and re-enter Canada at Sarnia and Sault Ste. Marie. Sarnia has gained enormously from this choice of routing because it has become the major refining centre of southern Ontario.

The recent show of pricing power by the Middle East countries and Venezuela has made clear the drawbacks involved in being too dependent upon foreign fuel sources. Plans have been made, therefore, to hook the Montreal petroleum refineries onto the trans-Canadian pipeline system to enable Montreal and provinces to the east to buy their oil from Alberta.

Again, a decision on routings has had to be made. The first route chosen has been the shortest and cheapest — that is, from Sarnia to Montreal — avoiding the Shield, but increasing the dependence on the lines which pass through the United States to reach Sarnia. Proposals have been made to build also a new, long, expensive line from Winnipeg across the Shield. Once more, in this vital matter, Canada faces the question of nationalism versus money.

Airlines.   Canada is a country well-suited to passenger air travel. The vast distances and the clustered pattern of population distribution make the use of aircraft desirable for all types of travellers, especially for administrators. The only way to get people in and out of the communities in the North is by air. Regularly scheduled runs operate between places with surprisingly small populations; these runs are supplemented by hundreds of bush pilots who handle emergencies and many other special flights.

Air freight is very expensive; therefore, airplanes carry only goods of high value and low weight or those needed quickly. Since this specification cuts out all the bulky goods, air's share of the total tonnage is well below one per cent. The government-owned airline, Air Canada, is one of the world's major lines and serves to "carry the flag" to many cities outside Canada. In the number of passenger-kilometres flown, it ranks just behind the huge Russian and American airlines and ahead of all the European airlines. The number of employees, on the other hand (Air Canada has fewer than Air France, British Airways, Lufthansa, and even Iberia), again points out the effects of geography. Within its own country, Air Canada deals with few cities and with great distances, whereas the European airlines fly short distances between many airports; hence, they must have hired help at all those airports. All traffic between Canadian cities must be handled by Canadian carriers, but international agreements are necessary for movements across the boundary. These agreements are usually arranged by exchanges. That Canada has so few large cities compared to the United States, Germany, or France means that the Canadian lines tend to be put at a competitive disadvantage. For example, every major Canadian airport is served by some American airline (often by several), whereas many American airports are not touched by any Canadian line. A Canadian flying to New Orleans or Kansas City would have to use a U.S. carrier for at least part of the way,

An aerial view of the Toronto International Airport.

Northway Survey Corporation Limited

but an American flying from there to any large Canadian city could use a U.S. carrier all the way.

The air network is very much like the rail network. Two major systems — the public (Air Canada), and a private (CP Air) — monopolize the long-distance traffic across the nation. (The scale of CP Air's operations is about 30% that of Air Canada.) Even more than with the railways is a focus on a few cities: Toronto, Montreal, Vancouver, Calgary, Winnipeg, Edmonton, Ottawa, and Halifax.

As with the rail and highway networks, a series of lines penetrate northward from the main corridor. These extensions can go much further than the railways or roads and have become the principal lines tying the North to the South. Three cities act as the jumping off points for these lines into the North. From Edmonton regularly scheduled flights go to Yellowknife, Inuvik, Cambridge Bay, and even Resolute Bay in the Arctic archipelago. From Winnipeg flights go northward to the communities along the western side of Hudson Bay. From Montreal the planes fly to Ft. Chimo, Frobisher Bay, and on to Resolute Bay. Thus, these three cities handle the air connections to the western, central, and eastern Arctic, respectively, with flights from Edmonton and Montreal ending up at Resolute. In addition, flights from Vancouver serve northern British Columbia, and from St. John's, the Labrador coast. Dozens of small airstrips in northern Ontario are connected to the towns further south.

A transport unity of all of Canada has been achieved, but at high cost. The railways and the Trans-Canada Highway have been built across the

Gulf Oil Canada Limited

A bush plane in flight. Note the skis used for landing on snow.

hard rock at great expense. In the North, the distances are so great, the climate so severe, and the problems of tundra and permafrost so difficult, that almost no attempt has been made to construct ground transportation. Under such conditions it is obviously much easier and cheaper to clear hundreds of airfields than to try to build roads to connect the widely scattered communities. On the other hand, air traffic under such conditions is very expensive, so the airlines are forced to charge rates higher than the air freight rates in effect between the southern cities. Once again we face the fact that Canada has been tied together, but at a price! Thus, the history of Canada has included a continual series of difficult decisions to invest large amounts of money in constructing transport routes across long stretches of empty land composed of difficult terrain.

COMMUNICATIONS: THE MEDIA   Transportation lines tie a country together physically, but communications enable the people to know of each other and to share common events, ideas, debates, and decisions. Communication is now felt to be of supreme importance in the development of a Canadian national identity.

By law, newspapers and periodicals in Canada must be Canadian owned and managed; with a couple of exceptions, this law has been effective. None of the great foreign newspaper chains has been able to establish itself in Canada. The newspapers, in particular, are important in helping Canadians know each other by emphasizing Canadian news. Thus, elections, disasters, and cultural events anywhere in Canada are printed far more often in Ontario papers than are similar happenings across the boundary in the United States. Torontonians know more of what is going on in Vancouver than in Buffalo or Rochester, just across the lake.

Canadian newspapers tend to be individual and regional. Each region has its own influential journals. Because the total number of major newspapers is small, each carries an impact on government affairs; none can be said to dominate in the same sense that the *New York Times* is the accepted leader in the U.S. The Toronto papers claim a kind of primacy, but it is doubtful that Canada can be said to have a true national newspaper; language and region are too strong to allow any Canadian newspaper to inform the entire country.

The airwaves are felt to be national public property; as such they have been under government regulation since 1932. As in the case of transportation, the policy was set up in response to American business pressure, to keep the airwaves under Canadian control. The Canadian Broadcasting Corporation (CBC) was set up by the federal government in 1935 to give Canada a national network, broadcasting in both English and French. Much like the British Broadcasting Corporation (BBC) in Britain, attempts have been made to keep the quality high and commercials few on the CBC. The federal government has also, from the start, regulated the content of all programs, whether on CBC or private stations. The principal concern of the Board of Broadcast Governors (BBG) from 1958 to 1968, and the members of the Canadian Radio-television and Telecommunications Commission (CRTC) since 1968, has been to push for more Canadian content in broadcasting. The Broadcasting Act (1968) states that the purpose of all Canadian broadcasting should be to *safeguard, enrich and strengthen the cultural, political, social and economic fabric of Canada*. The underlying problem was that popular music was at that time almost entirely a British or American importation; it was difficult for any Canadian artists to have a chance to be heard, much less to sell their records (if they could find a company to record with). In a sense, music was yet another example of nationalism clashing head-on with big money, this time in the entertainment business. As of October 1970, 30% of all music on AM radio had to be either performed, written, or composed by a Canadian, or recorded in Canada. Canadians began to hear a great deal of Anne Murray and Gordon Lightfoot.

Television is now felt to be the most important medium of communication. Surveys show that people obtain more of their news from TV than from newspapers; the amount of time spent by Canadians in front of "the tube" averages several hours a day. Canadian television policy has been an extension of the radio policy. The CBC television networks (French

A taping of a television program.

Robert C. Ragsdale Limited

and English) were set up; since October 1961 when CTV began, private networks have been permitted. The clash between government and "free enterprise" stations is lessened because all stations are subject to the careful checking of the CRTC, which has the power to cancel broadcasting licences.

Again, the issue of money versus nationalism has arisen. American television has enormous funds at its disposal; its programs are well and richly produced and are aimed carefully at what is popular. The Canadian systems simply cannot compete financially and thus they tend to buy many of the American shows. Only the Canadian government is in a position to protect a Canadian entertainment industry and help it to grow. Since 1970-71, the CRTC has stated that 60% of all programming should be Canadian.

Of course, many Canadians, especially in southern Ontario, can pick up American television directly, but the government hopes that this loophole will be covered by the gradual extension of cable systems. Under CRTC rules, cable companies are permitted to operate as local monopolies, provided that they allow all Canadian television stations, and even a local channel to have precedence over non-Canadian stations. The greatest difficulties with this system have been in the Toronto-Hamilton urban area where five Buffalo stations compete directly with seven Canadian outlets. In some cases, the cable companies have had to have stations share a channel at different times of the day. Without the CRTC regulations, the cable companies would be strongly tempted to give the popular American stations top priority, to the loss of some Canadian outlets.

Broadcasting is a fairly big business. The CBC employs a fulltime staff of about 10 000 persons. Since broadcasting is aimed at the larger groups of people, the principal studios and staffs are in the greater cities of each region. Montreal and Toronto are the two headquarters, for French and English, respectively, but programs also originate in Vancouver, Winnipeg, and Halifax. The CRTC offices are in Ottawa. The private radio and television stations employ almost another 10 000 persons, but these stations are more spread out across Canada. The CBC operates a shortwave service to the North; some native-peoples dialects are broadcast.

Somewhat less noticeable than the radio and television networks are the telephone, telegraph, Telex, Broadband, and Data-Phone services which rapidly send messages and data of all kinds. All of these are formed of groupings of various companies, notably the CN and CP Telesat, a mixed private-public corporation, which operates a satellite-based communications network. More than anything else, the ability to communicate instantly throughout the vast bulk of Canada ties the country together.

UNITY AND EQUAL OPPORTUNITY

Unity cannot be achieved as long as some regions, areas, or groups of people feel themselves to be especially disadvantaged. People nursing a grievance against the country cannot be expected to feel patriotic. This consideration plus an obvious desire for justice have led the federal government to the other major aim — to see to it that every Canadian has access to a decent standard of living.

The problems involved are immense and varied, but can be put into two classes: *spatial* and *cultural*. The spatial problems are both the easiest and the hardest to handle. They are easiest because they are fairly obvious; they are hardest because no amount of money put into an area seems to be able to overcome that area's poor economic location.

The existing concentrations of population produce an almost irresistible pull on all companies looking for a place to set up shop. The big cities have the labour force, in numbers as well as in the needed variety and skills. The cities have the largest pools of people with management experience, the decision makers. The big cities make the financial policy; they have the money, the technology, and the research capacity. A great city is an efficient concentrated market which sets the styles and what consumers will want to buy. And the cities, with their shops, restaurants, and theatres, are where the executives and their families want to live. Thus, an ore-resource site will usually have only the mines and the ore-concentration plants, whereas the headquarters and sales offices with their executives and office workers will be located in Toronto or Montreal. Toronto, as a well-known English-speaking money centre near the American border, has a great attraction for all U.S. firms wishing to establish branch plants in Canada; Montreal, with its more established cosmopolitan appearance, has attracted many branch plants as well.

So it happens that, despite the vast size of Canada, a few areas receive and control most of the wealth of the country: southern Ontario, Montreal, southwestern British Colubmia, and southern Alberta. All the economic trends which lead industry to locate near the richest markets, near the investment money, or near the oil fields favour these areas. In Canada, automation, new styles, and the concentration of business into bigger companies all tend to make the rich places grow richer and the poor get poorer.

Yet millions of people live outside these few fortunate areas. They cannot be allowed to starve, nor can their communities be allowed to fall apart through the loss of local tax funds. The young workers leave such areas and flock to the great cities, but such a migration leaves the non-workers at home, while it causes crowding and sky-rocketing land prices in places like Toronto.

Tables 11-5 and 11-6 show the enormous variations in house prices in Canada. Note in Table 11-6 the difference between the three wealthy provinces, Ontario, British Columbia, and Alberta, on the one hand, and the Atlantic Provinces and the North on the other. Table 11-6 shows the high costs of housing in the Toronto-Hamilton, Ottawa, and Vancouver-Victoria areas. A major part of house costs is the price of the land a house is built on. That the average house in Toronto costs twice as much as that in St. John does not mean that the Toronto house is twice as luxurious; the house *may* be somewhat better, but the land also probably cost much more. (To make Table 11-6 easier to read, a few cities have been left off. Numbers 11, 12, and 13 are Sudbury, London, and St. Catharines-Niagara, all in Ontario; numbers 18, 19, and 20 are Saskatoon, Regina, and Thunder Bay.) Both the depopulation of one place and the crowding of another are to be avoided as much as possible.

The federal government is committed to the attainment of prosperity throughout Canada. Attempts are made, therefore, to spread the wealth around. One of the simplest methods is to provide every eligible Canadian with the same amount, regardless of residence. This is done through family-support, old-age pensions, and welfare cheques. These payments

TABLE 11-5
Median Value of Non-Farm Housing, 1971

Newfoundland	$ 7 828
Prince Edward Island	9 454
Nova Scotia	10 829
New Brunswick	9 153
Quebec	14 667
Ontario	23 768
Manitoba	14 904
Saskatchewan	11 467
Alberta	19 933
British Columbia	23 502
Yukon/N.W.T.	8 639

Source: *Canada Year Book 1974.*

* More recent information indicates that house prices have shot up since 1971 in Calgary and Edmonton. House values in those cities may now be the highest in Canada.

TABLE 11-6
Median Value of Non-Farm Housing, 1971

1.	Toronto, Ont.	$32 408
2.	Vancouver, B.C.	26 702
3.	Ottawa, Ont.	25 758
4.	Hamilton, Ont.	25 172
5.	Victoria, B.C.	25 007
6.	Kitchener, Ont.	23 968
7.	Edmonton, Alta.*	23 665
8.	Halifax, N.S.	22 820
9.	Calgary, Alta.*	22 461
10.	Windsor, Ont.	22 327
. . .		
14.	St. John's, Nfld.	19 945
15.	Quebec, Que.	19 422
16.	Montreal, Que.	18 603
17.	Winnipeg, Man.	17 780
. . .		
21.	Saint John, N.B.	15 528

Source: *Canada Year Book 1974.*

tend to be more important to the poorer areas than to the wealthy; they have made a major impact on Newfoundland since it joined Confederation. Health and welfare payments were the biggest expense in the federal budget for 1974-75. In fact, that expenditure (20%) equalled half the revenue obtained from personal income taxes (40%). Such payments help the individual families, but they do not solve the underlying regional problems. In an attempt to relieve these hardships, the federal government distributes "equalization payments." In effect, money that has been collected from the three richer provinces is given out to the poorer provinces. In addition, some federal agencies have made studies of specific problem areas.

Specific public works and transportation accounted for over 7% of total expenditures in fiscal 1974-75. But, despite all the government's investment, the regional problems seem to remain virtually unchanged. Table 11-7 lists the amount of "equalization payments" made by the federal government to the provinces in 1972.

It is clear that the Atlantic Provinces are being helped greatly by money collected from British Columbia, Ontario, and Alberta. The "have" provinces, who do not wish to be continually paying for the "have nots," feel that this redistribution of funds should be limited. Ontario pays over 40% of the federal taxes in Canada. The Metro Toronto

TABLE 11-7
Equalization Payments to Provinces, 1972

	Equalization Payments ($ millions)	Provincial Population est. 1972	$/person
Newfoundland	120.5	532 000	227
Prince Edward Island	23.1	113 000	205
Nova Scotia	93.8	794 000	118
New Brunswick	97.2	642 000	151
Quebec	511.6	6 059 000	84
Ontario	0	7 825 000	0
Manitoba	58.6	992 000	59
Saskatchewan	115.6	916 000	126
Alberta	0	1 655 000	0
British Columbia	0	2 247 000	0

Source: *Canada Year Book 1974.*

area pays 20% by itself. Those who pay also wish to receive what they think is their fair share of benefits and services. Still, this system of redistribution is one of the clearest proofs of the fact that Confederation works.

The cultural problems are not as hard to solve, but are felt to be more dangerous to the sense of unity. Within the past fifteen years, Canada's self-image has changed, growing from one of British primacy, to a British-French partnership, to a cultural mosaic of all European groups, to the present cultural mosaic of all non-native and native groups.

In the 1960s, the main cultural issue was the status of the French language within Canada. The Francophones felt themselves to be at a disadvantage. The Quebec government reformed the education system and tried to make French the principal business and administrative language of the province. The activity of Quebec was followed by attempts from the Acadians of eastern New Brunswick to gain educational and legal rights, and later from Francophone communities in many Ontario cities who tried to obtain French schools. The federal government set up the "Bilingual and Bicultural Commission" to examine the status of French-speaking peoples across Canada. As a result of that study, bilingualism has been favoured in the civil service; the use of both English and French has become normal in all governmental regulations and notices, and in learned publications. Further, those areas of Canada which have either 10% or a reasonable number of Francophones have been designated as bilingual areas.

*Inuit girls at Coppermine,
Northwest Territories.*

Gulf Oil Canada Limited

Although the French-speaking Canadians outside Quebec still find it difficult to work or socialize in their own language, their right to do so is now widely accepted, at least in theory. Most Canadians accept the idea of "the two founding peoples" and the concept which follows from it that Canada is, to some degree, built on a French-English partnership. (Two important by-products of the tensions of the 1960s were the new Canadian flag and the swift popular acceptance of "O Canada" as the national anthem.)

The biggest cultural issue in the 1970s concerns native rights over lands and over northern development. Much of the area of Canada is beyond the limits of unbroken white settlement and is populated mostly by small groups of native peoples. These tribes or peoples lived in these areas before European settlement of North America. They can claim that they were there first, that they never gave up the land, and that they are still there. On the other hand, it is difficult for Canadian governments at all levels to accept the claim that a mere two per cent of the inhabitants of Canada own more than half the area of the country. Therefore, until the last few years the northern lands were treated as being essentially empty and owned by the Crown. Within the past decade, however, native claims to the North have been considered seriously, and even allowed. In their treatment of the peoples in northern Quebec or in the Mackenzie Valley, the present governments are acting very differently than the Canadian governments of the 1870s and 1880s did in their dealings with the native peoples of the Shield and the Prairies.

REGIONALISM AND PROVINCIALISM

Every country has a political structure which keeps it working together day by day. Canada's structure is a result of its physical and cultural diversity. It is a federal system, a union of strong self-governing units we call provinces. The provinces tend to be large in area and to extend from the settled South into the bush of the North. The exceptions are the three Maritime provinces which are small because of their history and the way in which arms of the ocean separate them from each other. (They are much like the small New England states of the U.S.) Two of the provinces, Ontario and Quebec, have together more than half of the population and taxable wealth of Canada; thus they have great political power. (In contrast, California and New York combined have less than 20% of the population of the U.S.A.) Since all ten provinces are theoretically equal, all the provinces tend to be in a position of strength when they face the federal government. All cities, towns, and townships, are considered to be internal divisions of the provinces, so the federal government must work with the provincial governments to deal with municipal problems.

Thus, in Canada, government is often seen as a struggle between two strong levels of government, the federal and the provincial. Major policies are often worked out in federal-provincial conferences, which look and sound much like summit meetings between heads of state. Most federal policies must be channelled down through the provincial governments to reach the people concerned. One result of this system is that urban policies and school systems vary from province to province. Only in the two territories does the federal government exercise direct control (with the cooperation of local councils).

One unfortunate result of this system is that the cities and towns, where most Canadians live, are caught in a money squeeze. They are expected to pay for local services, protection, streets, and (most of all) education, from their own income, and that income must come mainly from property taxes. This desperate need for property tax money makes many towns so eager to get new factories, shopping plazas, or high-rise apartments, regardless of planning principles. More and more cities are forced to beg the provincial governments for the money to meet the costs of education and of major construction projects. Increasingly, the cities are asking to be allowed to become partners in federal-provincial conferences.

Most of the money raised by taxation or tariffs in Canada goes to the federal government, so that even the provincial governments must turn to Ottawa for needed funds. Therefore, we have the awkward situation in Canada that the federal government collects the revenue, but some of the greatest needs are in the cities which are under the control of the provincial governments. In the case of Ontario, Ottawa hands some money back, but Queen's Park (the provincial government in Toronto) acts as the money handler: it decides how and where the funds are to be used within the province.

Political representation within the elected House of Commons takes into account the regional qualities of Canada. By general unwritten agreement, none of the provinces should have fewer than four members, the total for Prince Edward Island. Representation is required to be adjusted after every major census. There is, however, a great reluctance to take away seats from any province, even if that province has lost population. Consequently, the tendency is to take care of increases in population in the growing provinces by enlarging the total membership of the House. Since no politician wants to add too many new seats, the larger cities never seem to get their share of the seats. This is true in most countries of the world: while the cities are underrepresented, the non-urban areas are overrepresented. Within Canada, the populations of the electoral districts vary from a low of 22 010 in Malpeque (P.E.I.) to 193 156 in York-Scarborough (Ontario), with 80 000 being about average.

Representation always lags behind population growth; the provinces which pay the most taxes tend not to have their just share of representatives in Parliament.

The regional aspects of Canada show up politically in two other ways. There are interesting differences in party support. During the past few elections, it has been accepted as the rule that Quebec is almost always *Liberal*, and the Ontario cities and Newfoundland usually so (but with many exceptions); that the Prairies are *Conservative*; and that the *New Democratic Party* has its strength in British Columbia and some urban ridings in Ontario.

That, however, is only on the federal level. The other sign of regionality is that Canadians often have provincial loyalties different from their federal ones. On a provincial level, Ontario has been Conservative for over thirty years, and the four western provinces have tended to support Social Credit or the NDP (or its predecessor, the CCF). On the local level, meanwhile, elections are mostly non-partisan. Canadians, then, tend to approach politics on three distinct levels with three separate sets of loyalties. Clearly, a Conservative provincial leader will often support a Conservative federal leader, but there is no guarantee that the average

Ontario "Tory" (or "Grit") will do so. In Quebec, regionalism is so strong that the provincial and federal parties of the same name have traditionally avoided saying anything about each other as parties.

CONCLUSION

Canada has been called a triumph of politics over geography. By this triumph is meant that a prosperous unified country has been established and made to work despite the problems of size and terrain. Technology can be said to have been a major factor because the inventions of the past century and a half gave us the transportation and communications which have made our unity possible. Confederation came in the midst of railway building; by 1890 the railway and telegraph had joined all of Canada from ocean to ocean. The icebreaker helped make secure the Canadian claim to the northern archipelago; more recently, the airplane and radio-telephone have tied all of the North to the South. The lake steamer, pipeline, and "mile-long" freight trains have allowed us to ship our goods and fuels relatively cheaply over long distances. The Canadian success story is thus largely a result of the technological revolution since 1850.

But Canada has also been unified because the people have wanted to have a free and independent nation with its own sense of identity. Above all, Canadians do not want to be confused with any other North American people. Attempts are continually being made to help the various groups and regions to keep and develop their cultures. The national wealth is distributed to help the poorer areas. The federal system allows for local differences by giving the provinces wide powers in education and directing urban growth.

Canada can be said then to be a union of many different peoples who chose to use the great inventions of our era to build a united country, despite geographical and human problems in the northern half of North America.

QUESTIONS

1. List the divisive factors that make the unification of Canada so difficult.
2. List the unifying factors that help to mould the sense of Canadian identity.

3. "Nationalism vs. Money" is a recurring theme in Canada's economic development. In very simple terms explain the fundamental problem. Give as many examples as you can of this problem of conflicting goals

for Canadians.

4. Canadians have a country rich in resources in a world where the demand for these resources is growing stronger. Many foreign investors are prepared to buy these resources now. Do you think that Canadians should sell now, sell at a later date, or never sell the ownership of these resources? Justify your answer.

5. The St. Lawrence Seaway Authority has a problem. It charges tolls of 4 cents per tonne on the gross tonnage of a ship and 40 cents a tonne for bulk cargo and 90 cents for general cargo. This means that the average ship passing from Montreal to Lake Ontario is charged approximately $14 000 for the one-way trip. Despite these charges, the profits are not sufficient to repay the interest and capital-debt charges on the government loan that was made to construct the Seaway. The result is that the size of the Seaway debt is increasing each year and is now about $800 million. This is a very real problem and the possible solutions are obvious:

   (i) Close the Seaway as a financial failure.
   (ii) Raise the tolls until the Seaway system is paid for.
   (iii) Lower the tolls and encourage additional volume of trade.
   (iv) The government repays the debt with the taxes it collects from all Canadians.

A. Analyze this problem and write out the pros and cons of each proposed solution.

B. Which of the four proposed solutions would appeal to
   (i) a Saskatchewan wheat farmer?
   (ii) a Halifax dockworker?
   (iii) a Toronto industrialist?
   (iv) a Vancouver Island logger?

RESEARCH

1. Conduct a survey within your class to determine if the intent of The Broadcasting Act (1968) to "safeguard, enrich and strengthen the cultural, political, social and economic fabric of Canada," is being fulfilled. What is the most popular radio program in Canada? What is the most popular TV program in Canada? Where do these programs originate? Of the total time spent watching TV during one week by the members of your class what percentage was devoted to Canadian-made programs and what percentage was devoted to foreign programs?

2. Explain why, after 100 years of railway construction in Canada, Vancouver, Winnipeg, and Montreal are "the three great nodes on the transcontinental network." Make a list of the most important regional transportation nodes.

3. Make a list of Canadian entertainers you feel would be well known to Canadians from coast to coast.

12 | CANADA AND THE WORLD: GLOBALISM

CANADA AND THE UNITED STATES

In the eyes of the world, Canada is a developed country; it has a high standard of living, an enviable amount of space, and a promising future. In Europe, Canada is sometimes spoken of as a giant of the future. Within the Commonwealth it is seen as second only to Britain in wealth and prestige. The Latin American countries have often asked Canada to join the Organization of American States, partly to add another wealthy and technologically advanced country to the group, partly to help balance the great weight of the United States.

Yet, despite this bright evaluation of Canada, it is also true that Canada is a relatively unknown place to most of the world's peoples. The United States is so strong a figure on the world stage that Canada seems hidden behind it. Thus, it is not surprising that many Europeans consider Canada to be joined to the U.S. Also, because "American" has come to mean a citizen of the United States, it is hard to understand another nation of North Americans not being "American." In the minds of immigrants from Europe and Asia, the two large countries have usually been combined into one giant land of opportunity, with the country chosen being mostly a matter of the ability of immigrants to get in.

At its worst, this tendency to be lumped with the U.S. may lead other countries, such as France, to try to exclude Canada from international meetings for being too closely tied to the United States. On a less serious level, it can lead to Canadian feelings of annoyance at being taken for Americans overseas. Relations with the United States occupy much of the average Canadian's thinking about foreign affairs. That world giant cannot be avoided. It shares a continent with us and is in fact our only land neighbour. (When you consider how many land neighbours small countries like Switzerland (5), Czechoslovakia (6), or Israel (4) have, for example, you can see how remarkable it is to have over 5000 km of land boundary, but all with just one other country.) Canada and the U.S. share the St. Lawrence Seaway, are linked in North American Defense (NORAD), and have worked together in climatic and satellite research. Canadians have always been closely involved in many of the social movements and the styles of entertainment begun south of the border.

Probably nothing shows the closeness of the two countries more than the trade between them. As shown in Table 12-1, we are each other's main shopping partners: our total trade has reached almost $43 billion in 1974. Although the amount going each way is about equal in value, the significance to each country is not the same. Canada's share comes to about 66% of all our exports, whereas for the United States it is only 20% of their total exports. Obviously Canada is more concerned about ties with the United States than the U.S. with Canada! By the way, that figure of "66%" tells us that, despite all we may read about wheat and coal being sent to Russia or Japan, most of our money trade is really in auto parts and minerals to the United States. Except for oil, Canada pays little for raw materials or agricultural products from Asia, Africa, or Latin America.

Canadians also feel close ties with Great Britain, which is the home of the Queen, of our parliamentary system, and of many of our traditions. One language and many of the people who founded and built up Canada came from the British Isles. Until a few years ago Britain was our second

TABLE 12-1
Canada's Foreign Trade, 1974 ($ millions)

	Exports to	Imports from
United States	$21 325	$21 306
United Kingdom	1 903	1 127
European Economic Community*	2 087	1 815
Eastern Europe & U.S.S.R.	189	197
Middle East	320	1 315
Japan	2 229	1 428
Australia	308	335
Venezuela	206	1 291
Other	3 610	2 825
TOTAL	$32 177	$31 639

* In 1974, the European Economic Community included West Germany, France, Italy, Netherlands, Belgium, and Luxembourg.

Source: Statistics Canada 1974, External Trade Division. Published by authority of Ministry of Industry, Trade and Commerce.

most important trading partner. Although it has now been passed by Japan, the United Kingdom remains one of Canada's main export markets.

FOREIGN OWNERSHIP

During the past decade, Canadians have become worried about the ownership of the Canadian economy by non-Canadians. Foreign investment has always been heavy in Canada. Until World War I, British investment was the most significant, but since the 1920s the United States has held the lead. In 1967, non-resident long-term investment in Canada was calculated to total over $28 billion. Of that figure, 81% was United States–controlled, 10% British, and 9% mostly European. Since then, the total has increased, and the Japanese have entered the picture. By 1973, the total had reached $53 billion, or over $2400 for every Canadian man, woman, and child. Of this total, the United States control 79%, the British controlled 9%, and "other" controlled 12%.

Control may be too strong a word, however. By "control" is meant "the capital which is subject to foreign control." Capital is the money put into a business by the owners. Normally the owner can run the business as he or she likes — the owner "controls" it — but, of course, all businesses are subject to laws and regulations. And all "foreign-controlled" companies have to obey the rules laid down by the Canadian governments. On the other hand, many people fear that the companies which operate in several countries may become too strong for any one national government.

If we look at not just the factories and mines but also at all the other sectors of the economic life of Canada — banks, transportation, stores, schools, medical facilities, and all the kinds of office work — we see that foreign control is not as high as we might fear. The overall figure for foreign control was 34% in 1973. Hence, about one-third of the total economy of Canada may be under non-Canadian control.

Foreign ownership is most noticeable in a few parts of the economy, some of which are felt to be vital to the well-being of the nation. The automobile manufacturing industry is almost all foreign owned; the proportion of foreign control stands at about 77% in petroleum and natural gas, 58% in manufacturing, and 46% in mining and smelting. Many foreign companies, like the drug manufacturers, set up branch plants in Canada to compete for the Canadian market. If these companies take over the market, then we are said to have a branch-plant economy.

A branch-plant economy has some disadvantages. The major deci-

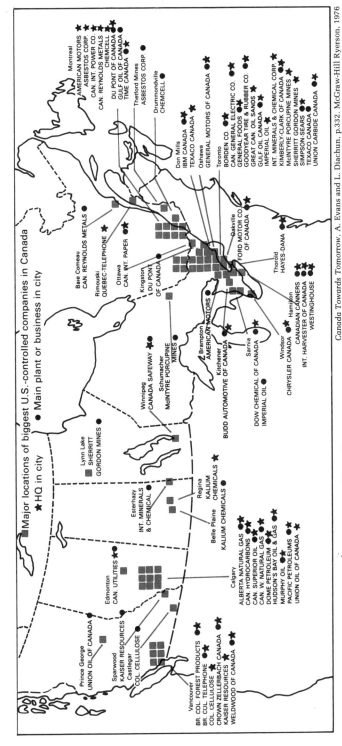

Figure 12–1:   American Investment in Canada

sions are made outside Canada. If the company owns factories in several countries, it can threaten to move its jobs to other places if workers demand more money, or when the government passes laws it doesn't like. Also, the high-income research work of the company is usually done in the home country, not in Canada.

Although Canadian nationalists tend to condemn the "takeover" of Canadian firms by foreigners, it must be pointed out that no takeovers would occur if Canadians were not willing to sell out. One reason for the large size of American investment is simply that Canadians in all kinds of business have been only too willing to sell at the high prices offered.

We come back, therefore, to the problem of nationalism versus money. It is a great temptation to sell Canadian land, resources, and businesses to those eager foreign buyers. Nationalists may condemn it, but many Canadian business people are happy to accept the best price offered, while others may find that they cannot find in Canada the money they need to expand. In addition, many believe that the great inputs of foreign money will help the economy to grow and will filter down to Canadians in general and as taxes to the government. The desire to pull in foreign money is so strong that Canadian interest and mortgage rates are usually kept higher than those in the U.S.A. and most European countries. (This lets the foreign investor gain higher profits in Canada than at home.)

One of the more interesting examples of the Canadian difficulty is in sports. As in all developed countries, professional sports command a large following in Canada. Some cities and towns identify strongly with their teams, like Hamilton with the Tiger-Cats, and Montreal with the Canadiens. But sports are also big business. The scale of operations, the needed facilities, the high salaries of players, all make the size of the market a critical factor. Only the largest cities can supply the number of fans needed to support the "big league" teams, and only Montreal and Toronto have a population equal to any of the twenty largest metropolitan areas in the United States.

Hockey has been a prime example of the victory of the market factor (money) over nationalism. As the National Hockey League (NHL) increased in its scale of operations, the smaller Canadian cities dropped out in favour of four large American cities near the border: Boston, New York, Detroit, and Chicago. Only Montreal and Toronto remained in a league full of Canadian players. A series of expansions have since scattered N.H.L. teams throughout North America, but the new teams have located in the larger cities (markets), almost all of which are in the U.S. The lone exception is Vancouver, but it is interesting to remember objections to Vancouver as being too small. (The metropolitan population of Vancouver is smaller than that of Buffalo.) Interestingly, almost half the clubs in the NHL's rival, the World Hockey Association (WHA), were located in Canada at the time of writing.

The lesson is obvious: any sports league based on the larger markets of North America will end up being a U.S. league. Faced with this fact, the federal government in 1974 passed legislation to assure that the only important Canadian sports league left, the CFL, would remain Canadian and not be overwhelmed by American money, even if it meant that the Canadian football teams would not be able to compete with the American leagues for the best players.

Slowly the federal and some provincial governments have made efforts to prevent the continued takeover of the economy by foreign interests. However, each move is opposed by those persons who believe sincerely in the free flow of money internationally and in selling at the best price possible. Besides, putting tight restrictions on the foreign-owned companies could annoy some of our friends abroad and cause their governments to retaliate. Nationalism versus money — it isn't easy!

In 1970, it was calculated that Canadians had an investment of almost $12 billion abroad, almost $6 billion in the United States. Thus, the average American had $160 invested in Canada, while the average Canadian had $275 invested in the United States! The big difference, of course, is that the U.S. has ten times the population of Canada: the smaller American average has swamped the Canadian economy, the larger Canadian average has remained a small part of the United States' economy.

Canadian money has been going increasingly to other countries too. In 1970 about 15% of our long-term foreign investment was in the United Kingdom, about 9% in other Commonwealth countries. Over 25% was invested in countries outside the British Commonwealth or the United States. Japan and the European Economic Community have become attractive places to invest. The fastest increases in investment have been outside the U.S. and the United Kingdom. Total investment in the United Kingdom has actually been dropping.

If we figure out all of the assets owned by Canadians outside of Canada and compare that total with Canada's total indebtedness to other countries, we get a difference of more than $32 billion (1973). Canada owes the rest of the world that much more than other countries owe us. Of course, that "debt" will not have to be paid off in huge lump sums.

Investment always means that the money stays put for a long time.

The big problem for Canada is that a debt of that size requires a lot of money every year just to pay for the interest charges or to send profits to the people who invested the money. And that problem is made worse by

The American Motors Company plant in Brampton assembles Gremlins for the Canadian and United States markets.

Russell Thompson Photographer

The Ford Motor Company of Canada, Limited.

Photo Courtesy of Ford Motor Company of Canada Limited

the great numbers of Canadians who spend their winter vacations in Florida and their summers in Europe. All that money flowing out has to be balanced somehow. Canada is often put into the position of looking for even more foreign money to be brought in to help match the money going out. Thus, Canadians both want and fear foreign investment.

Because of our small, scattered population and our high standard of living, Canadians have to look to the rest of the world for markets and money. More than most other industrialized countries, we are tightly hooked into the international flows of goods and money. So it is that foreign ties have a powerful affect on Canadian life, even though the rest of the world may often seem to be far away.

CANADIAN AID

At least since World War I, Canada has been an influential part of the Western world. Canada made large contributions in terms of money and goods (and blood in both World Wars) and was recognized as a major partner of the Western Alliance during World War II. The role of Canadian troops in freeing the Netherlands of enemy occupation, and of the Canadian government in offering asylum in Ottawa to the Dutch royal family, led to a long lasting friendship between the Dutch and Canadian peoples. The increasing emphasis on French culture within Canada has led to the redevelopment of close ties with France and, through France, with the Francophone community of nations.

Since the close of World War II, Canada has been a member of the North Atlantic Treaty Organization (NATO). Canadian forces have taken part in many army exercises. The stationing of about 5000 troops in Germany (and until a few years ago in France) has led to the development of close personal ties between Canadian families and the people of Western Europe.

Canada's closest connections with developing nations of the "Third World" have been through the framework of the Commonwealth. Because it was the first colony to gain independence, Canada has enjoyed a position of seniority and influence second only to Britain. The Commonwealth acts as a kind of channel directing Canadian aid and tourism to those tropical areas with a British tradition. Thus, Canadians tend to fly south in winter to Barbados or Jamaica, rather than to Puerto Rico or the Virgin Islands. To Canadians the Caribbean is English speaking, to Americans it is thought of as Spanish speaking. The great emphasis on Spanish in the schools of the United States is clearly not shared by the schools of Canada.

Canada gives over a billion dollars a year to foreign aid of all types. This is a large figure, but it is still only a half of one percent of the wealth the people of Canada create in a year (the Gross National Product).

Table 12-2 shows roughly how this money is divided up. Over a quarter of the total is "multilateral," which means that Canada deals with groups of countries. Under this heading would be the Canadian contribution to the World Bank, which helps to finance development and to balance the rates of exchange of the moneys of different countries. Canada also contributes to four Regional Development Banks, the Asian, Caribbean, African, and Inter-American, which supply money for development in their parts of the world.

About half the total aid is listed at "bilateral," which means that Canada deals directly with the country being helped. About half this money is given in grants, half in interest-free loans for 50 years. (Because of inflation, an interest-free loan of that length of time is almost a grant.) As you can see in Table 12-2, about 66% of this "bilateral" aid was channeled through the Commonwealth, almost 50% of it to the Colombo Plan countries.

The Colombo Plan is an overall program for the development of the densely populated countries of South Asia. It is named after the city of Colombo, the capital of Sri Lanka (formerly Ceylon), where the plan was first drawn up. Britain, Australia, and New Zealand joined Canada in setting up the plan in 1951. The United States and Japan have joined it since. Under this program, India and Bangladesh have obtained larger

TABLE 12-2
Foreign Aid, 1975-76

Multilateral (with several countries)	$318 560 000
Bilateral (Canada with individual countries)	525 710 000
Asia	257 810 000
Bangladesh	29 480 000
India	98 910 000
Pakistan	63 940 000
Francophone Africa	104 9990 000
Commonwealth Africa	108 320 000
Commonwealth Caribbean	21 900 000
Latin America	27 020 000
Other (relief programs, food aid, etc.)	256 400 000
TOTAL	$1 100 670 000

Source: *Canada and Development Cooperation, Annual Review 1975-76*, Canadian International Development Agency, 1976, pp. 124-136.

shares of Canadian aid than have any other parts of the world. Between 1951 and 1973, Canada gave almost two billion dollars in aid to Bangladesh, India, Indonesia, Pakistan, and Sri Lanka.

In Africa, Canadian aid has gone to the two groups of new states which were formerly colonies of Britain and France. Projects ranging from mining to beekeeping have been supported since 1960 in countries like Tanzania, Kenya, Ghana, and Nigeria. The ties to the Francophone community have been developed more recently. These ties were given a great urgency by the severe droughts of the early 1970s in Sahelian Africa (the grasslands along the southern edge of the Sahara desert).

Canada has given more aid *per capita* to the Caribbean than to any other peoples. The populations of the islands are so small compared to the Afro-Asian states that the money granted has been higher per person than elsewhere. In addition, Canadian banks and businesses have invested over $500 million in the British West Indies.

Two examples of practical Canadian aid are projects nearing completion in Ghana, West Africa. (Ghana was the first British Colony in Africa to gain independence and the first to receive Canadian aid.) Both projects are designed to supply the people with safe drinking water.

The importance of clean water was stressed by the famous British economist, Barbara Ward, at the Habitat Conference which was held in Vancouver in June 1976. Many of the worst diseases, parasites, and worms are carried in impure water. Farmers who suffer from these ailments cannot do normal work. They can raise only very little food for themselves.

A steady supply of clean water will not only make it possible for people to be strong enough to work well, but will also mean that water will be on hand to water the crops in dry spells. Clean water will make these people better able to take care of themselves and to earn money.

In northern Ghana, about one million people have already used safe drinking water for the first time in their lives. Around 900 wells had been dug in the area by the middle of 1976. Canadian and Ghanaian crews have worked together. The Canadian International Development Agency (CIDA) has paid the costs of about $8 million.

The water supply of the capital city, Accra, has been expanded. A dam, pumping station, and filtration plant have been built at Weija, near Accra, at a cost of $50 million. Like most capital cities in the "the Third World," Accra is growing fast. This dam will mean that the increasing population will not have to face water shortages. The project is a cooperative effort of the CIDA, the World Bank, and the African Development Bank. Canada's share of the cost has been around $10 million.

A Canadian drill rig at the site of a new well in northern Ghana. Canadian-aid funds are being used to supply one million people in the north with their first supply of safe drinking water.

Wilf Nerrie of Calgary (left) and John Paulsen of Winnipeg examine a hand pump in northern Ghana. Paulsen is project manager and Nerrie is in charge of the drilling operations of a multimillion-dollar Canadian-aid project to provide residents with their first supplies of safe drinking water.

Canada has provided about $10 million for the expansion of the Accra water supply system. Accra, the capital of Ghana, is threatened with water shortages if the work is not completed on schedule.

On the stage of the entire world, Canada has acted as a middle power. Despite its small population and its small army, Canada enjoys great prestige and influence because of its resources, its membership in NATO, its close ties to the United States, and its diplomacy in the United Nations. Canada is viewed as a country which understands the United States, shares its technology, yet manages to be independent of American foreign policy. Thus, Canada served on the International Commission for Supervision and Control in Vietnam, Laos, and Cambodia as the unofficial Western representative, from 1954 to 1974.

Above all, Canadians have looked on the United Nations as the setting where they can influence the world. The efforts of Lester Pearson for peace, which gained him the Nobel Peace Prize, have been looked upon as the ideal Canadian contribution to the world.

Canada, probably more than any other country, has tried in recent decades to act as a peacemaker and peacekeeper. Canadian troops have served in the cause of peace between the Egyptians and Israelis, and between the Greeks and Turks in Cyprus, with the costs being borne by Canada. Canadian diplomats have tried to thaw relations between the West and both China and the Soviet Union. Canadians, who are so worried about the lack of a national identity at home, have a clear image of themselves outside Canada as peacemakers.

This emphasis on peace is partly an outgrowth of Canada's internal life. Canadians are always trying to tie themselves together physically and culturally. We are concerned about the working out of problems between cultural groups, in the development of our poorer regions, and in the sale of raw materials to other industrial countries. We know about the problems caused by foreign money and by the huge multinational corporations which operate in so many countries that no one government seems able to handle them. The Canadian work for peace in this world can be seen as an extension of the work for peaceful development inside Canada. In the work for peace in the world, Canadians are able to find the identity which seems so hard to find inside this mosaic of regions and peoples we call Canada.

QUESTIONS

1. Why does Canada have such close ties with the United States? List all the reasons you can think of.

2. In what ways is a high level of investment by foreigners in Canada good and bad for Canada?

3. Study Figure 12-1 and discuss the types of American investment in Canada.

4. Where has most of Canada's foreign-aid money gone? Why has it gone to those countries?

5. What do you think Canadians feel has been their main contribution to the world since World War II?

RESEARCH

1. Find out the amount of Canadian investment in a Latin American country or on an island of the Caribbean.

2. How much did Canadian tourists spend in the United States and how much did American tourists spend in Canada in any one recent year?

3. Where outside Canada do Canadians go for vacations or business trips? Obtain the statistics for a recent year.

4. Which are the African states in the Francophone community?

5. List the members of the Commonwealth, by continent or part of the world.

6. For what actions was Lester Pearson awarded the Nobel Peace Prize?

7. Why are Canadian soldiers in Cyprus? How long have they been there? How much has it cost Canada?

INDEX